Criminal Psychology

Criminal Psychology

Topics in Applied Psychology

David Canter

HODDER
EDUCATION
AN HACHETTE UK COMPANY

First published in Great Britain in 2008 by
Hodder Education, an Hachette UK Company, 338 Euston Road, London NW1 3BH

www.hoddereducation.com

© 2008 **David Canter**

Hachette UK's policy is to use papers that are natural, renewable and
recyclable products and made from wood grown in sustainable forests.
The logging and manufacturing processes are expected to conform to the
environmental regulations of the country of origin.

The advice and information in this book are believed to be true and
accurate at the date of going to press, but neither the authors nor the publisher
can accept any legal responsibility or liability for any errors or omissions.

Every effort has been made to trace and acknowledge the owners of copyright.
The publishers will be glad to make suitable arrangements with any
copyright holders whom it has not been possible to contact.

British Library Cataloguing in Publication Data
A catalogue record for this book is available from the British Library

Library of Congress Cataloging-in-Publication Data
A catalog record for this book is available from the Library of Congress

ISBN 978 0 340 92892 9

2 3 4 5 6 7 8 9 10

Cover & section opener © Photodisc/Getty Images

Typeset in 10pt Berling Roman by Servis Filmsetting Ltd., Stockport, Cheshire
Printed and bound in Great Britain by CPI Group (UK) Ltd, Croydon, CR0 4YY

What do you think about this book? Or any other Hodder
Education title? Please send your comments to the
feedback section on www.hoddereducation.com.

Contents

Section 4: Areas of application 193

Contributors

David Canter, Director of the Centre for Investigative Psychology at the University of Liverpool, UK

Michael Davis, Lecturer in Clinical-Forensic Psychology at Monash University (Australia) and Forensic Psychology Co-ordinator of the Monash Clinical Psychology Centre

Louise Goodwin, completing a Doctorate at the Centre for Investigative Psychology at the University of Liverpool, UK

Paul V. Greenall, Researcher into Personality Disorder at the Adult Forensic Psychology Service, Prestwich Hospital, Manchester, UK

Laura Hammond, completing a Doctorate at the Centre for Investigative Psychology at the University of Liverpool, UK

Maria Ioannou, Research Fellow at the Centre for Investigative Psychology at the University of Liverpool, UK

Natalia Wentink Martin, recently completed a Doctorate at the Centre for Investigative Psychology at the University of Liverpool, UK

Sam Mullins, completing a Doctorate at the Centre for Transnational Crime Prevention at the University of Wollongong, Australia

Freya Newman, completing a Doctorate at the Centre for Investigative Psychology at the University of Liverpool, UK

Jonathan Ogan, completing a Doctorate at the Centre for Investigative Psychology at the University of Liverpool, UK

Kevin Rogers, Head of Forensic Psychology at HM Prison, Liverpool, UK

Mary Santarcangelo, completing a Doctorate at the Centre for Investigative Psychology at the University of Liverpool, UK

Katie Thole, completing a Doctorate at the Centre for Investigative Psychology at the University of Liverpool, UK

Shannon Vettor, completing a Doctorate at the University of Birmingham, UK

Michelle Wright, Professional Practice Developer for the National Policing Improvement Agency (NPIA), UK

Donna Youngs, Senior Research Fellow at the Centre for Investigative Psychology at the University of Liverpool, UK

Series preface

Psychology is still one of the most popular subjects for study at undergraduate degree level. As well as providing the student with a range of academic and applied skills that are valued by a broad range of employers, a psychology degree also serves as the basis for subsequent training and a career in professional psychology. A substantial proportion of students entering a degree programme in Psychology do so with a subsequent career in applied psychology firmly in mind, and as a result the number of applied psychology courses available at undergraduate level has significantly increased over recent years. In some cases these courses supplement core academic areas and in others they provide the student with a flavour of what they might experience as a professional psychologist.

Topics in Applied Psychology represents a series of six textbooks designed to provide a comprehensive academic and professional insight into specific areas of professional psychology. The texts cover the areas of **Clinical Psychology, Criminal Psychology, Educational Psychology, Health Psychology, Sports and Exercise Psychology**, and **Organizational and Work Psychology**, and each text is written and edited by the foremost professional and academic figures in each of these areas.

Each textbook is based on a similar academic formula which combines a comprehensive review of cutting-edge research and professional knowledge with accessible teaching and learning features. The books are also structured so they can be used as an integrated teaching support for a one-term or one-semester course in each of their relevant areas of applied psychology. Given the increasing importance of applying psychological knowledge across a growing range of areas of practice, we feel this series is timely and comprehensive. We hope you find each book in the series readable, enlightening, accessible and instructive.

Graham Davey
University of Sussex, Brighton, UK
September 2007

Preface

This book is very much a team effort. When approached by the Series Editor to write a book on psychology and crime I was fortunate to have around me a number of colleagues, many of whom had been or were currently studying with me, who were more than keen to contribute chapters. This provided a rare possibility of stage managing a book with people who shared a common vision of the many ways in which our understanding of crime and criminals could be informed by psychology.

The book is therefore rather more than a selection of diverse readings like many books of contributions. Instead it maps out a coherent set of perspectives on the psychology of offending. However, in my editorial role I have deliberately avoided imposing a strong, or limited theoretical structure on the work reviewed. That is more appropriate for the single authored textbook which complements the present volume that is published with my colleague Dr Donna Youngs, under the title *Investigative Psychology: Offender Profiling and the Analysis of Criminal Action*.

Criminal Psychology therefore provides a general map of the approaches that are taken by psychologists to help understand and explain the several aspects of offending, followed by a consideration of the processes that underlie different subsets of crimes as diverse as burglary, rape and murder. After these reviews of some of the fundamentals of the psychology of crime, consideration is given to the challenges that the police and courts face in obtaining effective evidence because of the vagaries of human memory and the more overt problems of deception.

The insights that psychological research provides for those who have to deal with crime and criminals are reviewed in the next set of chapters running from police investigations through the courts and into the prison system. The often neglected consideration of the victims of crime provides the penultimate chapter before the final review of where the study of the psychology of crime and criminals seems to be heading.

One of the major delights of academic life is being able to participate in the transformation of students into colleagues. The student caterpillars that weave their cocoons around their dissertations, often disappearing from view for a while, only to emerge with wet wings that they must shake dry before they spread them wide and fly free as independent scholars is the reoccurring marvel that teachers are privileged to watch. Most fly off like summer butterflies so it is most unusual to have been able to keep in contact with so many of them, augmented by others with whom I have cooperated on various projects, to work together on preparing this volume.

Organizing this range of contributors was quite a task so I am especially grateful to Louise Goodwin for the great assistance she has given me in monitoring progress on the production of the chapters and helping to bring them all together in a manageable form.

David Canter
University of Liverpool, UK
May 2008

1 | The basis of criminality

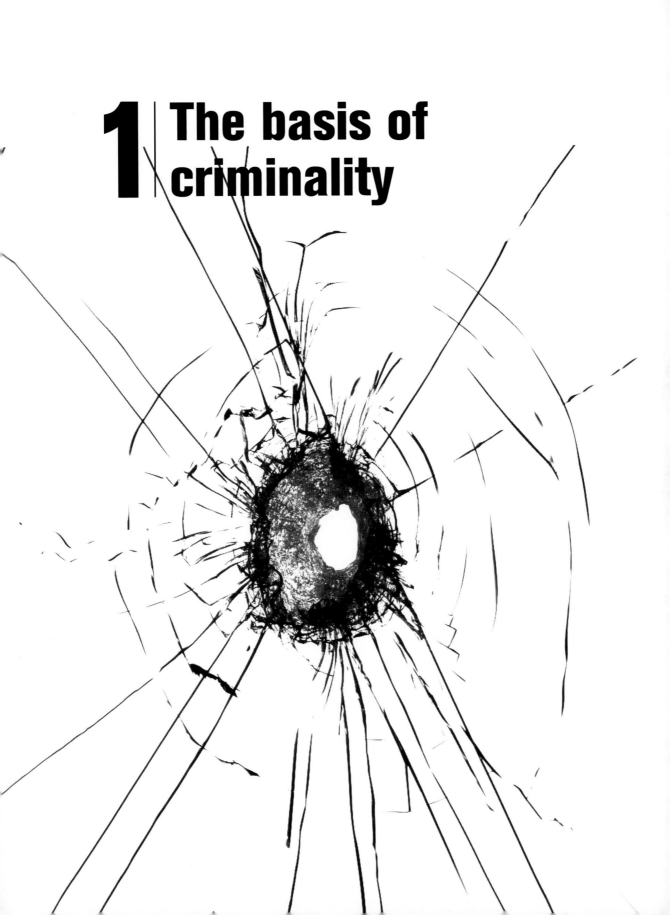

1 Psychology and the criminal process

David Canter

The wide range of psychological studies of crimes and criminals that have emerged over recent years are reviewed in this book. This introductory chapter lays the foundations for subsequent chapters by considering the process from crime to investigation, trial and imprisonment, then describes attempts to manage offenders in prison and help them out of criminality. This leads to exploration of the many different institutions and agencies that have to deal with crime and opens up the debate on the ways in which a psychological approach may differ from other ways of considering crimes. This includes an examination of such processes as those by which people become criminal; the variety of ways in which crimes are enacted; how an understanding of criminals' thoughts and actions can assist police investigations; factors influencing witness testimony, and managing and treating offenders once they are convicted. The gap between criminological studies of delinquency and psychologists' studies of rare and extremely serious crimes is highlighted. The study of all of these topics raises challenges in gaining access to appropriate data as well as legal and ethical demands on the researchers.

Learning outcomes

When you have completed this chapter you should be able to:

1. Recognize the range of topics that are dealt with by psychologists in the area of crime and criminality.
2. Understand the difficulties and challenges associated with research into crime and criminals, including practical, legal and ethical demands on study in this area.
3. Describe the various approaches to research that are utilized when studying criminal activity.
4. Acknowledge the many different disciplines within and outside psychology that contribute to our understanding of criminality.
5. Summarize the dominant theoretical perspectives that are drawn on in this area.
6. Discuss the differences in approaches to knowledge that distinguish psychology from law enforcement and other disciplines.
7. Recognize how the present book is organized from considering principles and theories in the early chapters to more practical applications in later chapters.
8. Acknowledge the wider range of topics that forensic psychologists deal with which are given greater emphasis in other publications.

The criminal process

It is useful to think of criminal activity as being part of a process rather than a particular action or an act committed by a particular type of person. The process starts when people carry out illegal acts, but even those acts are likely to have their roots in earlier experiences. Once the act has been committed there are then victims and witnesses, as well as other social processes that become associated with the act, most notably aspects of law enforcement. Thus an important aspect of the process that emerges if the criminality is recognized and reported is the police investigation. Furthermore, the criminal is likely to be part of various social networks that will also influence and be influenced by the crime. Other crimes may also be associated with the initial act so that the crime itself can become part of a developing process of criminality.

Psychologists focus on individuals rather than broader social, political or economic processes so the knowledge that is gained about the psychology of crime has to be gleaned in relation to the acts of offenders rather than general crime statistics. This means that the task of understanding the underlying cognitive, emotional and interpersonal aspects of **the criminal process** is very dependent on which crimes and criminals it is possible to obtain information about. Psychologists cannot glean very much from the sort of national crime statistics that are the stock in trade of those sociologists who study crime. To understand the individual and social psychological aspects of crimes, details of actual crimes and their perpetrators need to be obtained.

Yet, when considering criminals and their actions it has to be borne in mind that a very biased sample of people is being dealt with. For example, in many places, in less than 10 per cent of burglaries the offender is apprehended. There is thus an open debate on whether the burglars who get to court or are studied by researchers are typical of all burglars or are, possibly, the less competent ones who do not escape arrest. By contrast, around the developed world, as many as 95 per cent of murderers are caught. This means that studies of those who kill others may be more representative of the range and variety of homicides than is the case for other crimes, but it also means that there is more information on this very rare crime than for many other crimes that are far more prevalent.

Other crimes provide different forms of challenge in understanding what exactly is being studied. For example, arson that is committed as a carefully planned act to make money from insurance, as might be done by a failing business, is extremely difficult to detect. So 'arson for profit' is rarely studied by psychologists because there are so few people convicted of this type of arson.

Rape and sexual assault provide yet other kinds of limitation on the sorts of cases and people that become the focus for study. A conviction on these crimes is so dependent on a decision as to whether there has been consent to the offensive act that many of the social issues surrounding how such a conviction is obtained will inevitably cloud the picture of who rapists actually are. However, although in many cases psychologists do need direct contact with offenders to develop an understanding of crime and criminality, there is an emerging area of psychology known as **investigative psychology** (Canter and Youngs, 2008a) that pays particular attention to the actions of criminals. Information on these actions may be available from victim and witness statements as well as police and court reports independently of any direct contact with the offender, but the emphasis is still on understanding criminals rather than crime in general.

Crime and criminality, then, can never be considered in isolation from the processes by which the actions that are considered criminal come to notice and the route by which the offender emerges into view. The psychology of crime always interacts with the institution or agency that has recognized the criminal activity and the offending person. There are very many of these agencies and institutions, all of which deal with different kinds of events and individuals, having different objectives and carrying out different tasks. It is helpful to think of the initial agency being the police. They are most concerned with what the criminal act actually consists of and the evidence that can be found to bring the offender to justice. This moves on to the courts which, as Wrightsman, Nietzel and Fortune (1998) discuss in relation to the roles of psychologists, focus on making decisions about who is guilty, including judgements about the degree of seriousness of the offence. Beyond this are the prison authorities and other agencies that deal with criminals, such as the probation service and various forms of support services. These will include clinical services that attempt to assess or treat offenders and predict how dangerous they are likely to be in the future. Clinical psychologists have a particularly important role here in trying to help criminals who have, say, addiction problems, or need to manage their aggression, as discussed in detail, for example, by Blackburn (1994). He also draws attention to that special, rare subgroup of offenders who are regarded as being mentally disordered and require special attention in services that may often have a psychiatric as well as a psychological input. At every stage of this process there are crucial matters to be understood and acted on to which the psychology of crime contributes.

Figure 1.1 There is a lot of paperwork involved in any investigation.
Source: © Peter Casolino/Alamy.

Varieties of crime

It is unlikely that there will be one set of psychological explanations and procedures that applies to all criminal acts. To understand the psychology of crime it is important to take on board the great variety of actions that can be regarded as criminal. In every culture crime covers a great variety of very different sorts of activities, from fraud to serial killing of strangers. Even within a subgroup of crimes there are big variations. Burglary can include stealing a purse through an open window or breaking into a fortified warehouse to steal carefully selected works of art. Fraud can be signing a cheque from someone else's account or a complex abuse of pension funds. Murder can be a violent emotional outburst or a studied and prepared killing for profit. It seems unlikely that the same psychological issues are relevant for all these different forms of law-breaking. Indeed it would be expected that individuals who choose to act in rather different ways in pursuance of the same overt aim (e.g. obtaining funds) may be more distinct from each other than people who carry out actions that are given the same legal definition but do them in different ways.

To further complicate matters, crime is not one objectively defined, universal set of actions. It is the interpretations of actions that make them criminal. These interpretations come from the legal and cultural context within which actions occur. Even the most obviously offensive action of killing another person may not be criminal, for example when perpetrated by a soldier in a war or in defence of one's own life. As already mentioned, more complex and subtle issues surround crimes such as rape, where consent is a central factor. Even the action of theft usually is only considered criminal where intention to steal can be demonstrated. When it comes to fraud and other crimes typically associated with bureaucracies and professional work then what is illegal in one place may be common practice in another.

The problem of the variety of activities that can be criminal is compounded by the lack of any strong psychological basis to legal definitions of crimes. An arson attack carried out to hide the evidence of a crime would be classed as the same sort of crime to that which was an act of revenge. This is a problem of particular significance when reviewing published accounts of psychological research on crime. When studies are carried out of the characteristics of offenders they typically use the legal definition of the crime for which the offender was convicted, not some subtler exploration of what sort of actions were involved.

Because of these complications it will become apparent in later chapters that one of the challenges that criminal psychologists face is to get a clear account and classification of the differences between various illegal activities. It will not be enough just to discuss burglary, rape or even serial killing. It will always be important to determine if there are specific subsets of these offences that may well relate to different psychological processes.

Identifying subsets of crimes may be quite challenging because focusing on different aspects of crimes may give rise to very different ways of dividing them

Figure 1.2 Schematic diagram showing many of the disciplines that contribute to the study of the psychology of crime and criminals.

up. For example, the popular view that 'motive' is an important aspect of a crime turns out to be extremely problematic. This could be the justification a criminal has for a crime, such as revenge for a wrong done to him/her, or the need for money to feed his/her family. But it could also be interpreted in a more deeply psychoanalytic way, as when it is declared that a rapist was angry with women because of the way his mother had treated him so he was unconsciously projecting his anger with his mother on other women. Or motive could mean some benefit the crime had for the offender such as obtaining recognition from other members of his gang, enjoying the excitement of getting away with the illegal act, or carrying out what the offender considers to be a moral duty. All these different 'motives' overlap with each other and could all be applied to the same crime. Therefore in subsequent chapters there will often be some emphasis on being as clear as possible about what set of actions is being considered and how they can be distinguished from other apparently similar crimes.

Criminal psychology therefore relates to many and various aspects of human activity and as a consequence draws on many different disciplines, as varied as cognitive science and jurisprudence. The related social science disciplines that deal with aspects of criminality and the law are drawn on to understand the context and significance of offence behaviour. In addition there are other areas of study that consider the actions of criminals in terms of the forensic traces they leave, whether it be where crimes occur or aspects of the chemistry or physics of a crime that can inform the understanding of the patterns of criminal behaviour.

Explanations of crime

It is out of the differentiation of crimes and criminals that the various forms of psychological explanations of **criminality** emerge. An important point to get clear from the start is that there is no evidence that mental illness is the cause of criminality. The complexity and variety of criminal activity indicates that it is very unlikely that crime is produced by mental illness or, more generally, mental disorder. The emphasis that some psychologists such as Blackburn (1994) give to mental problems in criminals is partly a product of their focus being on clinical populations. This has also meant that the aspect of the examination of criminals that emphasizes a clinical psychological or psychiatric perspective has tended to be biased towards rather extreme and unusual subsets of criminals. In essence, the people studied by clinicians have been those who have been referred for treatment. They therefore are likely to be people who are obviously mentally disturbed or whose crimes have bizarre or extreme qualities to them, such as serial rape, or serial arson or violent serial homicide.

The clinical focus has produced the rather distorted picture that much of the psychological literature on offending is devoted to violent criminals and those whose actions are extreme and rare, whereas the broader criminological literature tends to explore the actions of delinquents and those who have carried out what is often called 'volume crime', such as burglary, theft and car crime. It is perhaps therefore not surprising that there is a difference in perspective between criminologists and clinical psychologists about the causes of crime because they are really talking about different populations.

The role of mental illness in criminality is remarkably difficult to determine, but Singleton et al (1998) report that mental disorder among prison groups ranges from 10 per cent to 78 per cent. Thus although this is a very wide range, showing how diverse different prison groups are, it is nonetheless rather higher than would be expected for the population at large, which Singleton et al (2001) put at no more than 19 per cent. The challenge here, though, is to disentangle cause from effect. The people assessed were in prison. As Haney (2008) has reviewed, prison can be very debilitating. Indeed, as Ly and Foster (2005) point out, a high proportion of people identified as mentally disordered find their way into hospital from prison. The issue may be clarified by a consideration of the nature of the mental disorder that relates to offending. Hodgins et al (1996) claim that a higher proportion of people diagnosed with schizophrenia and personality disorder commit violent crimes and are involved in general criminality than people without such disorders.

The interpretation of these general results requires the sort of close analysis that is often not possible from the way the broad statistics are presented. Perhaps people unable to cope in the way that is typical of schizophrenia are more likely to be caught or to find themselves in situations that are interpreted as criminal, or they may be drawn more readily from a crimogenic environment? Certainly Ly and Foster (2005) report that only a very small proportion of people diagnosed with a psychotic illness are criminally active.

The role of personality disorder is rather more problematic. It is widely demonstrated that people who are classified as psychopathic are more likely to commit serious crimes. Hare (2003), who developed the most widely used systematic procedure for assessing psychopathy, claims it is a very good predictor of offending violence. The difficulty in taking this claim at its face value relates to the nature of the assessment process and the way in which psychopathy is defined. Cooke (2008: 108) described psychopathy as 'a personality disorder, that is a chronic disturbance in an individual's relations with self, others and their environment which results in distress or failure to fulfil social roles and obligations … that is characterised by … an interpersonal style which is dominant, forceful, deceptive and grandiose, by … a failure to experience remorse or guilt, and by behaviour that can be described as impulsive or reckless'. Such a definition clearly describes a chronic criminal. There can be no surprise that impulsive, reckless people who do not feel guilt and tend to deceit and dominance may commit many crimes, including especially violent crimes. There is thus a need to consider whether the label of psychopathy is anything more than a description of a chronic criminal.

Activity 1.1

Gee Officer Krupke

Consider this following extract from the famous lyrics written by Stephen Sondheim for the musical *West Side Story* and discuss whether they exonerate hooliganism and delinquency. (The full lyrics of the whole song are available at www.westsidestory.com/site/level2/lyrics/krupke.html)

Dear kindly Sergeant Krupke,

You gotta understand,

It's just our bringin' up-ke

That gets us out of hand.

Our mothers all are junkies,

Our fathers all are drunks.

Golly Moses, natcherly we're punks!

Gee, Officer Krupke, we're very upset;

We never had the love that ev'ry child oughta get.

We ain't no delinquents,

We're misunderstood.

Deep down inside us there is good!

Do any other explanations of criminality implicitly exonerate offenders? What are the moral and legal implications of such proposals that criminality is caused by processes outside of the direct control of the offender? Do all psychological perspectives clarify or confuse this discussion to the same degree?

The discussion above about the difficulties in defining and differentiating criminals and the ways in which crime itself is socially defined draws attention to the need to consider the social psychological aspects of crime as well as characteristics of individuals. Most offending is part of a social process, whether it be a burglar entering the property of another person, a violent affray between a group of people, or the distribution and sale of drugs along a network of offenders. Thus many **explanations of crime** are deeply embedded in a view of criminals as growing up within or being absorbed into criminal society. For them breaking the law may be what they expect to do and is not really seen as immoral at all.

Such a social perspective on crime leads to rather different considerations than the clinical viewpoint. It draws attention to the offender's own understanding of the meaning and implications of his actions. The interpersonal interactions that the crime emerges out of will also be given much more prominence. For example, domestic violence may not be considered as entirely the product of an individual who has psychological problems but may be explored as a consequence of a dysfunctional relationship in which both parties hold a distorted view of what is appropriate behaviour.

The social psychology of crime also draws attention to the need to understand the social networks (Canter and Allison, 2000). The ways in which criminals contact each other, the formation of cliques and the role of significant individuals are all important in understanding what gives rise to an individual's offence activity. Yet this is an area of criminal psychology that has been little studied, partly because of the dominance of the clinical tradition in psychology generally.

Sources of information about crimes and criminals – evidence or data?

Crime is by its very nature very difficult to study. It is rare to be able to observe it in action and when it does occur there will be many pressures to keep it secret. People who commit offences will be reluctant to admit voluntarily that they have done so and often will go to some effort to hide what they have done. Therefore virtually all study of crime and criminals depends on accounts that are given after the event, often by people who are no longer in the situation in which the crime has occurred. It is therefore rather surprising that so much has been learnt about offenders and offending.

Self-reports

Over the years a large number of different sources of information have been utilized to build up a picture of crimes and criminals. These are often detailed interviews of offenders themselves, or their victims, often in a clinic, prison or other institutional setting. These may be formal questionnaire studies or more qualitative discussions with offenders about their crimes and life experiences. These self-reports have the advantage of direct contact with the perpetrators themselves. However, they depend on the person's memory of their offences, which may be weak after long periods of time (Kazemian and Farrington, 2005) and may be affected by concealment (Farrington, 1992).

There are also legal and ethical issues involved both in gaining access to offenders and in dealing with their accounts. At the most extreme, if an offender in an interview gave an account of a serious crime that he/she had not been convicted of or was intending to do, the interviewer could be regarded as an accessory to that crime if he/she did not subsequently report it. There may also be aspects of a crime and its investigation that are crucial to understanding what happened that are deliberately kept from public view for security or other matters of sensitivity.

If victims are the source of the information there will often also be legal constraints over the information that can be recorded and great care required in the storage and reporting of any accounts obtained. For example, in many countries the identity of a rape victim must not be made public. As a consequence there are often many barriers to gaining access to offenders or their victims.

Self-report data will also suffer from various biases because transient, difficult to find, uncooperative offenders will be under-represented (Farrington, 1987). There will be much more emphasis on people who are literally a captive audience for the research, being already incarcerated, leading to an over-representation of more frequent and more serious offenders (Farrington, 1992). Their imprisonment may itself distort what they are prepared to talk about or how they will present their actions.

Self-report data from offenders, and victim survey data on offences, have been used to supplement official records. However, many studies of crime rely heavily on official records, even though this means the 'dark figure' of crime (unrecorded and undetected) remains unknown. The collection of official statistics is not initially for the purposes of research but for the benefit of agency personnel (Farrington, 1992; Canter and Alison, 2003) and has with it inherent advantages and disadvantages.

Problems of remembering and deception

Given the nature of crime, **deception** and lying are recurrent issues that run through any consideration of the information available. This may apply to witnesses or victims as well as offenders. There has therefore been considerable interest in trying to develop systematic techniques for detecting deception. These have included purely verbal procedures as well as physiologically based systems – 'lie detectors'. None has proved foolproof, not least because a person who convinces himself he is telling the truth, or is very well rehearsed in his lies, will not be operating in any way differently from a genuine truth teller.

However, the accounts that may be suspicious are a product of what people remember. Therefore questions about the evaluation of the validity of testimony can include both the study of deliberate falsification and failures in remembering. The matter is further complicated by the fact that the accounts that are given emerge within the social context of the interview. There are therefore aspects of the interview process itself which may facilitate or hinder accurate recall or the recognition of falsehoods.

Victimization surveys and official statistics

Victimization surveys entail interviews with community samples concerning their attitudes and experiences of being victims of crime during the preceding 6 or 12 months, and can be carried out at the local or national level (Blackburn, 1994; Coleman and Norris, 2000). They can provide information about who the majority of victims were, and possible characteristics of their offender, with regards to age, sex, socio-economic status, ethnic background, etc. and the types of crimes they have become a victim of (burglaries, assaults, vehicle theft, harassment, property damage, etc.) (Farrington, 1987).

Like the other methods of obtaining information about crimes, victimization surveys also have their benefits and weaknesses. They are subject to sampling errors, accuracy of recall, willingness of victims to report their experiences, as well as interpretation of the coding of offences (Blackburn, 1994). Yet, while official statistics can provide information on the prevalence and incidence rates of crime, this fails to encompass the wide spectrum of crime that is actually being committed by individuals and groups – this is where self-report and victim surveys help to 'fill in the gaps' (Downes and Rock, 1982). They are also not reliant on police processing (i.e. reporting and recording procedures) and can often enlighten victims who are unaware they have even been victimized (Coleman and Norris, 2000).

An important disadvantage with official data is that only a small fraction of the actual amount of crime is recorded. Many of the records also deal only with those crimes where the offender has been identified and there is sufficient evidence against them (Farrington et al, 1988; Svensson, 2002). Two other major disadvantages include the variations in collection protocol leading to incomplete accounts, and the biases that may be present within the data reflecting personal agendas or incomplete or competing views (Farrington et al, 1988; Canter and Alison, 2003), although there have been improvements to unify the way police information is collected and maintained (Canter and Alison, 2003).

The main advantage of these records has been described in detail by Canter and Alison (2003) by exploring their parallel to what Webb et al (1966) called 'unobtrusive and non-reactive' measures. By their very nature and in their collection they do not influence directly the behaviour of the individual. The information is collected, in the main, either to help solve a case and bring it to court, in which case it is essentially thought of by various law enforcement agencies as evidence rather than data, or it is collected to provide official figures for various reports, guiding policy and the overall management of crime.

These records thus cover very many different sorts of information. Canter and Alison (2003) have argued that each needs to be assessed for validity and reliability using criteria specific to the source of the information. Each source also poses its own challenges to the researcher. Crime scene photographs, for instance, demand a very different approach to analysis to summaries of where crimes have taken place.

Reports in the media

An increasing number of researchers draw on published accounts of crime that occur in books and newspapers. These can be remarkably useful sources if treated with caution. Certainly when it comes to major crimes such as terrorist incidents or serial killing, then the published sources may be the only information publically available. They can therefore be drawn on to give accounts of the broad nature, developments and changes in these crimes. However, caution always needs to be exercised when using these sources because there will often be crucial information that the police and security services deliberately keep out of the public domain.

Focus 1.1

Data and methods used in crime psychology research

Official records

Around the world, police authorities and ministries of justice publish records of the crimes that have occurred. These are readily available and are the basis of much quantitative sociology.

Advantages

- The main advantage of these records is that they are unobtrusive in nature, and in their collection they do not influence directly the behaviour of the individual.
- Their official nature also gives them significance in policy-making, which gives added value to any study of them.

As well, they specify the exact dates on which the offences were committed and make it possible to determine the ordering of offences (Farrington et al, 1988).

Disadvantages

- Official data constitute a small fraction of the actual amount of crime recorded.
- It tends to be rather general with little detail or information on individuals or crimes of the form that is of value to psychological research.

Police data

These include victim and witness statements, police interviews, notes and photographs taken at the crime scene and any geographical information.

Continued ...

… Continued

Advantages

- Police data have not been derived under laboratory conditions. Therefore, findings from these studies will be high in *ecological validity*.
- There may be a lot of information about the details of the crime that is not available any other way.
- The information is collected in relation to the requirements of the law and so may be much more thorough than that collected as part of some forms of research.

Disadvantages

- Many crimes go unreported to the police.
- Police data are collected in order to collect evidence, or for official records, rather than for psychological research. Therefore, variables that psychologists may be interested in will not always be recorded in an easily extractable condition, if at all.
- Information is collected in different ways by different police forces and therefore comparison is often difficult.
- In general the police are extremely chary about making any data available to anyone outside of the police force.

Victim surveys

Researchers often use victim surveys as another data source. For example, the British Crime Survey (BCS) is the largest adult victim survey in the UK and is carried out annually.

Advantages

Anonymous surveys may offer a more accurate picture of the incidence of people being victims of crime.

Disadvantages

- Victim surveys may be subject to sample bias. Some populations are under-researched and difficult to study (for example, rape victims who are male or levels of rape within vulnerable populations such as prostitutes or homeless people).
- These surveys tend to have relatively little detailed information about the crime.
- The traumatic nature of the event itself may distort the victims' view of events.
- No information is available about the perpetrators.

Clinical studies of victims

Studies using medical notes from hospitals or special referral centres (as in Sexual Assault Referral Centres – SARCs), especially in violent crimes, can give a lot of detail about the victims and their experiences.

Advantages

As many victims do not report crimes to the police, the results from medical centres may provide a more representative account.

Disadvantages

- Such centres are often based in urban settings. Therefore, results derived from these contexts may not reflect the nature of rape in more rural areas.
- There are very significant problems of confidentiality which may limit access to researchers.
- Medical centres may have different methods of clinical evaluation. Therefore, variations in results between different centres may reflect different protocols.

Offender interviews

Offenders can be interviewed for research purposes, usually in a clinical or prison setting.

Advantages

- Interviews with offenders may provide a greater insight into the reasons why they carry out their crimes or how they may try to justify their offending behaviour.
- The findings may be useful in terms of designing an appropriate therapeutic programme for groups or individuals.

Disadvantages

- Offenders may distort events or lie in the hope that they may get a lesser sentence on conviction or early release from prison.
- Only known offenders, or those who are not transient, will be available for interview.
- Access to some offenders, for example terrorists, may be extremely difficult.
- Unless other records are made available, only the offender's side of the story will be available and the details of the crime may be very limited.

Court reports

The proceedings of courts are usually matters of public record following the famous saying 'Justice must not only be done but be seen to be done'. Increasingly the reports of courts are available online, although usually through subscription services, especially in the USA, e.g. at LexisNexis academic, or www.public-records.com/.

Advantages

- The details of the crime and of the offender are available.
- Information across many jurisdictions can be found.

Disadvantages

- Only the information considered appropriate and relevant to the court case will be recorded.
- Only those crimes that come to court will be available.

Continued …

... Continued

Published open sources in the mass media

Because of the huge interest in crime there are a great many accounts of crime in many different publications ranging from local newspapers to the autobiographies of criminals. A great deal of this information is, inevitably, now available in the World Wide Web.

Advantages

- This information is readily available.
- It covers crimes that occur all over the world and across history.

Disadvantages

- The information contained will relate to what is newsworthy and can be very patchy.
- The accuracy of the information always has to be checked.
- The cases selected will tend to be the unusual and sensational ones.

Areas of contribution

The numerous explorations of the psychology of crime find their way into an increasing range and quantity of contexts. It is perhaps easiest to understand the contributions psychologists are making in terms of the different sorts of institutional settings in which they work. In each of these settings they will be bound by different professional demands and codes of practice. This is leading to rather different professional disciplines emerging in these different areas even though they share a common requirement to understand criminals and criminality.

The area of activity for which crime psychologists are most widely known, which is popularly referred to as 'offender profiling', is actually still the most unusual role for them to take. 'Offender profiling' was always more of a mass media creation than an actual psychological contribution, being much more prevalent in fiction than in fact. The accounts that are given usually owe a great deal more to the adventures of Sherlock Holmes than to any real scientific activity. Nonetheless there is much that psychology can contribute to police and other investigations and it is out of this that the area of investigative psychology has been created, as reviewed extensively in Canter and Youngs (2008a).

Although the first writings on investigative psychology date back less than 20 years (Canter, 1989), the area has developed and expanded very rapidly. Of particular interest has been the emergence of a psychology of the police, especially of investigators. They often have to face very challenging tasks where decisions have to be made under conditions of considerable uncertainty. There is still very little known about how they actually face up to such tasks and the sort of people who are most able to handle them effectively.

Once a criminal comes before a court a new range of psychological issues must be dealt with. Some of these are very much within the realm of clinical psychology when the mental state and capabilities of the defendant are at issue. However, others relate more directly to the sort of cognitive processes that can help the court to understand memory processes. Psychologists take the role of expert witnesses who can comment on the value and validity of information presented before the court, but in most jurisdictions great care is taken to ensure that they do not offer opinions about the innocence or guilt of the accused. Legal systems differ from one area to the next and so the particular role of the psychologist and the sort of topics on which they can give evidence, and how it is required that evidence is presented, will relate very closely to what any particular jurisdiction finds acceptable.

It is probably the case that most criminal psychologists ply their trade with convicted offenders – assessing them and particularly the risk of them re-offending, providing support and treatment. Loosely these may be called prison psychologists, but there are many offenders being appraised and helped in many other institutions besides prisons. The task of these psychologists is an especially difficult one because they have to help people, eventually at least, to cope with the problems of their social environment and community, when the psychologist can have virtually no influence over that context. However, there are some signs that a basic understanding of criminal behaviour, how it emerges and how it is sustained, can give rise to productive interventions with offenders.

It is a moot point whether the experiences of those who suffer crimes, and ways of understanding those experiences and helping people to cope with them, should sit firmly under the heading of criminal psychology. But, as it turns out, many offenders are themselves victims. Furthermore, a great deal can be understood about crime by a careful consideration of who the victims are. Victims are no more randomly distributed through the population than are criminals.

The psychological perspective

Throughout the consideration of the psychology of crime it has been clear that it does not exist as an abstract, independent discipline which operates in a vacuum. At all points it interacts with the demands and processes of other institutions and disciplines and the perspective and constraints of the legal system and society at large. Therefore one of the greatest tasks that confronts psychologists working in this area is to bridge the gap between psychology and the other related legal disciplines. As Canter (2008) has expressed it, there are a variety of valid perspectives on crime and the challenge is to bridge the gap between them. Central to this is the need to deal with the tendency for the social sciences to look for causes of criminality outside of the direct agency of the person committing the crime, whereas the law and public debate puts great emphasis on the conscious intentions of the offender. Lawyers and those involved in the legal profession formulate the questions they consider it important to answer in quite a different way from social scientists. They are looking for definitive answers that relate to specific cases, as compared with the general trends that characterize the conclusions reached by psychologists. There are also differences in pragmatic issues that relate to the ways the different communities go about answering these questions. The courts and investigators look for evidence that will point to innocence or guilt. By contrast, psychologists look for statistical significance that emerges out of scientific studies. At the heart of these differences are very diverse attitudes towards the nature of evidence, as well as differences in the central models of what the nature of human beings is.

Conclusions

The psychology of crime covers a very wide range of human activity from the most mundane acts of minor theft, or the daily occurrence of deception, through to the outrages of serial killing and terrorism. It consequently connects with very many other disciplines across the spectrum of professions and sciences. The central challenges of the psychology of crime are, on the one hand, the access to valid, reliable, robust and representative data about crimes and criminals, and on the other the building of effective bridges with the many other perspectives for which the psychology of crime is relevant.

In a concise volume such as the present one it is impossible even to touch on all the very many topics that fit under this broad umbrella. Therefore, where reasonably up-to-date books already exist that deal with major topics such as psychology in prisons (Towl, 2006), or psychology in the courtroom (Lieberman and Kraus, 2008) or the considerable range of connections between psychology and the law (Brewer and Williams, 2005; Canter and Zukauskiene, 2008), then only a brief overview of these topics is given in the present volume. The considerable literature on clinical psychology applications in the legal context is also only touched on very briefly in the current volume. Roesch and McLachlan (2007) have brought together an encyclopaedic collection of papers dealing with these issues, emphasizing assessment and treatment. A more distilled set of accounts is provided in McGuire et al (2000).

This rapidly growing area of study and practise seems set to continue expanding into ever wider areas of research and application. This will in part be shaped by developments in criminality. It will also be influenced by the areas of success that psychologists have already had, leading to the opening of doors into as yet unseen areas of law enforcement and offender rehabilitation.

Key concepts and terms

Classification of crimes
Criminality
Deception
Explanations of crime

Forensic psychology
Investigative psychology
Sources of data
The criminal process

Sample essay titles

- What are the main differences between studying crime and studying criminals?

- Review the various sources of information for studying criminals with their strengths and weaknesses.

- Could you ever study crime under controlled laboratory conditions?

- What are the main ways in which psychology can contribute to the control and management of crime?

- What do you think are the main differences between legal testimony and research data and what implications do you think this has for the understanding of criminality?

Further reading

Books

Brewer, N., and Williams, K.D. (Eds) (2005). *Psychology and Law: An Empirical Perspective*. London: Guilford.

Canter, D., and Youngs, D. (2008a). *Investigative Psychology: Offender Profiling and the Analysis of Criminal Action*. Chichester: Wiley.

Canter, D., and Zukauskiene, R. (Eds) (2008). *Psychology and Law: Bridging the Gap*. Aldershot: Ashgate.

Wrightsman, L.S., Nietzel, M.T., and Fortune, W.H. (1998). *Psychology and the Legal System*, (4th Ed.). London: Brooks/Cole.

Journal articles

Canter, D., and Alison, L.J. (2003). Converting evidence into data: The use of law enforcement archives as unobtrusive measurement. *The Qualitative Report*, 8, 151–176.

Haney, C. (1993). Psychology and legal change: The impact of a decade. *Law and Human Behaviour*, 17, 371–398.

Monahan, J., and Walker, L. (1988). Social science research in law: A new paradigm. *American Psychologist*, 43, 465–472.

Otto, R.K., and Heilbrun, K. (2002). The practice of forensic psychology: A look toward the future in light of the past. *American Psychologist*, 57, 5–18.

2 Individualistic explanations of crime

Maria Ioannou

Explanations of how and why crimes occur can be broadly divided into those that, on the one hand, put the emphasis on processes within the person. These may be aspects of the person's biological and physiological makeup or more general psychological aspects of the offender, relating to their cognitive processes and personality. The present chapter reviews these individualistic explanations. The second group of explanations – those that look to the interpersonal and social processes of which a person is a part – are dealt with in the next chapter.

Learning outcomes

When you have completed this chapter you should be able to:

1. Understand the major biological approach to explaining crime.
2. Understand the evidence offered for these biological explanations.
3. Be aware of the dominant critiques of these explanations.
4. Know about the neurological and related explanations.
5. Understand the psychological explanations for crimes.

The biological approach explaining the causes of crime

Biological theories of crime and delinquency see the root causes in the 'nature' of the particular person; in their actual makeup and individual **psychology**. They assume, in their most simplistic form, that offenders are born, not made (Martin, 2005). Their crimes are seen as a product of their **heredity**. More generally, in extreme cases, it is argued that for example the crime of rape is part of human evolution, and thus in some senses a 'natural' phenomenon (Thornhill and Thornhill, 1987). These sorts of explanations are regarded as *reductionist* because they imply that complex human interactions can be reduced to basic biological causes. They are often also referred to as *deterministic* because they imply that the actions of people can be determined from an identifiable number of specific causes.

Some of the earliest versions of these theories gave rise to the view that if criminals were born there ought to be some indications in what could be observed about them to show their criminal propensity. Fuller and Thompson (1978) discuss how Johan Lavater's *Physiognomy* (judging character based on the expressions of the face) and Franz Gall's phrenology (the study of the shape and protuberances of the skull, used to reveal the character and mental capacity of a person) were used to suggest that personality abnormalities were apparent in what a person looked like. Furthermore, if criminality was embedded in human evolutionary past, then the indicators of criminal potential would be revealed in what they looked like.

Cesare Lombroso took this evolutionary idea so seriously that in 1887 he published *L'Homme Criminel* which contained 64 pages of pictures of what criminals were thought typically to look like, as discussed by Martin (2005). Lombroso (1876), an Italian physician and 'criminal anthropologist', linked facial features and criminality. He argued that criminals represented a genetically primitive species that had not yet evolved. He suggested this difference was obvious in their faces and physical abnormalities such as asymmetrical skull, large ears, flattened or crooked nose, fat lips, enormous jaws and high cheekbones. These ideas were enormously influential until some carefully conducted research by Goring (1913) showed that they had no validity at all.

Today, however, not even the most fundamentalist believers in the biological basis of criminality such as Rowe (2001) totally ignore other influencing factors such as the opportunities the environment provides and the social factors that influence what is thought to be criminal. Nonetheless the distinguishing feature of these explanations is the considerable emphasis they place on the role of the individual, the person's own characteristics being the primary cause of crime. These theories take the stand that some individuals are more likely to become criminals than others because of innate, congenital factors. Innate refers to genetic inheritance from parents. The congenital factors are taken to be what is present at birth together with influences of the uterine and perinatal environment. The constitutional aspects of the person are most readily understood as the phenotypic characteristics of the individual, such as morphology and physique, resulting from the interaction between the person's genetic makeup and the environment.

Constitutional theories

Despite the demise of Lombroso's claims there have been a number of other theories that suggest that the physical makeup of criminals distinguishes them from non-criminals. The most notable of these was Sheldon's (1942) constitutional theory. He described three basic body types which he believed were correlated with particular types of personality:

- Thin and bony ectomorphs, who were introverted and restrained.

- Large and heavy endomorphs, who were sociable and relaxed.

- Broad and muscular mesomorphs, who were aggressive and adventurous.

He argued, after studying criminals, that they were more mesomorphic and less ectomorphic, a finding supported by Glueck and Glueck (1956) who found that 57 per cent of their criminal sample were mesomorphic and 16 per cent ectomorphic, compared with 19 and 33 per cent, respectively, of controls.

Possibly more understandable has been the exploration of disfigurement in offenders. Masters and Greaves (1969) showed that 60 per cent of 11,000 prisoners had facial deformities compared with 20 per cent in a non-criminal population, and Agnew (1984) found that schoolchildren rated as unattractive self-reported higher delinquency. Thompson (1990) estimated that, in any given year, there are 250,000 disfigured offenders in US prisons. Recent research has focused on 'minor physical anomalies' (MPAs) such as asymmetrical ears or webbed toes, and there is evidence that these correlate with delinquency (Arseneault et al, 2000a). These more recent studies, though, do not claim that disfigurement is the direct cause of criminality. Rather it may be that some people who are facially unattractive or have MPAs are judged in negative terms and may not have the same opportunities or may react to the perceptions of others in ways that lead into offending. But it is also possible that offenders, especially those who have spent time in prison, may have suffered assault and poor diet and hygiene because of their incarceration, or indeed because of the social circumstances from which they emerge, so that their physique or appearance is a product of their criminal activity rather than a cause of it.

Genetic inheritance

The difficulties of disentangling genetic influences from environmental causes of crime have given rise to many studies that attempt to distinguish the different processes involved. The main research procedures for doing this have looked at families, twins and adoptees.

Family studies

Family studies compare criminal behaviour of the biological relatives of offenders and non-offenders. The argument is that if criminality is inherited, criminal families will tend to produce criminal children, as is consistently found in studies going back more than a century. In a major Cambridge study, it was found that boys with a criminal father were twice as likely to become delinquent as those with non-criminal fathers (West, 1982). Osborn and West (1979) showed that about 40 per cent of the sons of criminal fathers were criminals themselves compared with 13 per cent for sons of non-criminal fathers.

Research methods 2.1

The Cambridge study in delinquent development was conducted by Farrington and West (1990). It was a longitudinal study of the development of offending and antisocial behaviour aiming to examine whether teenage delinquents become adult offenders. The sample was 411 white working-class boys who at that time were all living in a working-class deprived inner-city area of South London. The boys were 8–9 years old in 1961 and were followed for 30 years with regular interviews.

Continued ...

... Continued

The study found that of those convicted of an offence between the ages of 10 and 16, 75 per cent were reconvicted between the ages of 17 and 24, and 50 per cent reconvicted between the ages of 25 and 32. The study also highlighted a number of common factors in persisting offending such as poor and large families, poor housing, parental neglect and parental criminality.

Note: There are more recent papers that report findings of the criminal careers of these boys up to the age of 50 (Farrington et al, 2006).

However, a correlation between parental and children's criminality does not prove that a causal relationship exists. It may be that environmental factors such as low income, large families, and social and psychological factors within the family are involved in the transmission of values and behaviour (Hollin, 1989) from generation to generation rather than genetic factors. More precise studies of twins have therefore been carried out in an attempt to determine more precisely the likely power of genetics in relation to environment.

Twin studies

Both identical (monozygotic or MZ) and fraternal (dizygotic or DZ) twins have been studied in an attempt to examine the relationship between inheritance and criminal behaviour. MZ twins develop from the splitting of a single egg at the time of conception and so share a very high proportion of the same genes. It is often thought that they are totally identical but there is the possibility for random variations and different influences in the womb that make them appear different. DZ twins, though, just like any other siblings, share about 50 per cent of their genes. So, when DZ twins share the same environment, any major differences between them are very likely to be due to genetic variation. Thus any differences between MZ and DZ twins are usually regarded as an indication of the power of genetics.

Lange's (1931) twin study was one of the first to demonstrate concordance (the degree to which related pairs of subjects within a study population display the same behaviour) for criminal behaviour. He reported 77 per cent for 13 pairs of identical twins and 12 per cent for 17 pairs of fraternal twins. Other studies have found differences in the same direction but not always to the same degree. In general, the average concordance rate for MZ twins is 55 per cent and for DZ twins 17 per cent (Bartol, 1999), favouring the idea of some genetic influence on criminality. These findings, though, are inconclusive in the absence of data on twins reared apart. Critics argue that the phenotypic similarities of MZ twins entail a closer relationship, more similar treatment by parents and therefore similar interests, behaviour and social responses. As a consequence it may be these social processes that give rise to the concordance rather than genetics.

Adoption studies

Another strategy that helps to determine the impact of genetics is to consider people who have been adopted and therefore brought up by people who are not their biological parents. The view is that to some degree this separates out the influence of genetics from the influence of family environment. This may not be as straightforward as may seem at first sight. The whole process of adoption and indeed how people come to be adopted into families that are criminal, or adopted from families that are criminal, raises many questions that go beyond genetics.

One of the first studies of criminality in relation to adoption was by Crowe (1974) who found that in a sample of adopted children whose biological mothers had a criminal record, almost 50 per cent of adoptees had a criminal record by 18 years of age, while only about 5 per cent of the adoptees whose mothers had no criminal record had been convicted for a criminal offence. In a much larger study Hutchings and Mednick (1975) looked at over 1000 adoptees. They found that 21.4 per cent of sons became criminal when the biological father was criminal, 11.5 per cent when the adoptive father was criminal and 10.5 per cent when neither father was criminal. However, if both fathers had criminal records the percentage of adoptees with criminal records was higher at 36.2 per cent. Mednick et al (1984), in their study with a sample of 14,427 adoptees, also showed that the percentage of criminal adoptees is higher when both fathers are criminal (Table 2.1). All these studies imply a modest genetic contribution to crime and show that interaction between genetic and environmental factors appears to be crucial.

Biological parents criminal	Adoptive parents criminal	Percentage of criminal sons
Yes	Yes	24.5
Yes	No	20
No	Yes	14.7
No	No	13.5

Table 2.1 Results from Mednick et al (1984)

In reality no one can predict the consequence of family history on likely criminality with any certainty. There are children with criminal parents who experience adverse environments and yet do not commit crimes, and there are children with non-criminal parents, raised in seemingly good environments, that become criminals. 'The question of just what is inherited remains unanswered; it is unlikely to be criminality as such' (Rutter and Giller, 1983: 179).

Comparison of twins reared together with those reared apart

Many researchers have pointed out that one further step towards unravelling the confounding variables that confuse studies of the influence of genetic processes is to compare MZ twin pairs who have been raised separately with those who have been brought up in the same family. As Ainsworth (2001), among others (e.g. Hollin, 1989), points out, the argument here is that if identical twins reared apart still show high concordance rates then this must be explained by reference to genetic factors. As Joseph (2003) points out, in an extensive review of genetic factors in psychology and psychiatry, there have not really been any major studies that make such comparisons.

One reason for this is the simple practical one that there are very few twin pairs who are separated at birth and, of those who are, relatively few will have developed criminal records. Case studies of individual pairs of twins reared apart do sometimes show dramatic similarities, but without knowing the frequency with which such similarities occur, it is always possible that they come to notice because they are so unusual. In one of the few studies relevant to criminality that did consider 32 MZ twins reared apart since shortly after birth, Grove et al (1990) measured a variety of 'subclinical manifestations of antisocial problems'. Grove found some concordance that indicated genetic influences for both childhood conduct disorders and adult antisocial behaviours (correlation of 0.28). However, the former produced a correlation of 0.41 which only accounts for around 16 per cent of the covariance. The adult behaviours were reported to correlate at 0.28, which is less than 8 per cent of the covariance. So although this does show some genetic influence for aspects of the individuals that may be a precursor to criminality the data suggest that environmental factors may be much more significant.

Chromosomal abnormalities

A fundamental problem with twin and adoption studies is that the genetic influence has to be inferred from a complex mix of environmental factors and interactions between the people and their surroundings. A much more direct genetic link can be claimed if some aspect of a person's genetic makeup can be observed directly. Examining a person's chromosomes would seem to offer the possibility of observing the genetic causes directly. The chromosome is a single long molecule of DNA which contains the genetic material that influences many of the individual's biological characteristics. Humans normally have 46 chromosomes in pairs: 44 autosomes (that determine the shape and constitution of the body), and two sex chromosomes (that determine the gender), XX for females and XY for males. A variety of chromosomal abnormalities exist, some of which involve the presence of extra chromosomes such as the XYY syndrome.

This extra Y chromosome in males has been linked to above average height, borderline intelligence and violent criminal behaviour. Sandberg et al (1961) were the first to associate the XYY syndrome and violent crime. Witkin et al (1976) examined 4591 men for the presence of the extra Y chromosome and identified only 12 cases. They also found that these men were more likely to be involved in crime (41.7 per cent) but not violent. Researchers are mixed in their conclusions. Not all the individuals with XYY syndrome are criminals and the vast majority of criminals do not have any chromosomal abnormality.

The XYY syndrome helps to illustrate that even if a particular chromosome or mix of chromosomes were found to exist in many offenders that would still be a long way from demonstrating that genetics was the cause of criminality. It would be essential to demonstrate that non-criminals did not have this genetic background and the biological mechanisms would need to be elaborated to show how the genetic makeup gave rise to the criminal actions. Since crimes are socially defined and there are many ways in which people can express their potential it does seem rather unlikely that a 'crime gene' will ever be found. However, there may be aspects of individuals that make the possibility of them becoming criminal more likely under particular circumstances, but those aspects are far more probable at the level of the person than something as specific as their genetic structure.

Biochemical explanations

Before considering more general psychological factors it is useful to review aspects of the person that relate to their **biology** at any point in time. This may have genetic roots but can also be a direct product of environmental factors at many stages in life from the womb through to matters such as diet and substance abuse in later life. Some research does indicate that criminal behaviour may be related to a range of such biological factors inherent in a person's biochemistry, for example their hormones.

The hormones that have been most commonly considered as relevant to criminality are those secreted by the gonads (androgens and oestrogens), the adrenals (adrenaline and noradrenaline) and the pancreas (insulin). Broadly speaking, there are suggestions from research studies that excessive androgen levels may increase the probability of antisocial behaviour, and higher testosterone levels have been found in aggressive prisoners. This would certainly help to explain the very great preponderance of men among criminal populations, except that there are many criminals who do not show high levels of hormonal activity.

Aspects of diet such as vitamin and mineral deficiency, levels of protein and carbohydrate, as well as allergic reactions and food additives have also been studied in relation to criminal behaviour. Hypoglycaemia (low blood sugar) may affect the functioning of the brain and contribute to violent behaviour (Virkkunen, 1986). In addition, environmental conditions, e.g. the presence of lead or radiation from artificial lighting, have been linked to criminal behaviour. Low levels of serotonin, a key neurochemical, have been associated with impulsive behaviour. A number of studies showed a link between low serotonin levels and aggression (Moir and Jessel, 1995). The difficulty with all these explanations is that there are often many other factors that are also associated with diet, such as general economic deprivation or membership of particular social subgroups, which may be the influential factors.

Neurological explanations

An apparently more direct exploration of the processes within the person that may be an important part of that person's antisocial or offending activity is to examine neurophysiological and neurological functioning. This is an area of study that is developing rapidly as ever more sophisticated ways of measuring brain functioning are becoming available. The relatively simple process of measuring the electrical activity of the brain using electroencephalograms (EEG) has indicated that there are high-frequency abnormalities relating to frontal and left hemispheric dysfunction in aggressive and psychopathic criminals (Blackburn, 1993). Other studies failed to show similar results (Pillman et al, 1999). However, the literature contains many inconsistencies, mainly due to unreliability and confusions in what EEG is actually measuring. It could be suggested that trying to understand what is going on in a person's brain by measuring the surface electrical currents is a little like trying to understand what is wrong with a car engine by listening to the noises it makes. Very obvious and specific faults may be apparent to the expert, but even then the expert can understand what is happening because he or she knows exactly how a car engine works. The same cannot be said of the infinitely more complex human brain.

Brain damage due to perinatal complications, head injuries, tumours and infections has also been linked to crime. Similarly, attention deficit hyper-activity disorder (ADHD), minimal brain dysfunction (MBD), dyspraxia or

Focus 2.1

The case of Charles Whitman

Charles Whitman (1941–1966) was the eldest of three brothers raised in Florida. At the age of six he had scored 138 on an IQ test, he was a pitcher on his high school's baseball team and took piano lessons. All three brothers served as altar boys at Sacred Heart Roman Catholic Church and at 12 Charles was the youngest ever to achieve Eagle Scout.

Figure 2.1 Charles Whitman.
Source: © Bettman/Corbis.

In 1959, against his father's wishes, he joined the Marines. Following his enlistment, he was accepted into the University of Texas mechanical engineering programme where he met and married his wife in 1962. In 1966, Charles was diagnosed with depression that he attributed to his parents' separation and his increasing strains at work and school. On 1 August 1966, while still a student, he shot and killed 14 people in a day and wounded 31 others, shooting them from a university tower. He did this shortly after murdering his wife and mother. He was eventually shot and killed by the police. Autopsy revealed that he had a large brain tumour in the amygdala.

developmental coordination disorder and epilepsy have also been linked to antisocial and criminal behaviour. Such conditions may cause dramatic personality and behavioural changes but cases like these are rare and it is not clear that they are the direct and only cause in cases of violent behaviour. In general, brain pathology is difficult to detect and diagnose. It is always associated with other forms of trauma that relate to life-changing circumstances, so even if there is a causal relationship it may well be confounded with interactions with environmental or other circumstances. Nonetheless there are striking case studies that show in very rare and unusual cases remarkable changes in people following brain damage, including the sudden emergence of special skills as well as extreme violence. From what is known of the brain it would be remarkable if there were not situations in which injury to it did not affect behaviour.

Psychological theories

All the genetic and biological explanations of crime deal with the individual very much as an organism with virtually no attention to thought processes, understanding of morality or emotional aspects of wrongdoing. Yet most attempts to explain what aspects of the individual are responsible for crime focus on these sorts of psychological factors. There is a great range of these forms of explanation. They run from those that are distinctly within the individual, assuming a profound psychological depth to the causes of crime, to those that are much more about how the person makes sense of and deals with the world.

Psychoanalytic theories

Psychoanalytic theories stress the role of inner processes, conflicts and childhood events as determinants of behaviour. Sigmund Freud's view that the child is motivated by pleasure-seeking and self-destructive impulses has been developed in order to explain adult criminal behaviour. While psychoanalytic ideas come originally from Freud, he had little to say about crime. Aichhorn (1925) was the first person to apply psychoanalytic ideas to the explanation of crime following his work with delinquent children. He proposed that criminal behaviour is the result of what he called 'latent delinquency', which is innate but also determined by the child's early emotional relationships. Aichorn's view was that each child is asocial in the early years and becomes more socialized, behaving according to social rules, with the emergence of the ego and the operation of the 'reality principle'. For some individuals this process does not occur and 'latent delinquency' becomes dominant, a state which Aichhorn describes as 'dissocial'. The criminal behaviour is therefore the result of a failure of psychological development (Hollin, 1989). Put at its most elementary, this theory is not quite as challenging as may first appear from its psychoanalytic trappings. It is really the notion that criminals, especially young ones, have not grown up properly and are still operating in a child-like search for immediate gratification without regard for the consequences.

Healy and Bronner (1936) use sublimation, another psychoanalytic concept, to explain crime. Sublimation is the process by which instinctual impulses are channelled into other thoughts, emotions and behaviours. Their belief was that criminal behaviour results from inner, unsatisfied desires that are a result of a failure to experience early emotional ties. Criminal behaviour is, therefore, a sublimation (acting out) of inner desires that cannot find expression in other ways. These may be the desire for status or feelings of self-worth, or more direct urges for gratification.

Bowlby's (1944) theory of crime being a result of breakdown in attachment between child and parents, especially the mother, has its roots in psychoanalytic theory but moves far beyond the reliance on hidden primitive urges. He argued that delinquency was linked to maternal deprivation and suggested that any disruption of the attachment bond between mother and child in the early years might lead to later deviance. He said this was mainly because of the consequent inability of the child to develop any meaningful relationships. He studied 44 juvenile thieves that were compared with a matched group of non-delinquents and found that 39 per cent of the former group had experienced complete separation from their mothers for six months or more in the first five years of their lives compared to 5 per cent of the non-delinquent group. The difficulty of accepting his conclusions from this study relates in part to his small sample, but more to the difficulty of matching children who have been separated and those who have not. The reasons for their separation, such as illness of the child or the mother, or more directly socio-economic reasons, may themselves have an influence on the child's development.

Over the century since Freud first outlined his theory of **psychoanalysis** there has been extensive criticism of the whole approach because of the difficulty of testing the proposals that derive from it or of measuring the inner mechanisms that are put forward to explain the purported processes. This has not prevented psychoanalytic vocabulary and assumptions pervading most aspects of modern discourse.

Eysenk's personality theory

Hans Eysenck devoted much effort to debunking psychoanalytic theories, claiming that subconscious urges should be jettisoned in favour of a mixture of biological and social factors that give rise to distinct differences in personality. Eysenck (1977) proposed that there are three major dimensions that underlie personality, each of which is independent of the others: neuroticism (N), extraversion (E) and psychoticism (P). Each of these dimensions is conceived as a continuum with most people falling in the middle range; comparatively few people fall at the extremes of each scale.

Eysenck suggests that 'In general terms, we would expect persons with strong antisocial inclinations to have high P, high E, and high N scores' (1977: 58). He believed that certain personality types were inclined towards crime and these individuals could be described as neurotic extraverts, sensation seekers, characterized by high levels of anxiety and depression, and aggressive, cold and impersonal behaviour (Eysenck and Gudjonsson, 1989). Offenders have been found to score highly on all three dimensions, although this finding is not consistent. In general, more research supports that offenders score high on P and N (e.g. Silva et al, 1986) but the evidence is mixed for E. Some studies reported high

Figure 2.2 The Kray Twins. Were these violent men created or born to control the London underworld in the 1950s and 60s? How was it that only one of these identical twins was diagnosed with schizophrenia?
Source: Popperfoto/Getty Images.

E scores in criminal samples, others found no difference between criminals and non-criminals, and a few studies reported lower scores in offenders (Hollin, 1989).

Cognition and crime

Many conclusions from psychoanalysis and from Eysenck's personality theory can be expressed in simpler and more focused ways as aspects of how the person understands their actions or typically interacts in relation to others. This has been reflected in a growing area of research that looks at offender's cognitions to explain criminal behaviour. The term **cognition** is used to describe how individuals think about people and their actions. Studies of cognition have led to the proposal that offenders may have ways of thinking or reacting to events, sometimes referred to as cognitive styles, which are different to non-criminals. This view is expressed most clearly and strongly by Yochelson and Samenow (1976) who describe the 'criminal thinking patterns' that they believe characterize all criminals. They list over 40 different styles and errors of thinking, such as concrete thinking, fragmentation, failure to empathize with others, lack of trust, an opinion of oneself as good, irresponsible decision-making, super-optimism, and perceiving themselves as victims, that define the criminal mind.

Other researchers have focused on particular aspects of offenders' modes of cognition, each giving emphasis to one dominant aspect:

Locus of control

This refers to the degree to which individuals perceive their behaviour to be under their own internal control, or under the control of external forces, such as luck, fate or authority figures (Rotter, 1966). Some studies have shown that offenders tend to have an external locus of control (not taking responsibility for their actions) while other studies failed to do so; the evidence is contradictory. The problem may in part be due to the attempt to generalize the results to all crime. Canter et al (2003b) have suggested that some offenders, such as those who carry out violent assaults, may believe they are at the mercy of the fates, whereas others such as burglars believe they are very much in charge of their lives, taking what they want.

Neutralization and attributional processes

Neutralizations are temporary excuses or rationalizations such as denial of responsibility (one's actions are a consequence of external factors, such as poverty, broken home or drunkenness), denial of injury (little harm is entailed), denial of victim (victim deserves it), condemnation of the condemners (critical of criminal justice system) or appeal to higher loyalties (e.g. peers) (Sykes and Matza, 1957). This includes a *hostile attribution bias*. Research has shown that offenders often have a hostile attribution bias. They see aggression and violence where there is none and are more likely to interpret ambiguous actions as hostile and threatening (Dodge, 1986). The difficulty of seeing these perspectives as the initial causes of crime is that the results have to be based on the accounts offenders themselves give, once they are caught. There is therefore likely to be a great deal of justification in their responses, attempting to explain away their actions.

Lack of empathy

This could be seen as another aspect of the same attributional process. It refers to a person's inability to see a situation from the perspective of others and the inability to respond to their feelings. A consistent finding with offenders is that they see situations only from their own perspective, not appreciating the view of the other person. Although it is presented as a relatively distinct explanation of criminality, there are parallels in Bowlby's (1944) concern with the inability of delinquents to form deep or lasting relationships. More recently the difficulty of relating effectively to others has been seen as a problem in *social skills*. Sarason (1968) was among the first to suggest that delinquents are deficient in socially acceptable and adaptive behaviour, and social skills training has become a popular technique in the 'treatment' of offenders. Indeed, the whole move towards what is known as 'restorative justice', in which offenders meet their victims and learn from them about the experience of suffering crimes, can be seen to be based in attempts to develop criminals' empathy and ability to understand how to interact effectively with others.

Self-control

Lack of self-control, impulsivity and inability to delay reward have been associated with criminal behaviour. This, of course, is a reflection of the sorts of processes that Aichhorn (1925) drew attention to when describing offenders as immature. However, it is much more likely to be present in younger offenders or substance abusers. It hardly describes a person who spends months carefully planning a bank raid or even a murder.

Problem-solving and decision-making

One debate in the literature is emerging, implicitly at least, between those psychologists who see criminals as having difficulties in *problem-solving* and those who propose that they actually make carefully thought through, rational *decisions*. The former argue that offenders lack the ability to make appropriate judgements in difficult social situations and to generate a range of solutions to social problems or ambiguous social experiences (Freedman et al, 1978; Higgins and Thies, 1981). Offenders, it is claimed, tend to show poorer cognitive skills here compared to non-offenders. The alternative perspective portrays offenders as rational decision-makers who weigh the possible consequences of their actions, both positive and negative, and take advantage of a criminal opportunity only if it is in their interest to do so (Cornish and Clark, 1986; Hollin, 1989). Opportunity, skills, resources (tools and equipment), risk involved (bystanders, intervention by police, detection), target (vulnerability, pay-off, etc.) and cost of offending are all considered. As is so often the case for opposing arguments, the chances are that both have some validity under different circumstances.

Cognitive scripts

Another line of research has concentrated on *cognitive scripts* (Huesmann, 1988). A 'script' is the details of how people should behave in a certain situation and what will happen if they behave that way. These are learnt from the environment in direct experience and from watching others, and from the media. But each 'script' is unique to an individual and resistant to change, especially when repeated and rehearsed over time. An individual with poorly integrated internal standards against aggression, or who is convinced that aggressive behaviour is a way of life, is more likely to incorporate aggressive scripts for behaviour. Canter (1994) and Canter et al (2003b) have developed this perspective further by exploring the personal or *inner narrative* that criminals have. These narratives are seen as encapsulating the concept the offenders have of themselves and their actions as played out in various episodes. These are reflected in the implicit, and sometimes explicit, roles they see themselves as playing, for example as a hero, or victim, professional or adventurer.

Activity 2.1

John is serving a sentence for assault. According to him the violence was justified as he was provoked by his victim. It all happened on a train when one man asked him to move from a booked seat. The man was insisting that the seat was his and after a while John moved to a nearby seat but not before verbally abusing his victim. After a while he noticed that the man who had asked him to move a while ago was now looking at John and laughing. John stood up and violently attacked him which resulted in his victim ending up in hospital with serious injuries.

- What cognitive style is John using?
- How does John justify his violence?
- What possible explanations are there for John's behaviour?

Moral development and crime

One particular cognitive perspective on criminals is to consider that they are just less morally developed than those who do not commit crimes. Kohlberg (1976) developed Piaget's (1959) theory of cognitive development and proposed that there were direct analogies in moral development. Kohlberg proposed three levels of moral reasoning, each having two stages (Table 2.2). He suggested that each stage is shaped by the one before and that an individual progresses from stage to stage sequentially.

Level 1: Pre-conventional morality: authority is outside the individual and reasoning is based on the physical consequences of actions
Stage 1: Moral behaviour is based on concrete rules; no internalization of moral standards; rules are kept in order to avoid punishment
Stage 2: Each person seeks the maximum return to him/herself; there is consideration of others only when it benefits itself
Level 2: Conventional morality: authority is internalized but not questioned and reasoning is based on the norms of the group to which the person belongs
Stage 3: Persons conform and adjust to others; socially acceptable standards are important
Stage 4: There is a respect for those in command, such as social and religious authorities; respect for law and order; obedience to authority
Level 3: Post-conventional morality: individual judgement is based on self-chosen principles and moral reasoning is based on individual rights and justice
Stage 5: The majority opinion of society is important
Stage 6: People assume personal responsibility for their actions based on universal ethical and moral principles which are not necessarily laid down by society; self-chosen ethical guidelines based on equality and respect for all

Table 2.2 Kohlberg's stages of moral development (1976)

Kohlberg regards moral reasoning as a very important mediator of moral action and concludes that delinquents are more likely to demonstrate pre-conventional reasoning. Some research has indeed shown that delinquents operate at lower levels of moral reasoning than non-delinquents (Brugman and Aleva, 2004). On the other hand, Thornton and Reid (1982) found that convicted criminals who committed serious crimes without financial gain (murder, assault, sex offences) showed higher levels of moral reasoning than those who offended for money (robbery, burglary, theft, fraud) suggesting the possibility that the crimes more likely to be associated with lower levels of moral reasoning are the less serious ones.

Intelligence

Many of the claims for deficiencies in cognitive abilities, whether it be inability to see the consequence of one's actions, the lack of empathy or the lower moral development, could all be seen as part of some general intellectual weakness on the part of offenders. This is supported by a number of studies that have revealed that the average criminal is below average intelligence. However, the findings are, as so often in studies of criminals, not as strong as might be expected.

Recent studies found that the average intelligence of offenders is only slightly below average with an average IQ of 92 compared to the average of the general population of 100. So although this is a statistically significant difference it cannot be the sole cause of criminality, and of course it implies that many offenders are above average intelligence and many people below average intelligence never offend. Earlier studies found average IQs of around 70 but there is doubt over the validity of these studies now (Brewer, 2000). The Cambridge study also found offenders to be of low intelligence. Of those who subsequently became delinquent, 39 per cent had an IQ of less than 90 at age 8, compared with 22 per cent of non-delinquents (West, 1982). More recent research reached the conclusion that IQ is only weakly related to criminality (Cullen et al, 1997). Other studies suggest that higher intelligence is a protective factor against criminal development in those who are at risk for criminality (Blackburn, 1993). Despite the fact that a link between crime and low IQ seems to exist, some offenders will be found to have high IQ scores, especially those involved in organized and corporate crime that require considerable skills. Reviews also have shown that juveniles with IQs over 115 are less often caught.

Conclusions

We have seen that in general terms criminals are seen as defective in some way. They have not bonded with their mothers, they are more neurotic, show less empathy, and have lower intelligence and fewer social and cognitive skills. They will tend to deny the role that society applies to their actions, regarding themselves as the victims not the people who suffer their crimes. There are attempts to link this to their genetic makeup, biology or hormones. This must be an over-simplification on a number of counts. Crimes are hugely diverse in their nature; most studies have relatively weak findings or are inconclusive, and reveal wide ranges of scores on any measures. Thus although there are without doubt aspects of people who commit crimes that, in very broad terms, distinguish them from the population at large, these individualistic explanations of crime cannot be the whole story.

Key concepts and terms

Biology
Cognition
Heredity

Psychoanalysis
Psychology

Sample essay titles

- What does it matter if crime is caused by nature or nurture?

- What are the implications for interventions with criminals of individualistic explanations for the causes of crime?

- Why is it so difficult to determine if crime is inherited?

- How might a person's cognitive processes give rise to criminality?

- Are criminals different from those who do not commit crimes?

Further reading

Books

Bartol, C.R. (1999). *Criminal Behavior: A Psychosocial Approach*. Englewood Cliffs, NJ: Prentice-Hall.

Blackburn, R. (1993). *The Psychology of Criminal Conduct*. Chichester: Wiley.

Hollin, C. (1989). *Psychology and Crime: An Introduction to Criminological Psychology*. London: Routledge.

Journal articles

Arseneault, L., Tremblay, R.E., Boulerice, B., Seguin, J.R., and Saucier, J-F. (2000a). Minor physical anomalies and family adversity as risk factors for violent delinquency in adolescence. *American Journal of Psychiatry*, 157, 917–923.

Mednick, S.A., Gabrielli, W.F., and Hutchings, B. (1984). Genetic influences in criminal convictions: Evidence from an adoption cohort. *Science*, 224, 891–894.

Sykes, G.M., and Matza, D. (1957). Techniques of neutralisation: A theory of delinquency. *American Sociological Review*, 22, 664–673.

Thompson, K.M. (1990). Refacing inmates: A critical appraisal of plastic surgery programs in prison. *Criminal Justice and Behaviour*, 17, 448–466.

3 Social explanations of crime

Maria Ioannou and Shannon Vettor

A common set of explanations for causes of crime relate to the person's interactions with others. At the heart of these theories is the view that people learn, either directly or indirectly, to offend. This may be direct learning of how to commit crimes as well as the absorption of a moral code in which criminality is acceptable. This can include recognition that others regard the person as criminal and therefore channelling actions to fit those expectations. The different stages in personal development at which people do enter into this criminal ambience may also affect how longstanding is their criminality.

Learning outcomes

When you have completed this chapter you should be able to:

1. Understand the role of learning in committing crimes.
2. Know about the major **social psychological theories of criminal behaviour.**
3. Be aware of the variations in criminality of different genders.
4. Understand the concept of a criminal career and development in criminality.
5. Know about the role of families and schools as causes of criminality.

Learning theories

Instrumental or operant

According to all learning theories human behaviour, whether criminal or not, is learned. The dominant forms of learning that are considered in the context of crime are instrumental or operant learning, and social learning. Skinner (1953) formulated the principles of operant learning which led to the emergence and growth of *behaviourism*. The basic principle of operant learning is that human behaviour and as a result criminal behaviour is learned and strengthened because of the reinforcements it brings. Behaviour that produces desirable consequences will be reinforced and therefore repeated. Behaviour that has negative consequences is said to be punished and therefore not repeated. Punishment should be distinguished from negative reinforcement, which is anything that stops an unpleasant experience. This strengthens behaviour and encourages repetition. Property crimes like shoplifting and burglary, or violent crimes like robbery, appear to be reinforced by the physical rewards achieved. However, they may also be prompted by a desire for social and psychological reinforcements such as increased status among peers, self-esteem, feelings of competence, or simply for the thrill of it (Bartol, 1999).

Social learning theory

While operant learning stresses the importance of environmental consequences on behaviour and maintains that behaviour is acquired through reinforcement and punishment from the environment, social learning expands upon the role of 'inner' processes in learning and holds that behaviour can also be learned at a cognitive level through observing the actions of other people. Although formulated by Rotter (1954), social learning theory is more generally associated with the American psychologist Bandura who contends that much of our behaviour is initially acquired by watching others, who are called 'models'.

According to Bandura, the more significant and respected the models, the greater their impact on our behaviour. Observational learning takes place primarily in the family, in the prevalent subculture, and through cultural symbols such as television and books which form part of the social environment (Bandura, 1976). Therefore explanations for crime will be found via the behaviour modelled within families, by peer groups, on television and so on. Once learned, the behaviour may be reinforced or punished by its consequences. In general, social learning theory suggests that through observation, especially if the model is someone regarded as successful or of high status, we learn at a cognitive level how to perform the observed behaviour which in turn is reinforced or punished, motivating future behaviour. Many studies report that observing aggression leads to hostility in both children and adults. People who observe aggressive acts not only imitate the observed behaviour but also become generally more hostile (Bartol, 1999).

Activity 3.1

Prepare a talk debate on the link between violence on TV and real-life violence.

1. What influence might violence on TV have on the actions of those who watch it?
2. What processes would underlie that influence?
3. Would younger children be more influenced than older? Why?
4. Would some people be influenced in different ways from others?

Differential association theory

Edwin Sutherland's **differential association** theory (Sutherland, 1947) is a general theory of crime encompassing the idea that **delinquency** is learned through a process of communication with other people – usually small intimate peer groups (Coleman and Norris, 2000). Thus, although it may be regarded as a sociological theory, differential association theory clearly assumes that behaviour is learned and may be seen as a development of learning theories to explore how offenders learn and from whom. The theory also broadens the notion of 'behaviour' to claim that attitudes, motives and rationalizations are learned, as well as the appropriateness of particular actions in given situations (Smith and Paternoster, 1987; Coleman and Norris, 2000).

Sutherland (1947) provides nine statements to explain how criminal behaviour develops and in what circumstance:

1. Criminal behaviour is learned.
2. The learning is through association with other people.
3. The main part of the learning occurs within close personal groups.
4. The learning includes techniques to carry out particular crimes and also specific attitudes, drives and motives conducive towards crime.
5. The direction of the drives and motives is learned from perception of the law as either favourable or unfavourable.
6. A person becomes criminal when their definitions of attitudes and actions favourable to breaking the law outweigh their definitions favourable to non-violation.
7. The learning experiences – differential associations will vary in frequency, intensity and importance for each individual.
8. The process of learning criminal behaviour is no different from the learning of any other behaviour.
9. Although criminal behaviour is an expression of needs and values, crime cannot be explained solely in terms of those needs and values.

The theory proposes that through contact with other people who hold favourable attitudes towards crime, similar attitudes are learned. The learning or criminal behaviour does not have to develop through association with criminals, but with people who are favourable to crime. For example, parents may communicate that it is all right to be dishonest by not informing a shop assistant if they receive too much change in error even if they constantly tell their children that it is wrong to steal.

However, as Blackburn (1993) for example discusses, in its most basic form differential association theory only accounts for the actual acquisition of criminal tendencies, and not necessarily their maintenance or performance. Furthermore, it says little about the differential receptivity of individuals to their associations – are we passive and empty participants into which different cultural norms and values are added (Coleman and Norris, 2000) or do some of the individualistic processes discussed in Chapter 2 predispose some people to accept and maintain the offending patterns they observe?

Family influences

Learning theory and differential association theory both raise questions about exactly who provides the reinforcement schedules that shape behaviour and the models which may teach people that certain sorts of illegal actions are acceptable. The family is one obvious source of such influence. Comparisons of the family environments of criminals and non-criminals indicate adverse conditions with some regularity.

Large family size is one correlate of delinquency. Research shows that only children are less likely to be delinquent, and delinquents are more likely to come from families with four or more children (West, 1982). There are many reasons why this may be the case. Large families are more difficult to discipline, and individual children may receive less supervision, individual attention and affection. A further possibility is that such families are more likely to live in poor and overcrowded homes which may result in greater stress, family disorganization and material deprivation (Farrington, 1991). Exposure to delinquent siblings is another important factor and this is more likely in large families where there may be a 'contagion' effect, with children relying more on siblings than parents as models and sources of appropriate and social behaviour.

One key set of family factors associated with the development of criminal behaviour are child-rearing practices, including discipline, positive parenting and monitoring. When parenting is described as lax, neglectful, erratic, inconsistent, overly harsh or punitive, it is found to be predictive of adolescent delinquency. For instance Jackson and Foshee (1998) found a relationship between how well parents responded to the child when they were needed (which they termed 'responsive parenting') and a parent's inclination to have rules and expectations (termed 'demanding parenting') and the development of antisocial behaviour. More responsive and demanding parents were associated with lower levels of delinquency in their children.

Hoffman (1984) identified three child-rearing styles as indicated in Table 3.1 and several studies suggest that delinquent families are more likely to use power assertion style whereas parents of non-delinquents use more induction and love withdrawal styles. In general, physical punishment, inconsistent punishment, poor parental monitoring, poor discipline and lack of family cohesion were found to be linked to violent delinquency. Beyond child-rearing practices, specific types of family interactions such as constant conflict, poor use of language and communication, mistrust of family members, indifference and low affection towards the children and a lack of shared leisure activities seem to be associated with the families of delinquents.

There has been some considerable debate on whether children from divorced or single-parent families are more likely to become involved in crime. One traditional view deriving from the work of Bowlby (1944), discussed in Chapter 2, and his notion of breakdown in maternal attachment, was that a 'broken home' was the cause of delinquency. In a number of studies it has been shown that offenders are more likely to come from homes 'broken' by the absence of one or both natural parents. Children from single-parent families are more likely to engage in antisocial behaviour (Bank et al, 1993). Overall, there seems to be a modest relationship to the absence of a biological parent on delinquency. This may be explained by reasons other than the lone parenting itself: a combination of problems are often associated with lone parents that lead to delinquency such

■ Power assertion – involves use of physical punishment, criticism, threats and material deprivation
■ Love withdrawal – involves the withholding of affection, for example by ignoring the child or threatening to do so, as a sign of disapproval
■ Induction – involves the parent developing empathic and sympathetic responses in the child by explaining what the consequences of their actions are for others

Table 3.1 Hoffman's child-rearing styles

as the traumas of divorce, distress, poverty and mental health problems of the parents. This is further supported in that the loss of a parent through death does not seem to be associated with delinquency in the same way a 'broken home' is (Rutter, 1971).

This variety of contradictory findings of the relationship of single-parent families to delinquency indicates that the 'broken home' concept is ambiguous. Studies tend to examine together families which have been single-parent from the birth of the first child with those which became single-parent after divorce or death without distinguishing between these two (Feldman, 1993). Changes in society, in which blended families and single-parent households are becoming much more common, also raise the possibility that there is much more social support for single-parent families and that they reflect a much more diverse range of family situations than may have been the case a quarter of a century ago and more, when a lot of the cited studies were conducted.

A further complication in understanding the impact of family life on criminality is the well-established fact that criminals are more likely than non-criminals to have criminal parents (West, 1982). For instance in the Cambridge study 37.9 per cent of boys who became delinquent had a parent with a criminal record, compared with 14.6 per cent of non-delinquents (Farrington and West, 1990). A century ago this was considered by many as evidence for the inheritance of criminality, but a much stronger relationship might have been expected if inheritance was the dominant influence. Although genetics cannot be totally ruled out, explanations based on learning are much more plausible. These include modelling of antisocial behaviour by parents, even to the point of involving their children in their criminal activities, failure of parents to provide models of normative and prosocial behaviour, poor supervision of children, and children modelling their behaviour on the behaviour of family members.

School influences

Beyond the family, the school is probably the most influential environment for children. Certainly academic failure is associated with increased risks of delinquency (Hirschi, 1969). Adult offenders are more likely to have a history of low educational attainment. This may be because the school fails to engage with challenging or less intellectually able pupils, who then opt out of the school and become involved in offending behaviour. However, the causal role of the school remains unclear. It is well established that schools vary widely in the rates of delinquency exhibited by their pupils, possibly reflecting parental choice of schools with better reputations and the socio-economic context of the school. Hargreaves (1980) identifies the features of a school which may contain high numbers of delinquent pupils and these include high staff turnover, low staff commitment, streaming, social disadvantage and a view of pupils as being of low ability (Harrower, 1998).

Peer influences

By the time young people reach the most frequent age for crime, in their mid teens, their main social contacts and influences are their peers. It is perhaps therefore not surprising that numerous studies find that one of the strongest predictors of delinquency among adolescents is the delinquency of close friends. Delinquent acts among juveniles are typically committed in groups and with co-offenders who live close to each other (Farrington and West, 1990). However, group offending is more common for non-violent than for violent crimes and most adult offenders offend alone.

Peer pressure alone cannot explain all juvenile crime as there are lots of offences committed alone. Agnew (1990) asked 1400 adolescents what had led them to engage in crime. Their answers indicated that peer influence was only one factor, the others being a rational choice to obtain money or kicks or a result of anger or provocation (Harrower, 1998). As with other correlates, a causal

Figure 3.1 Youths become involved in crime for many reasons.
Source: © 2004 TopFoto/John Powell.

effect is not established as we do not know how much such groups influence their members to engage in criminal behaviour (Blackburn, 1993).

Routine activities and crime

An important consequence of crime emerging out of the family, school and peer groups is that it is integrated with all the other actions in which an offender may be engaged, such as work and leisure. One implication of this is that criminal violations share many of the same attributes of, and are interdependent with, other legitimate routine activities (Cohen and Felson, 1979). People participate in legitimate routine activities daily to satisfy their personal needs, through work, child-rearing, shopping or leisure pursuits and it is these routine daily activities which determine where and when people are, and what they are doing, and hence the location and vulnerability of personal and property targets (Blackburn, 1993).

Cohen and Felson's approach serves to link illegal and legal activities and builds upon the concept of opportunity for crimes (Cohen and Felson, 1979; Coleman and Norris, 2000). As such, crimes, more specifically predatory crimes directed at people and their property, involve the convergence in time and space of 1) motivated offenders; 2) suitable targets; and 3) the absences of capable guardians. Under this approach crime and delinquency cannot be understood outside or apart from the ecology of everyday life (Sampson, 2001).

The influence of structural changes in societal routine activities such as the increased number of women working, people living alone, the size and weight of consumer items, the locations of shops and unsupervised play areas can be seen in the increase of crime trends in areas where conditions that are supposed to cause crime have lessened (Cohen and Felson, 1979; Blackburn, 1993; Sampson, 2001). Guardianship or some other form of protection against crime is sufficient to prevent the occurrence of a successful predatory crime, but the convergence in time and space of suitable targets and the absence of capable guardians can lead to increases in crime rates without any increase or change in the personal condition that leads individuals to engage in crime (Cohen and Felson, 1979; Blackburn, 1993).

A general limitation of the emphasis on routine activity is its focus on predatory criminal actions, such as illegal acts in which an individual intentionally harms another person or takes or damages their property. It seems less plausible as a significant component of non-predatory crimes such as prostitution or drug-dealing, or those crimes in which the location of the activity is determined by the target of the crime, as may be the case for a bank robbery. It offers little in the way of explaining deviant behaviour in general.

Social control theory

The general finding of the youthfulness of offenders (Smith, 2002) and the obvious relevance of the broad details of differential association theory, combined with many of the cognitive characteristics of offenders discussed in the previous chapter, raises questions about what it is that stops people offending rather than what it is that causes people to offend. Many young people who have the characteristics and life experiences we have considered do not become delinquent. Hirschi (1969) argues that youths refrain from committing deviant acts because of a bond to conventionality and conformity. They accept **social control**. There is a sense in which this proposal is self-evident, but it is developed beyond the obvious by claiming that social control implies restraining factors in the individual, in the form of internalized norms comparable to the superego and ego, and the controlling influence and authority of social institutions, such as the family, school or neighbourhood (Cusson, 2001; Sampson, 2001). The basic idea is that crime occurs through a lack of social controls to stop it, such as the social bonds of marriage or employment. Hirschi (1969) believes that the law is kept only when special circumstances exist in which the appropriate social training in being law-abiding can occur. The success of social training depends on attachments, commitments and beliefs.

This bond consists of four elements:

- Commitment: the rational element of the social bond; consists of investments in conventional goals, such as education or a future career.

- Attachment: the affective element of the social bond; consists of the emotional ties established with others in the form of conscience, internalized norms and caring what others think.

- Involvement: the time and energy invested in conventional activities; those heavily involved in conventional pursuits have less time and energy to be involved in deviant pursuits; incompatible with delinquent activities.

- Belief: the degree to which one attributes legitimacy to conventional moral prohibitions against deviant acts; in the moral validity of conventional values.

All of these vary considerably across adolescents and are strongly related to lower rates of delinquency behaviour (Blackburn, 1993; Coleman and Norris, 2000; Cusson, 2001; Sampson, 2001). This theory is concerned with criminality in general, rather than the commission of specific crime types, and is held to be consistent with the stability of **deviance** from childhood, the versatility rather than specialization of offenders, and the correlation of crime with other forms of social deviance (Blackburn, 1993).

The argument several theorists maintain against this theory is that the weakness of the social bond can only partially account for deviant behaviour. The theory offers the view that no special motivation is needed for the deviation from acceptable social norms (since everyone is exposed to some form of temptation) and says little about how the bonds with society develop or break down. Yet social control theorists argue that criminal acts are natural consequences of unrestrained human tendencies to seek pleasure and avoid pain, and are held to be the immediate gratification of common human desires, and require little planning, effort or skill. Their commission is purely opportunistic and based on temptations which are often closely related to other socially disapproved acts (i.e. drinking, smoking, illicit sex), which become more likely when people lack self-control (Blackburn, 1993). In the end, however, we still need an explanation as to why some young people fail to become bonded to the 'conventional' social order (Coleman and Norris, 2000).

Deterrence theory

The obverse of explanations drawn from a lack of social control is an emphasis on the power of **deterrence**. Beccaria and Bentham's deterrence theory is the notion that the frequency of crime will vary inversely with the certainty, swiftness and severity of punishment for that crime, inflicted on the individual by the state (Cusson, 2001). Deterrence works on the process by which people are influenced to act or refrain from an action for fear of external sanctions and negative consequences – when the calculated costs of punishment outweigh the subjective benefits or profits of a deviant act (Blackburn, 1993).

A distinction is commonly drawn between two types of deterrence: general deterrence and specific deterrence. General deterrence is the discouraging effect the punishments of offenders have on *other* would-be offenders, whereas specific deterrence is the effect punishment has to reduce recidivism in convicted and punished offenders (Blackburn, 1993; Cusson, 2001).

A common objection to the applicability of deterrence theory is that many crimes are impulsive or emotion based and involve very little, if any, consideration of the consequences. Also, people's perceptions of legal sanctions vary, and deterrence will only occur when these sanctions are seen as being reasonable and their severity as being equal to the crime committed. If they are 'unruly' or harsh, this works to diminish the credibility of the punishment and decreases the likelihood of general deterrence. A person's willingness to take risks and their objective circumstances will also affect how they perceive the 'costs' and 'benefits' of acting deviantly. Further, there are some groups of individuals (i.e. the young, learning disabled) that may be less susceptible to the threat of legal sanctions (Blackburn, 1993).

Labelling theory

A more sociological perspective on explanations for criminality than any considered so far is **labelling** theory. This proposes that the deviant is someone to whom the label of deviant has successfully been applied by those individuals who make the social rules (i.e. police officers, judges, psychiatrists, etc.) – those in a position of power (Coleman and Norris, 2000). Deviance is not seen as an internal quality of the act a person may commit, but as the consequence of the application of rules and sanctions by others upon that person. The focus is on official reactions to delinquent acts (Sampson, 2001) which are governed by the characteristics of offenders (i.e. age, race or class), rather than by characteristics of the offence (Cusson, 2001).

While the original or primary deviant norm violations are carried out for various reasons, further acts, or secondary deviance, are sustained by the adaptation to the stigmatizing reaction of society to the primary deviance. The initial act of norm violation (primary deviance) is largely incidental since it is only a problem when labelled as such. Therefore, the delinquent career is sustained by official labelling and sanctioning processes (Blackburn, 1993; Sampson, 2001) through a self-fulfilling prophecy (Cusson, 2001). In effect this is the view that a young person will say to her/himself, 'if you are going to call me a delinquent I will act like one'.

Labelling theory examines characteristics and sources of labels such as 'criminal', the conditions under which they are applied, and the effect that giving a deviant label has on an individual. It is characterized by three assumptions:

- Acts are not intrinsically deviant.

- Crime is a label that becomes attached to behaviour for social reasons, especially the interests of the powerful.

- Criminal justice agents are influenced by the characteristics of the offenders, such as age, race or class, rather than by the characteristics of the offence.

The central view is that being publicly labelled a criminal results in a deviant self-image, and therefore fosters a **criminal career** (Blackburn, 1993).

Becker (1963) argues that deviancy is a normal part of adolescence that would be a passing phase if it were not labelled as criminal. Social groups are those who define what is deviant and what is not. The initial act of violating a norm (primary deviance) is incidental since it is only a problem when labelled as such. For example, a minor theft (primary deviance) is labelled as criminal, and this causes the individual to continue stealing. Secondary deviance is when the individual accepts the label and sees him/herself as deviant. Therefore, labelling is a process that eventually produces identification with a deviant image and the adjustment to stigmatization from the agents of social control (Blackburn, 1993).

Labelling theory is criticized for focusing on the deviance of the 'underdog' and for oversimplifying the relation between attitudes, self-concept and behaviour. However, psychological studies of expectancy confirmation, or the self-fulfilling prophecy, have also demonstrated that labels and stereotypes can bias perceptions, which are communicated to and influence those to whom they are applied (Blackburn, 1993). Another criticism is that the labelling process is not totally arbitrary nor is it completely unrelated to the primary deviant behaviour and the characteristics of the labelled individual. The majority of those found guilty of a crime are really those people who committed the crime. So the question is: Does the label create a new social identity or does it just confirm a deviant identity already there (Cusson, 2001)?

Age and gender

There are two recurrent findings in all studies of criminality and delinquency that stand out above all others. One is that the great majority of crimes are committed by males. The second is that the great majority of these are in their mid teens. As Smith (2006: 1) reports in a recent study that reflects many earlier findings: 'Offending peaked around the age of 14 among both boys and girls'. He goes on to point out that after the mid teens there is a 'fairly steep and steady decline in the proportion of young people involved in broad delinquency among both boys and girls. Among those who continued to be involved, the amount of offending also declined'.

Further, Smith (2002) elegantly summarizes the implications of the many studies of the typical age of criminals:

> Crime is mostly committed by young people – by adolescents and adults in their twenties. Criminal offending, therefore, is closely linked to the life course. It is one of a number of psychosocial disorders that are characteristic of youth, in the sense that they rise in prevalence or frequency, or reach a peak, in adolescence or early adulthood. Other examples are problem drinking, use of illegal drugs, depression (especially in females), suicide (especially in males), and eating disorders. (Smith, 2002: 701)

The emergence of crime and its unfolding across the life course raises many questions about what the underlying processes may be that give rise to crime. There must be some aspect of maturation that is having an influence, as touched on in the previous chapter, but it is also the case that societies are so structured that what it is possible for people to do, the contacts they have and the expectations of them also vary considerably as people emerge from childhood into adolescence on into young adulthood. Therefore many theories of criminality focus upon the life experiences of offenders and the opportunities offered to them to learn criminality. Many of the social processes discussed above, such as labelling and differential association, relate most strongly to particular stages in an offender's life.

Criminal career development and its relation to delinquency

The peak frequency of offending in the mid teens carries implications for considering the psychological processes involved in crime over the lifespan of an offender.

Many offenders do commit many crimes such that the longitudinal sequence of offences committed by an individual offender who has a detectable rate of offending over some period is often referred to as a 'criminal career' (Blumstein et al, 1988; Farrington, 1992; Svensson, 2002). The term 'career' is not a very precise one in this usage. It does not usually imply a training phase, graduation and eventual supervisory and management roles, with ultimate retirement, as is usually understood by a 'career'. It is simply a shorthand term to cover the sequence of crimes committed by one individual over his life.

Two predictors of the length and intensity of a criminal career have emerged in the literature: age of onset and chronic offending in adolescence (Stattin and Magnusson, 1991; Piquero and Buka, 2002; Svensson, 2002; Piquero et al, 2004; Kazemian and Farrington, 2005). Moffitt encapsulated the impact of age of onset with the distinction between temporary and persistent antisocial behaviour (Moffitt, 1993). The theory makes two main distinctions between types of offenders: 1) life-course persistent antisocial behaviour; 2) adolescent-limited antisocial behaviour.

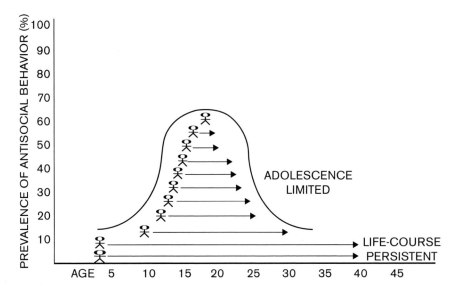

Figure 3.2 Moffit's developmental taxonomy. This shows the changing prevalence of participation in antisocial behaviour across the life course. The solid line represents the known curve of crime over age. The arrows represent the duration of participation in antisocial behaviour by individuals.
Source: Moffitt, 1993.

Life-course persistent antisocial individuals exhibit a changing manifestation of antisocial behaviour influenced by the new social opportunities that present themselves throughout different points in development (Moffitt, 1993). Moffitt argues that this type of behaviour has roots in both earlier neurological deficits and in exposure to environmental risks (i.e. poor parenting, parental antisocial behaviour) (Moffitt, 1993; McCabe et al, 2001). These two risk factors aggravate each other's impacts. Neurological deficits can lead to difficult temperaments, which in turn leave the child vulnerable to poor parenting, and poor parenting can then lead to a poor neurological development (McCabe et al, 2001). From this point of view the causal factors for life-course persistent offenders are most likely to be located early in their childhood and support the continuity of their antisocial behaviour throughout their lives (Moffitt, 1993).

On the other hand, those individuals with adolescent-limited antisocial behaviour, as the name suggests, begin their offending and antisocial behaviour in adolescence and desist once they reach young adulthood. This group of offenders makes up a large percentage of all delinquent offending. Moffitt (1993) sees the antisocial behaviour within this group as caused by a gap between biological maturity and social maturity. The adolescent-limited antisocial individuals may begin their antisocial behaviour as a result of the limitations their age places upon them. They may engage in antisocial behaviour in order to gain access to adult privileges, and because of peers who have seemingly gained autonomy from their parents through such antisocial behaviours. This type of adolescent-limited antisocial behaviour will cease to occur during early adulthood as autonomy becomes less significant (McCabe et al, 2001).

Moffitt's theory predicts that life-persistent offenders will partake in a variety of types of crimes, including those that demonstrate autonomy and those offences that are more violent and aggressive and victim-oriented. Adolescent-limited offenders, in contrast, will engage primarily in crimes that symbolize adult privilege or those that demonstrate autonomy from parental control. Such offences would include, but are not necessarily limited to, vandalism, public order offences, running away, truancy and theft (McCabe et al, 2001).

Gender and deviance

Because the majority of offenders are male, the majority of empirical work in the area of delinquency has been conducted with samples of male adolescents (Smith and Paternoster, 1987; Goodkind et al, 2006). Thus it could be argued that traditional theories of deviance are only appropriate for understanding the deviant behaviours of males, although without more detailed study of female offenders this is an open question. Changes in the role of women in society are doubtless also being reflected in changes in their criminal roles.

Theorizing about female involvement in deviant behaviour has generally been characterized by qualitatively different sets of explanatory factors (e.g. victims of personal maladjustments, psychological disturbances, home and family factors). A typical explanation for female delinquency is that of the inability to adjust to a poor home situation (Smith and Paternoster, 1987). However, in their 1987 study, Smith and Paternoster tried to address this deficiency in the literature. They explored differential association, social control, deterrence and strain theories for gender specificity and found that the relationships between variables derived from these traditional theories of deviance and marijuana use were not gender specific.

Focus 3.1

Are female criminals different from males?

'Girl gang' in vicious assault on woman, 19

Angus Howarth, *The Scotsman*, Monday 28 August, 2006

A young woman may have been left permanently scarred after being slashed across the face in an unprovoked attack by a 'girl gang' in Glasgow at the weekend. The 19-year-old victim was subjected to a vicious assault outside a pub as she made her way home in the city's east end at 1am yesterday.

Four girls, who are not thought to have known their victim, pounced as the woman alighted from a bus at Broomfield Road in the Balornock area.

The gang then ran off leaving the badly injured young woman, who lives locally, lying on the ground near the Broomfield Tavern.

When the word 'gang' is mentioned, most will associate it with a male-dominated group, yet there are increasing numbers of females who are becoming a part of the gang culture – some will form 'girl only' gangs, while others will join the 'traditional' male gangs.

Female gangs stem from the same reasons that the male gangs develop – economic deprivation, peer pressure, excitement, money, drugs, friendship, self-affirmation, fear, threats and intimidation. The gang 'family' promise to provide for their members all the things they want or need or believe that they lack in their lives, as well as providing an escape from what they may be experiencing in their own family homes (Moore, 1991).

Female gang members have been documented as participating in all of the criminal acts and violence associated with their male counterparts, but they commit fewer violent crimes and are more inclined to commit property crimes and status offences (Moore and Hagedorn, 2001). Female gang members are no longer just 'appendages' of male gangs, and have been developing their own gang culture and 'taking care of their own'.

Many aspects of female gang members' lives and the functioning of these female gangs remain a mystery as relatively few researchers believe the female gangs worthy of empirical study. As well as this bias, access to female gangs is a serious obstacle with gang members being extremely wary of researchers and only participating in unusual circumstances (Moore and Hagedorn, 2001).

Processes within society

While the focus of the present book is on psychological processes within crime, it is essential to acknowledge that the majority of explorations of crime are within a much broader social and legal framework. Most books on criminology discuss the prevalence of crime in terms of the effectiveness of the law or particular forms of punishment or aspects of the way society operates. Very briefly, two aspects of these **explanations of crime** will be mentioned because they both have clear psychological implications.

Strain theories

Strain theories assume people to be naturally conforming unless forced into deviance by their experiences in society that come from the structure of society. These ideas often draw directly on the concept of 'anomie', originally described by Durkheim in the 19th century. Durkheim argued that if we cannot regulate people's aspirations, then they will develop aspirations that cannot be fulfilled, particularly in periods of economic crisis. This would result in a state of social instability, 'anomie', which would correspond to periods of high suicide rates and personal crisis.

Building on Durkheim's work, Merton (1969) believed that anomie occurred because the society put particular pressure or strain on the individual to have unrealistic aspirations or to behave in a non-conformist manner. Anomie is the result of the particular goals and means of a society. Merton (1969) conceives of anomie as 'a disjunction between the cultural goal of success and the opportunity structure by which this goal might be achieved. Since the lower strata were discriminated against in educational and occupational market places, this was the group least likely to realize the American dream ... No wonder that from these strata so many pursued deviant activities; only such activities offered an available route to success'. Legitimate desires which cannot be satisfied by socially acceptable behaviour 'force' lower-class persons into delinquency. Cohen (1955) expresses this slightly differently; many working-class children experience status problems because they cannot meet middle-class standards of successful school performance. Frustration is the consequence and they deal with it with 'reaction-formation', rejecting middle-class values and expressing contempt towards property evident in their destructive acts.

One crucial source of strains in society is the uneven distribution of wealth. Thus the economic approach to the explanation of crime is that when society has rid itself of poverty, unemployment and major inequalities of income, crime will diminish sharply. It is commonly assumed that delinquents tend to come from family backgrounds which are 'deprived' because of poverty, poor housing, overcrowding and dependence on welfare. Farrington and West (1990) found that the most persistent offenders had worked in stable paid employment least or changed jobs most often, and low family income was a predictor of later delinquency. Witt et al (1999) analysed data from 42 police forces in the UK and found that property crime was associated with increasing male unemployment. Hirschi (1969) also found a relation between self-reported delinquency and the father's unemployment. However, the causal association of unemployment and poverty with criminal behaviour is still not clear. If persistent offenders are often without a job it may simply be that they are less employable because of fewer job-related skills. Also, psychological effects of unemployment include depression, anxiety and low self-esteem (Blackburn, 1993) and these might influence behaviour.

Conclusions

While interest in crime has always been high, understanding why it occurs and what to do about it has always been a problem. Our inability to prevent crime is partly due to our problems in understanding criminal behaviour. In this chapter we reviewed the major social **theories of crime**. No single explanation is adequate in accounting for all crime, especially as there are many types of crime and many types of offenders. Maybe it is better to think about multi-causal models or a combination of different factors in order to understand criminal behaviour. Whatever the case, increased understanding of criminal behaviour is critical both in terms of predicting future offending and successfully intervening for changing criminal behaviour.

Key concepts and terms

Criminal career
Delinquency
Deterrence
Deviance
Differential association
Explanations of crime

Labelling
Social control
Social psychological theories of
    criminal behaviour
Theories of crime

Sample essay titles

- 'Criminals are born not made'. Discuss.

- Why do you think most crimes are committed by males in their mid teens?

- Identify two social factors that might account for criminal behaviour.

- Critically discuss the learning theories offered to the explanation of criminal behaviour.

- Discuss how familial factors might have an effect on criminal behaviour.

- Evaluate the evidence for a criminal personality.

- What psychological processes do sociological theories of crime assume?

Further reading

Books

Bartol, C.R. (1999). *Criminal Behaviour: A Psychosocial Approach*. Englewood Cliffs, NJ: Prentice-Hall.

Blackburn, R. (1993). *The Psychology of Criminal Conduct*. Chichester: Wiley.

Brandt, D. (2006). *Delinquency, Development, and Social Policy*. New Haven: University Press.

Cassel, E., and Bernstein, D. (2007). *Criminal Behaviour*. Hillsdale, NJ: Lawrence Erlbaum.

Feldman, P. (1993). *The Psychology of Crime*. Cambridge: Cambridge University Press.

Harrower, J. (1998). *Applying Psychology to Crime*. London: Hodder and Stoughton.

Hollin, C. (1989). *Psychology and Crime: An Introduction to Criminological Psychology*. London: Routledge.

Journal articles

Agnew, R. (1990). The origins of delinquent events: An examination of offender accounts. *Journal of Research in Crime and Delinquency*, 27, 267–294.

Celio, M., Karnik, N.S., and Steiner, H. (2006). Early maturation as a risk factor for aggression and delinquency in adolescent girls: a review. *International Journal of Clinical Practice*, 60(10), 1254–1262.

Osborn, S.G., and West, D.J. (1979). Conviction records of fathers and sons compared. *British Journal of Criminology*, 19, 120–133.

Ozbay, O., and Ozcan, Y.Z. (2006). A test of Hirschi's social bonding theory – Juvenile delinquency in the high schools of Ankara, Turkey. *International Journal of Offender Therapy and Comparative Criminology*, 50(6), 711–726.

Wilson, M., and Daly, M. (2006). Are juvenile offenders extreme future discounters? *Psychological Science*, 17(11), 989–994.

4 Mental disorder and crime

Maria Ioannou and Paul V. Greenall

This chapter addresses the relationship between **mental disorder** and crime. The various forms of mental disorder are considered, especially distinguishing between personality disorders and mental illness. Whether people with these disorders have particular relationships to offending when compared with those who do not suffer these problems is examined. In so far as there are relationships, the difficulties of distinguishing between mental disorder as a cause as opposed to being a consequence of crime and criminality are explored. How mental disorder is dealt with in court is briefly considered, but a fuller account is given in Chapter 14.

Learning outcomes

When you have completed this chapter you should be able to:

1. Understand the major forms of mental disorder relevant to criminality.
2. Discuss the possibilities of links between mental disorder and crime.
3. Appreciate the role of mental disorder in some **criminal behaviour**.
4. Understand how mental disorder is handled within the criminal justice system.

Mental disorder and crime: Exploring the link

On 15 May, 1800, in the Drury Lane Theatre in London, James Hadfield tried to assassinate King George III. Although the facts were beyond dispute, Hadfield was later found Not Guilty by Reason of Insanity (NGRI) as the court accepted his actions were the result of his deluded mind. Consequently, Hadfield was detained under the hastily enacted 'Act for the Safe Custody of Insane Persons Charged with Offences' and the seeds of how we presently deal with **mentally disordered offenders** were sown (O'Reilly-Fleming, 1992).

The link between mental disorder and crime can be explored by examining the levels of known criminal activity among mentally disordered people, the level of mental disorder among known offenders and the importance of having a mental disorder on predicting the likelihood of future offending. Each one will be considered in turn.

Criminal activity among mentally disordered people

Research by Singleton et al (2001) suggests that levels of mental disorder among adults in Britain range from 0.6 to 13.5 per cent in males and 0.2 to 19.4 per cent in females (see Figure 4.1).

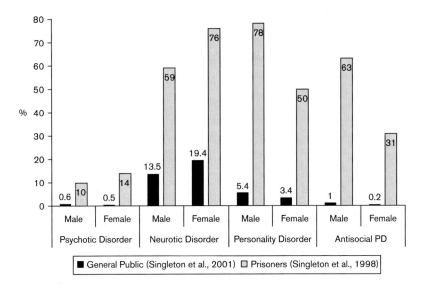

Figure 4.1 Highest rates of mental disorder among the general public and prisoners.

With a UK population of approximately 60 million, these findings suggest there are about 300,000–360,000 people with a psychotic disorder such as schizophrenia and 8–11 million people with a neurotic disorder such as anxiety, phobia, obsessive-compulsive disorder or depressive episodes. Additionally, there will be about 2–3 million people with a personality disorder (PD) such as avoidant, schizoid, paranoid or borderline PD, including 120,000–600,000 with antisocial PD. Levels of **psychopathy** within the general population are unknown, although Hare (2003) estimates the rate to be about 1 per cent. This means there are about 600,000 psychopaths in Britain.

Focus 4.1

Psychopathy and the Psychopathy Checklist – Revised (PCL-R; Hare, 1991, 2003)

Psychopathy is a form of personality disorder characterized by serious deficits in a person's ability to interact effectively with others, lack of remorse or guilt, pathological lying, callousness and lack of empathy, poor behavioural controls, impulsivity, aggressive narcissism, and early behavioural problems. As such, it is an important clinical construct within the criminal justice system and is a potent risk factor for violence and offending. The current gold standard for the assessment of psychopathy is the Hare Psychopathy Checklist – Revised (PCL-R). This comprises

20 items, each of which is scored on a three-point ordinal scale (0 = no, 1 = maybe, 2 = yes). The PCL-R provides a dimensional score that represents the extent to which a person matches the 'prototypical psychopath' (Hare, 2003: 30). While there is no official 'cut-off score', scores of 30 or above have been used in the bulk of research to lead to a person being designated as a 'psychopath', based on Hare's (1991) suggestion that this would be one standard deviation above the mean.

In addition to the total score, the PCL-R also comprises factors that underpin the higher-order construct of psychopathy. The original PCL-R manual reported two correlated factors. Factor one reflected a selfish, callous and remorseless use of others, while factor two described a chronically unstable, antisocial and socially deviant lifestyle. Nonetheless, Cooke and Michie (2001) argued on the basis of factor analyses that just 13 items reflected a three-factor model (arrogant and deceitful interpersonal style, deficient affective experience, impulsive and irresponsible lifestyle). They posited that the remaining items were secondary characteristics or a consequence of psychopathy (Cooke et al, 2004). However, since the second edition of the PCL-R manual, Hare (2003) and colleagues (Neumann et al, 2005) have argued that a hierarchical model comprising two factors and four facets (interpersonal, affective, lifestyle and antisocial) has strong empirical support. This essentially places the three-factor model of Cooke and Michie (2001) within the original two-factor model and incorporates further items into an antisocial facet. All 20 items still contribute to the total, overall PCL-R score.

PCL-R Items in the hierarchical two-factor, four-facet model

Factor 1: Interpersonal/affective

Facet 1: Interpersonal

Glibness/superficial charm

Grandiose sense of self-worth

Pathological lying

Cunning/manipulative

Facet 2: Affective

Lack of remorse or guilt

Shallow affect

Callous/lack of empathy

Failure to accept responsibility

Factor 2: Social deviance

Facet 3: Lifestyle

Need for stimulation/proneness to boredom

Parasitic lifestyle

Lack of realistic, long-term goals

Impulsivity

Irresponsibility

Facet 4: Antisocial

Poor behavioural controls

Early behavioural problems

Juvenile delinquency

Revocation of conditional release

Criminal versatility

Items not loaded onto any factor or facet

Promiscuous sexual behaviour

Many short-term marital relationships

Official statistics provide an indication of how many mentally disordered people are criminally active. For example, during 2004, 1986 people were admitted to a psychiatric hospital for committing a crime. Further, the population of restricted patients in hospital for committing a crime was 3282 (Ly and Foster, 2005). As a proportion of mentally disordered people in Britain, these figures suggest only a small minority are criminally active. This point is supported by data for 2004/05 which show that, while there were 26,800 formal admissions to hospital under the Mental Health Act 1983, only 6 per cent were admitted from court or prison (National Health Service, 2006). However, mentally disordered people may be responsible for proportionately more crimes than their numbers warrant. For example, people with schizophrenia and psychopathy have been found to have higher rates of convictions for violence and general criminality (Hodgins et al, 1996; Hare, 1999, 2003; Fazel and Grann, 2006) than those without such disorders.

Activity 4.1

Read one of the many autobiographies written by gangsters or other people who have committed crimes. Review the sorts of explanations and justifications they give for their crimes. Do these owe more to some sort of mental disorder, the types of cognitive processes discussed in Chapter 2 or the social processes discussed in Chapter 3?

Mental disorder among offenders

Research by Singleton et al (1998) suggests that levels of mental disorder among prisoners range from 10 to 78 per cent in males and 14 to 76 per cent in females, which by comparison are considerably higher than within the general public (see Figure 4.1). These findings suggest that a link between mental disorder and crime may exist, as many known offenders appear to be mentally disordered. Indeed, Singleton et al (1998) found only 10 per cent or less of their sample showed no evidence of any of the five disorders (i.e. personality disorder, psychosis, neurosis, alcohol misuse and drug dependence) considered in their survey. Additionally, compared to the estimated 1 per cent of the general public who are psychopaths, Cooke (1998) reports levels of psychopathy in British prisoners ranging from 8 to 22 per cent, and Coid (1992) found a rate of 77 per cent among violent prisoners. Such is the level of mental disorder among prisoners that the Government recently acknowledged 'we continue to imprison too many people with mental health problems' (Home Office, 2006a: 26) and many prisons have psychiatric 'in-reach' facilities to deal with such offenders (Department of Health, 2001). However, this is not a problem unique to Britain, as Fazel and Danesh (2002) found similarly high rates of mental disorder among prisoners in their meta-analysis of 62 surveys from 12 countries.

Although high levels of mental disorder exist among prisoners, it is not clear whether their mental disorder was related to their crimes or developed subsequently in prison. This point is supported by Ly and Foster (2005) who found that 21 per cent of mentally disordered offenders were admitted to hospital from prison. One further area to consider therefore when exploring the link between mental disorder and crime is whether or not mental disorder is important when predicting future offending.

Re-offending and risk assessment

Although percentages vary across samples studied, some offenders are very likely to re-offend once released (Councell, 2003). To help identify those most likely to re-offend, psychologists often conduct risk assessments of offenders. Risk assessment is a 'process of evaluating individuals to characterize the likelihood they will commit acts of violence and develop interventions to reduce that likelihood' (Hart, 1998: 122). To assist in this process, various risk assessment tools exist that rate an individual on the absence or presence of a list of variables that differentiate recidivists from non-recidivists (Cooke, 2000). Acknowledging the link between mental disorder and crime, several risk assessment tools include factors like mental illness, psychopathy and personality disorder in their assessments of physical (Webster et al, 1997) or sexual (Hart et al, 2003) violence risk, as they have been shown to be important predictor variables.

Some disorders, however, appear more important in risk assessment than others. For example, such is the link between psychopathy and violence that Hart (1998) suggests that a failure to consider it in a risk assessment may be professionally negligent. However, mental illness does not appear to have the same impact, as recidivism rates among mentally ill offenders are lower than among those with personality disorder (Jamieson and Taylor, 2004) and some argue that schizophrenia is negatively correlated with future offending (Quinsey et al, 1998). It should nonetheless be kept in mind that Quinsey and colleagues' research was conducted on samples of high-security forensic psychiatric patients.

Figure 4.2 The public image of mental disorder still harks back to the early asylums, but is this relevant to how we think about mental disorder and criminality?

Source: © Select Images/Alamy.

The protective role of schizophrenia may reflect the fact that many people in their sample had a personality disorder. Indeed, people with schizophrenia are generally found to be at a higher risk for violence when compared to the wider population, and this risk increases with concomitant substance abuse (see Wallace et al, 2004). However, the fact that risk assessment tools include variables other than mental illness or personality disorder suggests that other factors are important when assessing future risk (Powis, 2002), even among mentally disordered offenders (Bonta et al, 1998). Indeed, although he argues its importance to future violence, Hart (1998) suggests that it would be negligent to base a risk assessment on psychopathy alone.

Mental disorder and criminal behaviour

Given the link between mental disorder and crime, how do these factors interact and what do we know about mentally disordered offenders?

Mental disorder and the aetiology of crime

Research suggests that some people with a psychotic disorder such as schizophrenia offend in response to the positive symptoms (i.e. delusions and/or hallucinations) of their illness. This process, called 'psychotic drive' by Smith (2000), usually results in serious offences being committed (Taylor, 1985; Taylor et al, 1998). For some, this may be due to the persecutory nature of their delusions (Taylor et al, 1998) and/or the tendency to perceive the world as threatening (Arsenault et al, 2000b). This 'symptom approach' to explaining why some

---

Focus 4.2

Paranoid schizophrenia and homicidal delusions

In May 2001 a schoolgirl was stabbed to death in broad daylight in front of shoppers in Birmingham's busy Centenary Square. She had been sunbathing with friends when she was attacked in the middle of the afternoon. In Court, her assailant Inderjit Kainth, denied murdering the girl but pleaded guilty to manslaughter on the grounds of diminished responsibility. The Court was told that Kainth believed his life was in danger from Birmingham Education Authority and the Civil Service and the only way he could save himself was by killing a woman.

Consequently, he had spent weeks before the stabbing carrying a 'dagger of revenge'. On the day in question, Kainth sat beside the girl and pulled out a kitchen knife that he had hidden inside a shampoo bottle and stabbed her. Psychiatrists agreed Kainth was a paranoid schizophrenic who was suffering from delusions. Kainth was considered to present a serious danger to the public and he was ordered to be indefinitely detained at Ashworth High Security Hospital near Liverpool. (Source: www.bbc.co.uk)

schizophrenics offend has been applied to other crimes including sexual offending (Smith and Taylor, 1999) as well as property crimes, breaching probation and 'mischief' (Hodelet, 2001). Other research focusing specifically on sexual offending has highlighted the disinhibiting effect of psychosis (Phillips et al, 1999), which breaks down a person's normal inhibitory controls and leaves them unable to look beyond their immediate aim to the nature and consequences of their impulsive actions (Craissati and Hodes, 1992). This is underpinned by research that suggests that opportunism and sexual desire are important motivating factors among mentally ill rapists (Smith, 2000; Greenall and West, 2007).

Psychopathic offending can be viewed as the result of the basic features of this disorder, e.g. callousness, impulsivity, egocentricity, grandiosity, irresponsibility, lack of empathy, guilt or remorse (Hare, 2003). Compared to other offenders, psychopaths begin offending at an earlier age, commit a wider variety of crimes, pose serious management problems while incarcerated and violate parole and/or re-offend sooner once released (Hare, 2003). The relationship between psychopathy and violence is particularly important, as psychopathic violence appears more instrumental, dispassionate and predatory. Further, psychopathic violence appears motivated by factors such as greed, vengeance, anger, retribution or personal gain, and is mostly directed against strangers (Hare, 1999). Several of these aspects are present when psychopaths sexually offend. For example, research has found that, along with opportunistic impulsivity, anger/hatred and sexual deviancy (i.e. sadism) are important motivating factors among psychopathic rapists (Brown and Forth, 1997; Greenall and West, 2007). Further, sexual homicides committed by psychopaths have been found to be more gratuitous and sadistic, with victims tending to be strangers (Porter et al, 2003). Psychopathic offending, however, does not result from a deluded mind but as Hare states, 'from a cold, calculating rationality combined with a chilling inability to treat others as thinking, feeling human beings' (1993: 5).

Mentally disordered offenders

Having examined the link between mental disorder and crime and illustrated how some mental disorders interact with criminal behaviour, we now take a brief look at mentally disordered offenders themselves.

Research into mentally disordered offenders illustrates the demographic, psychiatric and criminological features of this population. For example, a recent study into the needs of over 1200 patients in the English high-security hospitals (i.e. Ashworth, Broadmoor and Rampton) found that the men were on average 40 years old and had been in hospital for an average of 9.8 years. By contrast, women were younger (mean age 37) and had shorter lengths of stay in hospital. Most men and women were single and from a white ethnic background and their mean IQ was 86. Most had several previous psychiatric admissions and the most common mental disorders were schizophrenia (61 per cent) and personality disorder (45 per cent); a minority had affective disorder (12 per cent) and mental retardation (10 per cent) (Harty et al, 2004). The diversity of offences committed by mentally disordered offenders is illustrated by Ly and Foster (2005) who found they included homicide (20 per cent), other violence (29 per cent), sexual offences (12 per cent), burglary, robbery, theft and handling stolen goods (9 per cent), criminal damage (16 per cent) and other offences (14 per cent).

Given the range of mental disorders among offenders and the variety of crimes committed by them, what determines whether an offender with a mental disorder is sent to prison or hospital? This will vary considerably between jurisdictions, but for the UK some insight is provided by Shaw et al (2006) who found that, generally, both a verdict of diminished responsibility and being sent to hospital were related to severe mental illness and abnormalities of mental state, especially psychosis, at the time of the offence. Factors like alcohol or drug dependence, personality disorder and previous convictions for violence reduced the chances of being sent to hospital. Although as Shaw et al (2006) suggest, this is justifiable in a system that aims to identify those whose illnesses are most serious and most treatable, they also found that a small number of offenders with acute and severe mental illness were sent to prison, even after a verdict of diminished responsibility.

Mental disorder and the law

Mentally disordered offenders pose special problems for a legal system that incorporates the notion of *mens rea*; that is, it must be shown that the individual acted with criminal intent, exercising free will and can therefore be held responsible for the crime they committed. Consequently, the courts have long sought to distinguish the sane from the insane. However, insanity in this regard is a legal not a psychiatric or psychological concept and its legal definitions have changed over time.

Presently, the main piece of legislation dealing with mental health in England and Wales is the Mental Health Act 1983 (as amended by the Mental Health Act 2007). This Act covers the assessment, treatment and rights of people suffering poor mental health and it provides for their compulsory detention and treatment in hospital as necessary and with appropriate safeguards. Under the 1983 Act, mental disorder included mental illness, psychopathic disorder, mental impairment and severe mental impairment. However, these categories have been replaced by the 2007 Act which defines mental disorder more broadly as 'any disorder or disability of the mind'. Additionally a new 'appropriate medical treatment' test replaces the previous 'treatability' test.

The Mental Health Act extends to mentally disordered offenders who can be detained in hospital before trial while on remand, during trial and after conviction, either by specific direction of the court or if their mental state deteriorates once in prison. This not only shows the problem of defining a 'mentally disordered offender' but it illustrates that the presence of a mental disorder is considered important at various stages in the criminal justice process. To illustrate this point, each one will now be considered in turn.

Unfitness to plead

Some persons charged with a crime are considered so intellectually and/or psychologically impaired that they are unable to understand the charges against them or the judicial process that is dealing with them, or they may be unable to cooperate rationally with their legal representative in their own defence. In such cases the defendant may be considered under English law, Unfit to Plead (the American equivalent is Incompetent to Stand Trial). In determining fitness to plead it is necessary to determine whether the defendant is able to:

- defend him/herself;

- challenge a juror;

- understand the substance of the evidence and

- the nature of the charge;

- follow the proceedings in court; and

- understand the difference between pleading guilty and not guilty.

Traditionally, those considered Unfit to Plead were detained in hospital; however, since the enactment of the Criminal Procedure (Insanity and Unfitness to Plead) Act 1991, innocent individuals go free and a range of disposals are now available for those who have acted as charged (Ormerod, 2005).

In **unfitness to plead** deliberations, the question essentially is, 'What is the defendant's state of mind at the present time, or at the time of the trial?'. An individual who was seriously mentally disordered at the time of an offence may be fit to plead by the time of their trial. Conversely, a person may be mentally stable during an offence, but may later become disordered and be determined Unfit to Plead.

The insanity defence

The McNaughton Rules

When insanity is raised as a defence, the question being asked is 'What was the defendant's state of mind at the time the offence was committed?'. The most famous and influential insanity trial is that of Daniel McNaughton in 1843. McNaughton attempted to assassinate the Prime Minister but mistakenly shot and killed his private secretary. In his defence it was pleaded that he suffered from paranoid delusions, one of which was that the Tories were persecuting him and that at the time of the offence he had lost control and was unable to resist his delusions. McNaughton was found NGRI and was among the first patients transferred to Broadmoor, where he remained until his death 22 years later. However, the original decision gave rise to the McNaughton Rules (West and Walk, 1977).

The Rules state that a person is not responsible for a criminal act if at the time of committing the act, the party accused was labouring under such a defect of reason, from disease of the mind, as not to know the nature and quality of the act he/she was doing; or if he/she did know the nature of the act, he/she did not know that it was wrong (Ormerod, 2005). The rules, therefore, emphasize the cognitive elements of being aware and knowing what one was doing at the time of the criminal act or knowing right from wrong in the moral sense (Bartol, 1999) and are recognized in several jurisdictions outside of England, including Australia, Canada, the Republic of Ireland and most US states.

The Durham Rule

The Durham Rule was created in 1954. Monte Durham, a 26-year-old resident of the District of Columbia, had a long history of mental disorder and petty theft. He committed burglary but he was acquitted because his act was considered to be 'the product of a mental disease or mental defect'. While the McNaughton Rules focus on knowing right from wrong, Durham assumes that someone cannot be held responsible if a criminal act is the product of mental illness. However, it soon became apparent that definitions of 'mental illness' are vague and subjective and it was later rejected by the same court that created it in favour of the Brawner Rule.

The Brawner and Ali Rule

The Brawner Rule is another rule for determining insanity shaped by the American Law Institute (ALI) in 1962. According to the Rule, a person is not responsible for criminal conduct if at the time of such conduct as a result of mental disease or defect, he lacks substantial capacity either to appreciate the criminality [wrongfulness] of his conduct or to conform his conduct to the requirements of the law. It therefore incorporates both cognitive and volitional tests. However, unlike the Durham Rule, it recognizes partial responsibility for criminal conduct as well as the possibility of an irresistible impulse beyond one's control. However, it excludes any repeated criminal or antisocial behaviour. Thus those who are psychopathic or who have antisocial personality disorders cannot claim that their condition is a mental disorder under the law.

The Brawner Rule formed the basis for the defence of John Hinckley who shot President Reagan in 1982 and who, despite disagreement between expert witnesses, received a NGRI verdict. This provoked a public demand for reform and led to President Reagan signing the Insanity Reform Act in 1984, which states that 'as a result of mental illness, the defendant lacks the capacity to appreciate the nature and quality or wrongfulness of the act'.

Diminished responsibility

The Homicide Act of 1957 introduced the defence to murder of diminished responsibility, which if accepted leads to a conviction of manslaughter. Section 2 of the Act states a defendant shall not be convicted of murder 'if he was suffering from such abnormality of mind (whether arising from a condition of arrested or retarded development of mind or any inherent causes or induced by disease or injury) as substantially impaired his mental responsibility for his acts and omissions...'. The meaning of 'abnormality of mind' was determined in a case of sexual homicide, as summarized in Focus box 4.3.

Focus 4.3

Diminished responsibility for a sexual psychopath: *Regina v. Byrne* (1960)

In December 1959 a woman was found strangled in a YMCA hostel and her dead body had been subjected to what were described as horrifying mutilations. In Court, Patrick Joseph Byrne admitted to killing his victim and claimed that in doing so, he was suffering from diminished responsibility. Three medical witnesses testified that Byrne was a 'sexual psychopath' who had suffered from violent perverted sexual desires from an early age and which he found difficult or impossible to control, such that in some cases he had indulged them. These impulses or urges were stronger than the normal impulse or urge of sex and the killing was done under such impulses or urges. Indeed, when not under the influence of such desires, Byrne was considered normal. All three doctors considered the killing was done under the influence of Byrne's perverted sexual desires. Although not amounting to insanity as defined by the McNaughton Rules, his sexual psychopathy could properly be described as partial insanity. Byrne's diminished responsibility plea was accepted and he was convicted of manslaughter ([1960] 3 All England Reports 1).

Mental disorders as defences

A number of special mental disorders have been used to support a claim of diminished responsibility or to free someone from criminal responsibility.

Dissociative identity disorder

Dissociative identity disorder (sometimes known as multiple personality disorder) is 'the presence of two or more distinct identities or personality states that recurrently take control of behaviour' (American Psychiatric Association, 2000: 526). Each personality state may be experienced as if it has a distinct personal history, self-image and identity, including a separate name. Periodically, at least two personalities take full control of the individual's behaviour. The change or transition from one personality is often very sudden (seconds to minutes), and is generally triggered by stress or some relevant environmental stimuli. Dissociative identity disorder has been claimed as an excusing condition for criminal responsibility. One of the most well-known cases in which this was tried involved serial killer Kenneth Bianchi, known as the Hillside Strangler, but he was still convicted.

Amnesia

The essential feature of dissociative amnesia is an inability to recall important personal information, usually of a traumatic or stressful nature that is too extensive to be explained by normal forgetfulness (American Psychiatric Association, 2000: 520). It refers to complete or partial memory loss of an event, or series of events, either due to physical trauma, neurophysiological disturbance or psychological factors. The loss is temporary and restricted to a specific event or incident. In general, the courts have not been receptive to amnesia as a valid condition in either the **insanity defence** or as a condition that promotes incompetence to stand trial. One reason for this is the suspicion that the defendant may be faking the memory loss. It is easy for people to say they cannot remember committing the crime and it is difficult for psychologists to determine whether a person can or cannot remember. Claims of amnesia are made in a substantial portion of homicide cases.

Post-traumatic stress disorder

Post-traumatic stress disorder (PTSD) is 'the development of characteristic symptoms following exposure to extreme traumatic stressor involving direct personal experience of an event that involves actual or threatened death or serious injury, or other threat to one's physical integrity; or witnessing an event that involves death, injury, or a threat to the physical integrity of another person; or learning about unexpected or violent death, serious harm or threat of death or injury experienced by a family member or other close associate' (American Psychiatric Association, 2000: 463). The precipitating event is usually experienced with intense fear, terror and helplessness. A successful PTSD defence usually results in a verdict of diminished responsibility, rather than NGRI.

Personality disorders

The American Psychiatric Association has over the years produced what is known as the *Diagnostic and Statistical Manual of Mental Disorders* (DSM). This lists different categories of mental disorders and the criteria for diagnosing them. It is widely used by clinicians and researchers as well as insurance companies, pharmaceutical companies and policy makers to put labels onto many different mental conditions. Despite its wide use it has attracted controversy and criticism, mainly because it treats mental problems as if they were distinct illnesses. It has gone through many revisions, the current version being the text revision of the Fourth Edition, referred to as DSM-IV-TR.

The manual divides the conditions along what are referred to as 'axes', there being five in all. Of particular note is that Axis I deals with 'clinical disorders', distinguishing them from 'personality disorders and mental retardation', which are referred to as Axis II. The personality disorders are generally characterized by 'an enduring pattern of inner experience and behaviour that deviates markedly from the expectations of the individual's culture, is pervasive and inflexible, has an onset in adolescence or early adulthood, is stable over time, and leads to distress or impairment' (American Psychiatric Association, 2000: 685). (See www.personalitydisorder.org.uk)

A term that has caused controversy among the medical and legal profession is 'dangerous and severe personality disorder' (DSPD, see: www.dspdprogramme.gov.uk). The UK government first introduced this term in a consultation paper

(Home Office and Department of Health, 1999), which suggested ways to detain and treat a small minority of personality disordered offenders who pose a significant risk of harm to others and themselves. Specialist services to deal with these people, most of whom are thought to have the potential for being serious violent and sex offenders, were proposed in the White Paper *Reforming the Mental Health Act* in December 2000 (Department of Health, 2000). The DSPD term was the result of high-profile cases such as that of Michael Stone, who in 1996 attacked Josie Russell and killed her mother and sister several years after his personality disorder was deemed untreatable. Personality disorders have often been used as a defence in court.

Conclusions

In this chapter we have focused on the relationship between mental disorder and crime. Although research suggests that only a minority of mentally disordered people offend, many offenders have a mental disorder. However, how this disorder interacted with their crimes varies, and in some cases the disorder may have developed in prison after conviction. Regardless of this fact, the presence of a mental disorder either at the time the offence was committed or when the offender is on trial, can be an important factor and the Law has several ways of dealing with this. In a recent expert paper on mental illness, Taylor (2002) argued there is no longer any doubt that there is an association, albeit a modest one, between violence and some mental disorders, including mental illness. Additionally, in the Second Edition of his revised psychopathy checklist, Hare (2003) provides a compelling body of evidence for the strong link between psychopathy and crime and his view that psychopathy is the single most important clinical construct in the criminal justice system. Consequently, the presence of a mental disorder is an important factor when considering the likelihood of future offending and how the risk posed by such individuals can be adequately managed once they are in the community.

Key concepts and terms

Criminal behaviour	Mentally disordered offender
Insanity defence	Psychopathy
Mental disorder	Unfitness to plead

Sample essay titles

- Does having a mental illness help to predict future criminality?

- Describe the legal concept of insanity and the various standards for the insanity defence.

- What is a psychopath?

Further reading

Books

Bartol, C.R. (1999). *Criminal Behaviour: A Psychosocial Approach*. Englewood Cliffs, NJ: Prentice-Hall.

Blackburn, R. (1993). *The Psychology of Criminal Conduct: Theory, Research and Practice*. Chichester: Wiley.

Hare, R.D. (1993). *Without Conscience: The Disturbing World of the Psychopaths Among Us*. New York: Guilford.

Ormerod, D. (2005). *Smith and Hogan Criminal Law*. Oxford: Oxford University Press.

Journal articles

Hare, R.D. (1996). Psychopathy: A clinical construct whose time has come. *Criminal Justice and Behaviour*, 23, 25–54.

Hart, S.D. (1998). The role of psychopathy in assessing risk for violence: Conceptual and methodological issues. *Legal and Criminological Psychology*, 3(1), 121–137.

Hodgins, S., Mednick, S.A., Brennan, P.A., Schulsinger, F., and Engberg, M. (1996). Mental disorder and crime: Evidence from a Danish birth cohort. *Archives of General Psychiatry*, 53(6), 489–496.

Sahota, K., and Chesterman, P. (1998). Sexual offending in the context of mental illness. *Journal of Forensic Psychiatry*, 9, 267–280.

Taylor, P.J. (1985). Motives for offending among violent and psychotic men. *British Journal of Psychiatry*, 147(5), 491–498.

2 | Varieties of crime

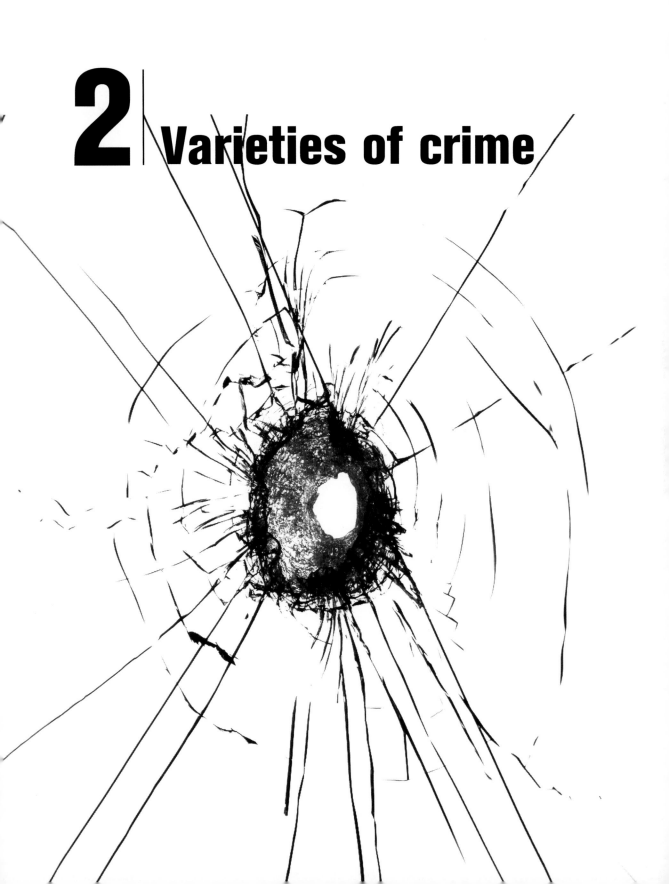

5 Burglary

Louise Goodwin

This chapter covers the major areas of research into the psychology of **burglary**. It considers the impact of being burgled then goes on to review the legal and psychological definitions. The prevalence of burglary will be presented and the demographics of burglars will be briefly explored. This will be followed by a discussion as to why people commit burglary and, when they do, how they choose their targets, including the spatial behaviour of burglary offenders. The next section will cover the attempts at classifying burglars based on their offence behaviour.

Learning outcomes

When you have completed this chapter you should be able to:

1. Appreciate the psychological, emotional and financial effects of burglary on crime victims.
2. Understand the legal definition of burglary and have knowledge of the prevalence of burglary in the UK.
3. Appreciate the demographics of burglars and the factors that contribute to a burglar's decision to offend.
4. Understand the decision-making processes of burglars that make potential targets attractive.
5. Comprehend the classifications of burglars and the utility and limitations of classification models.

The experience of being burgled

The feelings of violation following an incident of burglary are often compared to the intrusion felt by victims of rape (Bennett and Wright, 1984). Victims of burglary report increased levels of anxiety, depression and hostility, and fatigue and experience more psychological stress (Beaton et al, 2000). Although the emotional and psychological ramifications are shorter lived than the effects of violent crime there is a clear cost above and beyond the loss of possessions or damage to property (Maguire and Corbett, 1987). In the 2006 British Crime Survey (Walker et al, 2006):

- 86 per cent of burglary victims reported being emotionally affected;

- 56 per cent said anger was experienced;

- 46 per cent reported feelings of annoyance;

- 28 per cent experienced fear;

- 10 per cent experienced depression;

- 11 per cent experienced anxiety or panic attacks.

Bennett and Wright (1984) report that many victims feel that they became paranoid and distrustful even of neighbours and friends. They have an overwhelming sense that the crime was committed by somebody known to them. This is not an unfounded paranoia, as the 2006 BCS reports that 52 per cent of offenders are known to the victim in some capacity.

In terms of the financial cost of the crime to the victim, the median cost of a burglary was reported to be £330. In 31 per cent of offences no items were stolen. Where theft did occur, the items that were stolen were:

- money, usually from a purse/wallet (43 per cent);

- electrical goods/camera (24 per cent);

- jewellery (23 per cent);

- DVDs and CDs (22 per cent);

- computers and computer equipment (15 per cent); and

- mobile phones (10 per cent).

In less than 8 per cent of cases the resident suffered graffiti, soiling or damage to furniture; most damage was caused by forced entry. Budd (1999) reports that 80 per cent of households had an insurance policy covering home contents, with economically disadvantaged groups being far less likely to have insurance – the very group that is most at risk of victimization. Twenty per cent were victimized more than once in a year (Budd, 1999). It is thought that over a short period of time people may be subject to repeat victimization with offenders returning to a familiar house to take items they could not remove the first time round. However, it is likely that factors that made the property attractive as a target in the first instance still remain. See Pease (1998) for a discussion on repeat victimization.

These results show that this common crime is usually very disturbing for people and often has significance far beyond the value of the property stolen. Burglary is experienced as an intrusion and a violation. As we shall see, this may be relevant to understanding the psychology of the burglar as well as the experience of being burgled.

Definition and prevalence

Burglary is categorized as a **property crime**, along with other offences such as car crime, vandalism and theft. However, as we have noted, there is also undoubtedly an interpersonal element to burglary. A home is usually considered to be a sanctuary and stronghold. Intrusion into this highly personal space is a violation second only to rape. The legal definition of burglary was revised in England and Wales following the 1968 Theft Act to include not only entry by force into a property with the view to procure goods but any entry into a property without legitimate reason or appropriate consent. Forcing entry is no longer considered a defining prerequisite to the crime, neither is the theft of goods – in fact the British Crime Survey for 2000 demonstrated that one in three burglaries result in no loss of property to the victim (Kershaw et al, 2001). The Home Office figures include reported burglaries of all buildings, although they make a distinction between domestic and non-domestic burglaries. Domestic burglaries include break-ins to all inhabited dwellings. Non-domestic burglaries include burglary of businesses, including hotels, and burglaries of sheds and out-houses that are not connected to the main dwelling. Aggravated burglary is where an offender, armed with a firearm, weapon or explosive, enters a building as a trespasser to steal or commit grievous bodily harm. This is not to be confused with commercial burglary, which involves theft from a place of work, corporation or organization. Commercial burglary likely involves a new set of issues and a wider body of literature and will not be dealt with in this chapter.

In 2005/06 the police recorded 300,555 domestic burglaries and 344,563 non-domestic burglaries. Overall there was a 5 per cent decrease from 2004/05 (Walker et al, 2006). However, many people fail to report burglaries to the police for a variety of reasons. In a study by Budd (1999), reasons cited included: did not believe the offence to be serious enough; that the police would not be able to do much about it; and that the police were unlikely to care. The British Crime Survey (BCS) offers a more realistic measure of burglary, capturing those crimes that fail to be reported to the police. In 2005/06 the BCS estimated 733,000 domestic burglaries alone. The median cost of burglary per household was £330 with 56 per cent incurring damage costing under £500.

The demographics of burglars

Research on criminal specialization by Youngs (2004) demonstrates that burglary is part of a general criminality. A wide variety of offenders commit burglary while specializing in other specific subsets of criminal activity, such as drug crime or violent crime. This would suggest that burglars are unlikely to be drawn from a homogeneous population. The fact that burglary is a common crime indicates that there will be a high volume of offenders, resulting in a wide variation in the characteristics and behaviours of those offenders. This is not to say that burglary research does not make attempts at describing the sample of offenders in terms of age, ethnicity and socio-economic status. Research more often than not concludes that the average offender is male, unemployed and living in an area of social and financial deprivation. The 2005 BCS reports that

82 per cent of offenders are male and 56 per cent of offenders are aged 24 or under. Additionally, as part of an extensive project, probation officers and social workers interviewed all offenders convicted of burglary living in the Rochdale area in 1986: the majority of offenders were found to be male (95 per cent), living in council accommodation (95 per cent) and unemployed (70 per cent) (Forrester et al, 1988).

However, these demographics are often characteristic of other types of offenders and are not particularly useful in differentiating between burglars and other offenders. Despite this, some differences between burglars and violent offenders have been reported. For instance it is generally accepted that violent crime has a younger 'retirement' age than property crime, resulting in a broader age range in property crime offenders. A study by Farrington and Lambert (1994) compared the demographics of burglars and violent offenders and found that violent offenders were more likely to be male and were likely to be younger. Burglars were more likely to have prior convictions and were more likely to have previous convictions of 10 or more offences. Over half the burglars had previous convictions for burglary compared to one-quarter of the violent offenders. Additionally half the violent offenders, compared to one-third of the burglars, had previous convictions of violent offences. The study was conducted over a nine-month period and during this time recidivism was recorded. Burglars were found to be more prolific, and when re-offending the crime was more likely to be burglary.

The decision to offend and target selection

Why do people commit burglary and why do offenders choose one target over another? Studies of burglars, most of which take the form of semi-structured

Figure 5.1 Burglars chose the property they target.
Source: © Sally and Richard Greenhill/Alamy.

interviews, have attempted to ascertain the motives behind the offence. This may seem a somewhat obvious question with the immediate answer being that burglaries are committed purely for financial gain. However, research would suggest that burglars, as with fraudsters, do not offend out of any desperate financial need or abject poverty (Rengert and Wasilchick, 1985). Many offenders cite financial gain as a reason for committing a crime, but it would appear that there are other important precipitating factors in the decision to offend. Additionally it would seem that in choosing a suitable target offenders are on the look-out for far more than rich pickings. This section will first explore the factors that trigger an offender to commit a burglary and second the characteristics of a target that are attractive to a burglar.

The decision to offend

Home Office research (Wiles and Costello, 2000) listed, in order of importance, the factors in the decision to offend as need for money, being drunk/drugged up, good opportunity and, lastly, influence of mates. In their extensive interviews with offenders Bennett and Wright (1984) revealed the various triggers that prompt the decision to offend. The responses of offenders fell into six main categories in order of importance. Unsurprisingly the primary need was instrumental. Just under 50 per cent of offenders cited a need for money as a precipitating factor to committing a burglary. Some claimed that they only offended when short of money. Many stated that the need for money determined their rate of offending – the more extensive the 'loot', the longer the subsequent period before re-offending. Burglary was used to finance everyday needs and also recreational activity such as drug taking, drinking and gambling.

Second, 46 per cent of their sample stated that the influence of others was an important factor in the decision to offend. Some offenders took an active and some a passive role in the decision-making process. This opens up issues of the social psychology of the group, which are considered in Chapter 9.

The third type of decision was precipitated by presented opportunities. Twenty-two per cent stated that, instead of having a prior motivation to offend and actively seeking out a burglary opportunity, the decision to commit a crime arose as they came across an opportunity too good to miss – the classic 'opportunity crime' – or they received a 'tip off' of a suitable criminal opportunity.

Twenty per cent committed burglary on such a regular basis that they claimed that there was no precipitating factor in their decision to offend. It was simply an established part of their routine. Fourteen per cent of offenders claimed that there was an expressive need that triggered an offence – offending was described as a source of fun and excitement, a recreational activity. Lastly alcohol was cited as an important factor by 10 per cent of offenders. Some offenders saw the consumption of alcohol as a direct cause of the offence while others claimed that they drank after the decision to offend had been made, giving them the courage to go through with the offence.

It would appear then that there is more than a simple financial factor involved in the commission of a burglary. In fact Maguire and Bennett (1982) report that many of their sample had employable skills. They were not offending out of desperation with no other means of supporting themselves and their dependents. Maguire and Bennett, among others, report that some offenders actually gave up jobs due to their working hours interfering with their criminal activity (Maguire and Bennett, 1984; Rengert and Wasilchick, 1985).

Focus 5.1

Burglary and drugs

The need to obtain funds in order to feed a drug addiction is commonly accepted by the public as a major cause of burglary (Charles, 1998, cited in Mawby, 2001). There has been extensive research into the links between drugs and crime and there is undoubtedly a relationship between the two. A study by Ball et al (1981) demonstrated that many heroin addicts commit crimes almost every day of their addicted lives. Rengert and Wasilchick (1985) in their extensive work with burglars report similar findings. Bennett (1998) reports the high incidence of drug use in arrestees. This is supported by a recent Home Office study (Wiles and Costello, 2000) that reported that 69 per cent of burglars were hard drug users (mostly heroin).

However, research would suggest that this relationship is not as simple as once assumed. Cromwell, Olson and Avary (1991) cited in Mawby (2001) reported that a large proportion of their sample were drug users, with cocaine and heroin being the most common drugs of choice. However, many stated that offending behaviour pre-dated their drug addiction. Some of the expendable proceeds were spent on drugs and alcohol, which over time led to addiction, driving the need to offend in order to support a habit. It was also found that drugs were used to aid in the success of an offence, with depressants such as cannabis and heroin calming the nerves and helping the offender to attend and respond to stimuli more effectively. In contrast, cocaine, a stimulant, detracted from the success of the offence by making the user feel disinhibited and consequently more likely to take risks. In conclusion, the evidence for an association between drug abuse and burglary is strong. However, drug abuse does not necessarily precede offence behaviour. It should also be taken into consideration that there are any number of alternative activities that could be used to support a drug habit. Some of these are criminal such as drug dealing, trafficking, fencing and fraud, but many drug users survive in ordinary jobs paying for their illegal drugs with money obtained legally.

Research pre-dating Bennett and Wright (1984) details combinations of precipitating offence factors. Chappell (1965) collected his data from a variety of sources and cites the primary influence on behaviour as monetary gain but also highlighted the role fun and excitement played in the decision to offend; this was almost exclusively noted in the younger offenders in the sample. Scarr (1973), through interviews with victims, non-victims, court personnel and burglars, identified four distinct motivations to burglary: financial gain, the need to satisfy drug and alcohol addiction, social needs such as peer approval, and finally idiosyncratic and eccentric reasons such as excitement and pitching oneself against the authorities. Again, Reppetto (1974) claims need for money was the prime motive in committing an offence with excitement, revenge, curiosity and group solidarity being found commonly in younger criminals.

Target selection

Most of the understanding of burglary **target selection** comes from interviews with offenders or research where offenders are asked to 'recreate' their burglary choices. The suitability of a target must be considered both in terms of the general area in which a burglar chooses to offend and also the specific target that is chosen from that area. A report by the Home Office (Wiles and Costello, 2000) states that overwhelmingly burglaries are opportunity crimes. This may be the case but, even so, offenders must recognize what an 'attractive' opportunity is when they see one. The findings in this research area have been heavily drawn upon to inform crime prevention and crime reduction initiatives.

Cohen and Felson's (1979) much quoted model of offence behaviour states that in order for a crime to occur three components must be present: a motivated offender, a suitable target and the absence of a guardian. So, once we have our motivated offender, what is considered to be a suitable target? It could be argued that the third component of Cohen and Felson's model – the absence of a guardian – is in fact an important element of what constitutes 'a suitable target'.

There are many studies on target selection. Typically offenders comment that the absence of a guardian is paramount in target selection. It would seem that most offenders go to great lengths to ensure that a property is unoccupied before they attempt unlawful entry. Rengert and Wasilchick (1985) stated that offenders fear, above all things, coming into contact with the occupants of a property. Elaborate techniques are reported such as looking through the local paper to find advertisements of weddings and funerals, where the residents are sure to be away from the home. This is a rather predatory and morbid practice that a minority of offenders may use, however many offenders do claim to take measures such as repeatedly ringing the door bell or calling the house phone of a property to ensure the house is empty. Some people choose to make their private telephone numbers ex-directory for this very reason.

Burglars also use visual cues to determine if an occupant is at home – are the lights or television on? Is there a car in the drive? Has the post been collected? Contrary to popular belief many burglaries are not committed at night under the cover of darkness but in the daytime when occupants are out of the house. This is increasingly the case as a woman's role is no longer in the home and many houses are left unoccupied for the majority of the day (see Rengert and Wasilchick, 1985, for a discussion on time sequencing).

The affluence of an area is also regularly cited as a factor in target selection. Offenders claim that they choose to offend in middle or upper middle class areas, because these properties are more likely to yield items with a high market value (Bennett and Wright, 1984). It has also been reported that offenders prefer to target areas that are only moderately affluent so that they do not look out of place in their surroundings (Carter and Hill, 1979; Rengert and Wasilchick, 1985). Targeting higher income areas seems logical; however, this does not explain why most burglaries are committed in areas of low socio-economic status. As we have seen from the earlier section on demographics, offenders themselves tend to live in areas of high crime and unemployment.

Despite poor detection rates, studies have addressed the relationship between offenders' homes and their offence sites. Results demonstrate that there is a high correlation between the two (Forrester et al, 1988; Bernasco and Luykx, 2003). Mawby (2001) makes the point that the disparity between what offenders claim they choose in a target and the actual crime figures may be due, in part, to a process of 'rational reconstruction'. He states that offenders may overestimate how much planning, organization and rational choice actually goes into their decision to offend. In terms of routine activity theory (Cohen and Felson, 1979) it would make sense that burglars commit crimes in their local areas, as they are more likely to come across opportunities in the places that they regularly frequent, live, work and socialize. Brown and Altman (1981) demonstrated that offenders largely preferred to offend in areas that were familiar to them. In addition to this, Bennett (1998) found in his sample of offenders that many offended on their journey to buy drugs, a transaction which will, more often than not, take place within a low-income area.

Another factor that offenders claim to be on the look-out for is an area of low social cohesion. Burglars want to operate in an environment where there is a poor sense of community. If everybody knows their neighbours then a new face on the block will not easily go unnoticed (Brown and Altman, 1981; Nee and Taylor, 2000). Statistically, houses on the corner of a street are targeted more than the houses in the middle of the street. This is because end houses are less physically overlooked by their neighbours, but also because people living in end houses tend to have less interaction and socialization with other members of their immediate community (Whyte, 1956). Burglars claim that ideally an area suitable for targeting will have lots of 'through traffic' of strangers where the neighbours are used to seeing new faces for legitimate purposes, for example housing situated next to a business/industrial estate or a shopping centre (Rengert and Wasilchick, 1985). However, this does of course conflict with the notion of guardianship and the offender not wishing to be seen actually breaking into a property. The offender may thus be making a subtle judgement between remaining anonymous and being out of sight of possible witnesses.

The proximity of the crime location is also cited as a major influence on target selection. A recent Home Office study (Wiles and Costello, 2000) claimed that many studies overestimated the distance that offenders were willing to travel, with many offenders committing crimes very close to their homes. In addition Barker (2000) demonstrated that urban burglars tended to travel shorter distances than rural and rural/urban mix offenders. This is likely due to a greater availability of targets within the urban areas and possibly the increased anonymity of being in an urban location.

A variety of studies (reviewed in Canter and Youngs, 2008b) have shown that burglars tend to select targets within two miles of their homes, but that this does vary in relation to the overall population density of an area. Furthermore, evidence would suggest that ease of access and escape routes are an important aspect in the target selection of an area. Bevis and Nutter (1977) demonstrated that target selection was related to the degree of access afforded by street design. Additionally Luedtke (1970) found that houses near a major highway were more likely to be selected as targets than houses far away from major routes.

In terms of the individual property that the offender chooses as a target, houses that offered rear access were preferred as the offenders felt they were less likely to be seen breaking into the property. Unsurprisingly, houses that had overgrown hedges and shrubs, providing cover to the offender, were preferred. It has also been demonstrated that houses where access can be gained through low windows or patio windows are more likely to be targeted by burglars (Bennett and Wright, 1984; Rengert and Wasilchick, 1985; Budd, 1999). Offenders claimed that there was much variation in the 'quality' of opportunities even within the same street or neighbourhood. Offenders claimed to look out for signs of expendable income such as antiques or big entertainment systems on display through windows (Bennett and Wright, 1984). Offenders also highlight the deterrents of other risks, such as visible alarm systems, dogs, heavy-duty locks and security systems, which can be time consuming to negotiate (Budd, 1999). The research on target selection has informed many crime prevention initiatives; see Mawby (2001) for a discussion on their effectiveness in reducing crime rates.

Parallels have been drawn between target selection and optimal foraging, where the offender strives to acquire the greatest gains for the least effort and risk of apprehension (Johnson and Bowers, 2004). This was demonstrated by Thompson (2001) who carried out multiple sorting tasks on 62 burglars for 27 houses. The sample identified 18 constructs that could be divided into four regions relating to risk, place, skill and rewards. It was demonstrated that offenders weighed up the risks and rewards of committing an offence and acted accordingly, making rational decisions about their environment.

Recent research from the Netherlands (Bernasco and Nieuwbeerta, 2004) has taken our understanding of target selection a step further by considering the aspects of target selection that are most salient to different subsets of offenders. This paper is important as it recognizes that offenders will not behave and react to situations in the same way. It was hypothesized that the target selection of younger offenders would be more greatly influenced by proximity compared to older offenders, who are more likely to have transportation available to them. Second, it was hypothesized that non-native offenders would be more influenced by the ethnic heterogeneity of an area, reasoning that these offenders are more likely to be inconspicuous in an ethnically heterogeneous area compared to their native colleagues. The results support the papers second hypothesis but not its first. The results of this study also showed that there was no difference in the spatial activity of offenders of different age groups. However, in Canter and Youngs' (2008b) review it is clear that this is not always the case. So there are likely to be a number of local factors that influence different offenders' target selection and journey to crime. The following section will explore the attempts that have been made to classify offenders based on the variation in their behaviour.

Activity 5.1

How secure is your neighbourhood?

Take the time to consider the macro and micro characteristics of where you live. Consider the features of your area and your individual property in the context of burglary risk assessment and crime prevention. What improvements can be made to your property and neighbourhood to make it burglar proof? How well do you know your neighbours? Would you recognize a stranger prowling your street if you saw one? Find out if you have a local Neighbourhood Watch Scheme and get involved if you can.

Activity 5.2

What does it feel like to be burgled?

If you know someone who has been burgled, discuss with them the experience and whether their feelings relate to the value or 'instrumental' significance of what was stolen or to some other emotions.

Classifying offenders – is there such a thing as a professional burglar?

At the beginning of the chapter we briefly explored the demographics of burglars and how they differ from other offenders. Research into the specialization of offenders would suggest that the crime of burglary is part of a general criminality that a wide range of offenders partake in during their criminal careers. This would indicate that burglars are unlikely to be a homogeneous group. Due to the sheer volume of burglars there is likely to be wide variation between offenders and the behaviours that they exhibit. Accordingly there has been much research into the variation between offenders, all of which refers to the relative '**professionalism**' of offenders as a means of differentiating between them.

A number of early researchers postulated categorization models of burglary. Black (1963) explored the level of skill involved in an offence and discriminated between burglars with the labels 'crude', 'run of the mill' and 'professional'. Maguire (1982) attempted to develop a typology of offenders based on the level of skill or professionalism that they displayed when committing an offence. Offenders were presented as subgroups existing along a linear continuum relating to level of professionalism. They were categorized as low, medium or high professionalism, which determined their resultant pattern of offending. Elaborating this typology, Shover (1991) goes on to present the likely offender characteristics of perpetrators associated with each level of skill. Low professional level offenders are often co-offending juveniles who partake in opportunity crime and display an absence of planning to their offence. Mid-level professionalism is characterized by an older offender who is more likely to work alone and whose increased experience results in more focused target selection and resultant higher yield. High levels of professionalism are characterized by offenders who often work in conjunction with another offender and whose attacks are selective and often planned well in advance of the event.

Bennett and Wright (1984) distinguished between three different types of offenders: first 'opportunistic offenders'; second 'search offenders' where the decision is made to offend and a search is made of the area to select a suitable target; and third 'planned offences' where there is a time gap between the choice of target and the execution of the offence. The authors argue that very few from their sample could be described as opportunistic offenders, with just over half of their sample being categorized as 'planners', although it is possible that this is a product of their sample population and study of juvenile offenders may yield different results.

Although these earlier works provide some useful insight into the possible beginnings of behavioural typologies of offenders, the ideas hold no unified encompassing structure and lack any systematic empirical validation of the proposed categories. The population that the majority of these early studies are drawn from is of convicted and often incarcerated offenders. As such the sample is inevitably biased. It is likely that there are significant differences between those offenders who are convicted of their crimes and those who evade detection. Additionally, as highlighted by McIntosh (1975), the term 'skill' is used interchangeably with professionalism and relates to a poorly defined set of constructs which are somewhat arbitrary, including the technical skill and intelligence of the offender, the offender's motivation and determination to offend, organization (membership of a group/network, contacts) and status, demonstrated by respect from others and measurable success of arrest and scale of rewards.

There is an almost mythical idea of the 'professional' burglar. The 'professional' burglar is often talked about in papers and books but how they differ from the 'average' burglar is rarely defined. If the true 'professional' offender does exist then they are unlikely to fall within the radar of the researcher who relies on data from the cohort of apprehended offenders! A recent study by Wiles and Costello (2000) mentions 25 'professional' offenders in the South Yorkshire area, identified as such due to their prolific offending. There are of course other criteria by which 'professional' offenders could be identified. Nevertheless there was no difference in the target selections, distances travelled or reasons for offending to differentiate these 25 offenders from the 'non professional' cohort.

In order to develop these earlier theories, more recent research has empirically tested the variation among offenders by analyzing real burglary crime scene data. Interestingly this research does find evidence for variation in professionalism among offenders. In addition variation is also found on a further dimension – an interpersonal element in the crime. Burglary has long been considered a crime against property alone. It is only in recent years that it has been recognized as holding an interpersonal significance for both the victims of crime and the perpetrator.

Burglary was first presented as a crime that holds an interpersonal element by Canter (1989), where the perpetrator and victim become 'intimate strangers' as a product of the intrusion into the resident's personal space (Merry, 1995). The effects of burglary on the victim are discussed earlier in the chapter, where it can be clearly seen that the psychological and emotional consequences of victimization are testament to the interpersonal nature of burglary. By widening the perspective of the crime, embracing concepts of emotion and goals peripheral to that of economic gain, research now encapsulates the notion of the interpersonal significance of burglary. This has facilitated the development of understanding into the multifaceted structure of the crime, differentiating it from earlier research that focuses on a single isolated element of the offender such as level of skill.

Some ideas apparent in recent research into the thematic structure of burglary such as that presented by Merry and Harsent (2000) can be seen in the earlier research literature. Walsh (1980) introduced ideas of a classification based on offence styles and the assailant's primary goals. The study distinguishes between interpersonal (expressive) and instrumental aspects of offender behaviour. Walsh includes technical craft and interpersonal factors in his typology of offenders. He distinguishes between 'challenge burglaries', which are motivated by destructive and revenge seeking actions, with expressive behaviour as the primary goal, and 'dispossessive burglary', which is motivated primarily by instrumental gain. Although the inclusion of ideas of expressive elements to burglary is progressive, Walsh's **classification system** does not allow for the presence of both expressive and instrumental elements in a single offence. Also Merry and Harsent (2000) drew attention to the very low occurrence of such destructive revenge seeking behaviours in actuality.

Merry and Harsent (2000) present the home as a central part of our everyday lives, a sanctuary from the world and its stresses and problems. The home and its interior are seen as the highly personal and idiosyncratic extension of the occupier's lifestyle, personality and tastes depicted in decor and furnishings. Merry and Harsent hypothesized that burglary has an interpersonal element and that the role of the victim is relevant to the offender's goal. The study analyses the actual behaviours present in burglary including the mode of entry, the features of the crime and the type of property stolen. Two facets emerge which define the crime: the interpersonal narrative or script of the offender and the craft/ability of the offender. The interaction of these elements creates a four-way thematic model of residential burglary. Each of the four facets is a combination of low or high skill level and implicit or explicit interpersonal interaction.

Therefore the evidence would suggest that there does seem to be variation in the level of professionalism that offenders display. There is also a further interpersonal dimension to offence behaviour that is of importance when attempting to differentiate between offenders. These empirically derived multifaceted models of burglary help to reveal the variety of psychological processes involved in carrying out a burglary. They point to distinctions not only in the overt reasons for the burglary but also in the different interpersonal styles that differentiate between those who break into other people's homes.

Conclusions

Most people who commit a number of crimes and are part of some form of criminal community, being typical of those people most readily labelled by the population at large as 'criminals', commit some form of burglary or theft at some time during their criminal careers. This makes burglary the essence of criminality. However, the direct instrumental gains of burglary are no more the sole purpose of carrying out the act than are the consequences for the victim purely financial. Burglary is most productively thought of as reflecting both styles of relating to other people and certain forms of cognitive skills. From this perspective, then, burglars can be of great interest to psychologists who wish to explore the processes that shape how people interact with each other. Yet there are very few studies of burglars that have been carried out to examine these issues.

Key concepts and terms

Burglary
Classification systems
Professionalism

Property crime
Target selection

Sample essay titles

- Why is burglary sometimes compared to rape?

- Compare and contrast the different classification models of burglars. Is there such a thing as a 'professional' offender?

- Burglary is primarily about illegally acquiring money and goods of value from others. Discuss.

- What are the macro and micro characteristics of a property that may attract a motivated offender?

Further reading

Books

Bennett, T., and Wright, R. (1984). *Burglars on Burglary*. Aldershot: Gower.

Canter, D.V., and Alison, L. (Eds) (2000a). *Profiling Property Crimes*. Aldershot: Ashgate.

Canter, D., and Youngs, D. (2008). 'Geographical offender profiling: Applications and opportunities.' In: D. Canter and D. Youngs (Eds). *Applications of Geographical Profiling*. Aldershot: Ashgate, 3–24.

Maguire, M. (1982). *Burglary in a Dwelling*. London: Heinemann.

Journal articles

Cohen, L.E., and Felson, M. (1979). Social change and crime rate trends: A routine activity approach. *American Sociological Review*, 44, 588–608.

Farrington, D.P., and Lambert, S. (1994). Differences between burglars and violent offenders. *Psychology, Crime and Law*, 1, 107–116.

Youngs, D. (2004). Personality correlates of offence style. *Journal of Investigative Psychology and Offender Profiling*, 1, 99–120.

6 Domestic violence

Maria Ioannou

This chapter begins by discussing what **domestic violence** is and its different forms. Theories of domestic violence and classifications of offenders will then be examined. Stalking as a separate crime and as a form of domestic violence is briefly described. Finally, the chapter examines risk factors associated with domestic violence, **risk assessment** measures that are used to assess the risk of future violence and interventions for domestic violence that various agencies carry out.

Learning outcomes

When you have completed this chapter you should be able to:

1. Know what domestic violence is.
2. Understand the theories that explain domestic violence.
3. Comprehend classifications of domestic violence.
4. Appreciate the link between stalking and domestic violence.
5. Be aware of approaches to risk assessment and interventions for domestic violence.

Defining domestic violence

The identification of domestic violence as a major social, legal and health problem has led to considerable research in this area during the past three decades. Despite the current prominence of domestic violence, historically it was viewed as very much a private matter. Men were expected to be dominant in households and the use of power – emotional, verbal, financial or physical – was acceptable in many places in the past and still is in many parts of the world today. This perception changed in Western Europe and North America due in part to research that increasingly demonstrated the prevalence of and damage resulting from domestic violence. '... people are more likely to be killed, physically assaulted, hit, beaten up (and) slapped ... in their own homes by other family members than anywhere else, or by anyone else in our society' (Gelles and Cornell, 1985: 12). The true extent of partner violence was acknowledged in the 1970s, mostly as a result of the women's movement.

Domestic violence is defined as 'threatening behaviour, violence or abuse (psychological, physical, sexual, financial or emotional) between adults (aged 18 or over) who are or have been intimate partners or are family members, regardless of gender or sexuality' (Home Office, 2005a).

The terms **intimate partner violence** (IPV), domestic abuse, wife abuse, spouse abuse, spouse battering and family violence are often used synonymously. Domestic violence occurs in all types of intimate relationships, whether heterosexual or homosexual, and in all cultures and socio-economic classes. It is perpetrated by both men and women; however, the majority of cases involve male perpetrators and female victims. Because the literature on domestic violence has focused on male partners perpetrating violence on female victims, we have focused our review of the literature on violence in those relationships.

As we can see from the definition, domestic violence has many forms (see Table 6.1). Stalking is another form of domestic violence that will be discussed in a separate section of this chapter.

- *Emotional/psychological violence:* Includes humiliating, ridiculing or intimidating the victim, controlling what the victim can and cannot do, withholding information from the victim, deliberately doing something to make the victim feel diminished or embarrassed, isolating the victim from friends and family, yelling, swearing and accusing him/her of having affairs, putting him/her down, name-calling, playing mind games, making him/her feel guilty and to blame for causing the abuse, using looks, actions, gestures, weapons to make him/her feel afraid, attempts to undermine self-worth, threats, denial of reality (e.g. saying the victim is mentally ill).

- *Financial/economic violence:* Controlling the victim's money and other economic resources (this involves putting the victim on a strict 'allowance', withholding money at will and forcing the victim to beg for the money until the abuser gives them some money), preventing the victim from finishing education or obtaining employment, stealing from or defrauding a partner of money or assets, exploiting the intimate partner's resources for personal gain, withholding physical resources such as food, clothes, necessary medications or shelter.

- *Physical violence:* Infliction of physical pain and/or injury, e.g. pushing, shoving, slapping, hitting, pulling hair, biting, grabbing, choking, shaking, arm-twisting, kicking, punching, hitting with objects, throwing things, burning, stabbing, shooting, poisoning, indirect physical violence (destruction of objects/property).

- *Sexual violence:* Any exploitative or coercive sexual contact without consent, including fondling, intercourse, oral or anal sodomy, attacks on the sexual parts of the body, involuntary viewing of sexual imagery or activity and treating someone in a sexually derogatory manner.

Table 6.1 Forms of domestic violence

In both the USA and the UK domestic violence occurs in 25–28 per cent of married couples at some time in their marriage (Browne and Herbert, 1997). British criminal statistics have determined that domestic violence accounts for one-quarter of all violent crimes (British Crime Survey, 1998) and half of all female homicides recorded by the police. According to the British Crime Survey (Finney, 2006), 28 per cent of women and 18 per cent of men experience domestic violence and it is more likely than any other criminal behaviour to involve repeat victimization.

It is difficult to estimate the true extent of domestic violence, especially since victims are often unwilling or unable to report the incident. Many acts of domestic violence are never reported or do not come to the awareness of law enforcement or social service agencies. Estimates of the extent of domestic violence have relied heavily on the data collected from women who have come into contact with women's agencies and the police. It is widely believed that there is serious under-reporting of domestic violence, not only on the part of victims but also by official agencies. On average, a woman is assaulted 37 times before telling someone for the first time (Harrower, 1998). Reasons for not reporting domestic violence are very varied. Some victims believe that it is too trivial to bother the police, underestimating the frequency and severity of the abuse, or they think it is a private or family matter and not police business, or that the police can not do much. Others believe that it will result in more violence because often they experience pressure and intimidation not to report the attack. Feelings of fear, shame, embarrassment and low self-esteem prevent many women from reporting violent incidents.

Theories of domestic violence

What causes domestic violence? Many theories of domestic violence have been offered by a number of researchers but it must be noted that no single

Figure 6.1 Police campaign poster against domestic violence.
Source: Courtesy of Northumbria Police.

theory or discipline has been adequate in thoroughly explaining this phenomenon.

Biological theories

As discussed in Chapter 2, biological theories of violence and aggression focus on the genetic, congenital or organic roots of behaviour. Researchers focus on genetics, neuropathology, head injury, brain infections and other medical illnesses, changes in the structure or function of the brain or endocrinological factors to explain domestic violence. For example, high levels of testosterone or low levels of serotonin have been associated with violence.

Psychological theories

These theories attempt to explain why particular individuals engage in physical aggression and others do not by assuming that some characteristic or combination of characteristics (individual personality traits) of the individual increases the risk that the individual will engage in partner violence. Some examples are social learning, psychopathology models, impulse-control problems, low self-esteem, attitudes regarding acceptability of violence, personality, the role of attachment (e.g. men that experience pathological levels of dependency, jealousy and fear of rejection resulting from childhood experiences with caregivers), etc. Impulsivity, suspicion of others, antisocial behaviour and compulsivity have often been associated with violence.

Social learning theory

As discussed in Chapter 3, according to the social learning perspective, children observe the consequences of the behaviour of significant others and learn which behaviours achieve desired results. When behaviours are modelled and reinforced these can become entrenched and replicated in other social interactions. During childhood, children observe how parents behave towards each other and this behaviour is viewed as acceptable. The social learning perspective asserts that the batterer learns to respond violently to situations by imitating the behaviour of family members, peers and significant others in his life. In other words, this theory links two variables: exposure to violence in the family of origin in childhood, and violence towards partners in adulthood. A child who grows up in a home where its members exhibit aggressive behaviours is at greater risk for exhibiting the same aggressive behaviours in adulthood.

Violent men are assumed to have observed the use and reinforcement of marital violence in their family of origin, learning to use violence and failing to learn non-violent methods for resolving marital disputes. Therefore, violence is a learned behaviour. Also, this ability to dominate through violence generates a feeling of success, which reinforces the behaviour and increases the likelihood that abuse will continue to be used as a method to satisfy such needs in the future. Therefore, following learning, violent behaviour is reinforced, therefore maintained and repeated, because it produces desirable consequences.

Feminist theory

The philosophical foundation of the feminist model is the belief that men are ordained with power and control by a patriarchal society and that they use their culturally dominant position to control the behaviour of women. Women are thus the victims of male abusive control. The notion of patriarchy has been used to emphasize that domestic violence reflects the unequal distribution of power between men and women in society, the family and their relationships (Dobash and Dobash, 1992). This views men as having the exclusive right to exercise power and control over their partner through the systematic use of violence, economic subordination, threats, isolation and other control tactics. Male abuse of female intimates is viewed as coercive control, growing out of a threat to male superior status in the marital relationship. Husbands who acknowledge and relate positively to their wife's autonomy are least at risk for violent behaviours (Yllö, 1993).

Systems theory

Family systems theories propose that the aetiology of marital violence lies in family interaction patterns (Lane and Russell, 1989). According to the systems approach the family is a dynamic organization made up of interdependent components (individual members) that continually interact with one another. The behaviour of one member and the probability of a re-occurrence of that behaviour are affected by the responses and feedback of other members. For example, an aggressive action by a man towards his wife results in a reaction by another family member. This reaction, in turn, affects the probability of aggressive behaviour in the future.

From this perspective violence is maintained through the roles, relationships and feedback mechanisms that regulate the system. If the system rewards violence then it is likely that it will re-occur. Therefore, researchers look at the communication, relationship and problem-solving skills of couples where violence occurs. They believe that both partners play some role so intervention must involve both or the whole family rather than one individual.

Sociological theories

A broader viewpoint considers the life events or social stress paradigm. Life events research has indicated that negative life events, especially those threatening the status of the traditional male role, are related to spousal abuse. According to stress theory, domestic violence is a reaction to stress, frustration and blocked goals. Men with lower incomes, poorer marital quality, bad housing, lack of job opportunities, unfavourable working conditions, less social support and alcohol abuse have been found to be most vulnerable to violent reactions (Gelles, 1994). Marital quality can serve as both a stressor and resource in the aetiology of domestic violence. Inability to communicate and negotiate conflict has been found to be highly related to physical violence between spouses (McKenry et al, 1995).

Social support, in general, is a major insulator from family violence. The ability to call on friends, family and community for assistance appears to mediate violent reactions to stress. In general, the more a family is integrated into a community, the less likelihood there is of violent behaviours (Strauss et al, 1980).

Classification of domestic violence offenders

Recent research has focused on identifying different types of batterers and has found that violent partners vary along a number of dimensions, including severity of violence, alcohol use, anger, depression, etc., thus showing that they are heterogeneous. Researchers developed a number of different typologies in an attempt to systematically examine how and why different men use violence against their partners. This increases the understanding of partner violence and facilitates effective identification, assessment and intervention. The assumption behind all these different typologies is that a valid typology of batterers could be used to match different types of abuse to different forms of intervention.

Research models have differed in their emphasis on behavioural traits, form and severity of violence or personality characteristics, motivation, causation, actions and victim–offender interaction. All these inconsistencies have made interpreting results, comparing findings and drawing conclusions problematic. As a consequence there have been numerous typologies developed in the domestic violence literature. Despite many commonalities, no single profile has emerged that completely and reliably distinguishes batterers from non-violent men. It must also be noted that the typology approach to classification that seeks to identify strict categories has been criticized. Such typological systems require that each individual belongs to only one 'type'. This rigidity denies the possibility of variation in an individual's behaviour and of more complex multidimensional aspects of the offending as well as ignoring the potential for development or change in someone's actions.

Johnson (1995) reviewed data gathered from large-sample survey research and shelter populations and distinguished four patterns of partner violence based on patterns of control that are present throughout the relationship: intimate terrorism (IT), violent resistance (VR), common couple violence (CCV) and mutual violent control (MVC).

- *Intimate terrorism* (IT) is violence utilized as part of a general pattern of control. One partner uses violence along with emotional and psychological abuse to maintain control over the other. It is more likely than other types to be frequent and to escalate in seriousness. Intimate terrorism is much less common than common couple violence, but probably dominates samples collected from different agencies such as police, courts and hospitals.

- *Violent resistance* (VR) is violence by one partner in the context of the relationship where the other partner is violent and controlling – violence used in resistance to an intimate terrorist. Sometimes it is self-defensive, sometimes more like payback, sometimes the act of an entrapped victim who sees no other way to escape a violently abusive relationship.

- *Common couple violence* (CCV) is violence that exists within the context of a specific argument in which one partner physically attacks the other. This arises out of conflicts that escalate to arguments and then to violence. CCV is not connected to a general pattern of control. It is less likely to escalate over time, less severely violent and more likely to be mutually violent. Although it is less serious than intimate terrorism, in some cases it can be frequent and/or quite serious, even life-threatening. This is probably the most common type of intimate partner violence and dominates general surveys, student samples and even marriage counselling samples.

- *Mutual violent control* (MVC) is where both partners are violent and controlling.

Holtzworth-Munroe and Stuart (1994) in a review of 15 batterer typologies proposed that batterer subtypes can be classified along three descriptive dimensions:

1. severity and frequency of marital violence;
2. generality of the violence (i.e. family-only or extrafamilial violence); and
3. the batterer's psychopathology or personality disorders.

These dimensions were used to identify three major subtypes of batterers: family-only, dysphoric/borderline and generally violent/antisocial.

- *Family-only* batterers are the most likely to feel remorse, admit having marital problems and seek help for such problems. They are the least violent group and the least likely to engage in psychological and sexual abuse. The violence is generally restricted to family members; they are the least likely to engage in violence outside the home or to have related legal problems. Also they evidence little psychopathology and either no personality disorder or a passive-dependent personality disorder. Approximately 50 per cent of batterer research samples are in the family-only subgroup.

- *Dysphoric/borderline* batterers engage in moderate to severe partner abuse, including psychological and sexual abuse. Usually the violence is confined to the family but sometimes they may engage in extrafamilial violence and criminal behaviour. They are the most dysphoric, psychologically distressed and emotionally volatile. They experience delusional jealousy and cannot tolerate separation from their partner. They may evidence borderline and schizoidal personality characteristics and may have problems with alcohol and drug abuse. These men make up about 25 per cent of research samples.

- *Generally violent/antisocial* batterers feel little remorse and are most likely to blame their victim. They engage in moderate to severe violence, including psychological and sexual abuse, and they are the most violent subtypes. They engage in high levels of partner and extrafamilial violence and have the most extensive history of related criminal behaviour. They are likely to have problems with alcohol and drug abuse and be most likely to show the characteristics of antisocial personality disorder or psychopathy. This type constitutes 25 per cent of batterer research samples.

Other typologies include Elbow (1977), Gondolf (1988), Saunders (1992), Hamberger et al (1996), Cavanaugh and Gelles (2005) and Chiffriller et al (2006).

Focus 6.1

Domestic violence case example

Figure 6.2 O.J. Simpson.
Source: Ron Galella/WireImage/Gerry Images.

O.J. Simpson was a very successful sportsman who then became a media star. In 1992 he and Nicole Brown divorced and in 1994 Nicole and her friend, Ron Goldman, were found murdered. The American public was shocked when O.J. was charged with the murders. During the trial it became clear that he had been violent to Nicole on several occasions, the police had been called out to their home at least nine times and in 1989 he had been charged with spousal assault and convicted. It was also revealed that for several months after they separated he hung around outside her new home, he called her trying to persuade her that they needed to work things out, brought her flowers and left them on her doorstep, and showed up at neighbourhood restaurants they used to go to in the hope of seeing her there. O.J. Simpson was eventually acquitted of the murder charges but was ordered, in the subsequent civil case in 1997, to pay $33.5 million to the relatives of Nicole Brown and Ron Goldman. He has since then written a book called *If I Did It* that somewhat ambiguously implies that he may well have committed the murders.

Stalking and domestic violence

The term **stalking** is used to describe the willful, repeated and malicious following, harassing or threatening of another person. The state of California was the first in the USA to pass an anti-stalking law in 1990. In Britain, stalking was legally recognized by the introduction of the Protection from Harassment Act in 1997.

Stalking typically consists of a broad range of behaviours. Stalkers most often persecute their targets by unwanted communications, which can consist of frequent (often nightly) telephone calls, letters, e-mail, graffiti, notes (e.g. left on the target's car) or packages (e.g. gifts, pictures). The offender may camp outside the house or workplace of the victim. Somewhat more extreme forms include ordering goods and services in the victim's name and charging to the victim's account, placing false advertisements or announcements, ordering funeral wreaths, spreading rumours about the victim and destroying or moving their property. The perpetrator may threaten the victim with violence and actually assault, rape and murder. In many cases innocent parties and the target's circle of friends and associates become victims of the stalker's behaviour (Table 6.2).

In a study of stalking victims conducted by the National Institute of Justice and the Centers for Disease Control and Prevention, 8000 women and 8000 men were contacted by telephone and asked whether they had ever experienced any number of acts of stalking. The report indicated that 8.2 per cent of the women

■ Posting cards or other cryptic messages
■ Breaking windows, breaking into or vandalizing partner's home
■ Taking partner's post
■ Leaving things such as flowers on doorstep or at work
■ Watching partner from a distance
■ Hang-up calls on the telephone
■ Following partner with a car
■ Following partner on foot
■ Hiding in bushes or other surveillance of partner's home
■ Surveillance of partner at work
■ Other trespassing
■ Vandalizing partner's property
■ Destroying property to scare or intimidate partner
■ Stealing things from partner
■ Breaking into partner's house or car
■ Filing numerous pleadings in court cases
■ Filing for custody of children regardless of their needs
■ Not respecting visitation limitations
■ Harassing telephone calls or notes
■ Violation of restraining orders

Table 6.2 Common domestic violence stalking acts (Sonkin, 1997, in Meloy, 1998)

in the sample and 2.2 per cent of the men had been stalked at some time in their lives and that an estimated 1 million adult women and 0.4 million men are stalked annually in the USA (Tjaden and Thoenness, 1998).

Stalking gained major media attention by the high-profile cases involving celebrities. However, research shows that most cases of stalking take place between ordinary people who had a prior intimate relationship or were acquaintances (Meloy, 1996). Emerson et al (1998) found that of women victims, a total of 48 per cent reported being stalked by a partner/spouse or ex-partner/spouse, 14 per cent by dates or former dates, 19 per cent by acquaintances and 23 per cent by strangers. Most men victims, about 70 per cent, were stalked by acquaintances or strangers.

Therefore research shows that the largest victim group of stalking is female ex-intimate partners (Meloy, 1998), establishing an association between stalking and domestic violence. In general, a high correlation has been found between domestic violence and stalking. However, very few studies have examined what factors predict the occurrence of stalking in relationships characterized by domestic violence or provide direct data on the link between stalking and previous domestic violence. Those that have been conducted suggest that between 30 per cent and 65 per cent of stalking cases that involve former intimates also involved a previous violent relationship (Tjaden and Thoennes, 1998). Approximately 50–60 per cent of all stalking cases may be considered 'domestic' in the sense that cases involve former intimates. About half of this domestic stalking group involves previous violent relationships (Douglas and Dutton, 2001). It is estimated that between 29 per cent and 54 per cent of all female murder victims are battered women, and in 90 per cent of these cases stalking preceded the murder. This has led many to conclude that stalking in intimate relationships is a form of domestic violence.

One other finding that seems to emerge from the research is that persons who stalk ex-intimate partners tend to display more violence towards their victims than do persons who stalk others. Meloy and Gothard (1995) determined that threats made by stalkers were more common where the victim was a former intimate partner. Similarly, research found that violent stalkers were more likely to have a prior attachment to their victims (80 per cent) than were non-violent stalkers (55 per cent) (Schwartz-Watts and Morgan, 1998). Generally, findings suggest that men who stalked their former intimate partners after a break-up were more likely than other men to have been abusive in the relationship. Violence is common in the past relationship and is common during the stalking episode. Findings suggest that the co-occurrence of stalking and domestic violence increases the risk of serious violence and murder.

Risk factors associated with domestic violence

Risk factors or risk markers refer to characteristics associated with an increased likelihood that a problem behaviour, in this case, violence, will occur. It should be noted that the presence of one or more risk factors is not equivalent to a causal relationship. It means that the odds of an associated event, in this case domestic violence, are greater when one or more risk markers are present. While it may be an indicator of which groups of people are most vulnerable, a risk factor is not the same as the cause of the violence since it might be correlated with something else that is associated with the underlying cause.

Most of the work examining factors associated with domestic violence has focused on identifying differences between men who have engaged in violence against their partners and those who have not. Numerous risk factors for domestic violence perpetration have been identified by this means.

Many studies have found that men who perpetrate violence against their wives are more likely than non-violent comparison groups to report that they experienced violence in the family of origin, either as a witness to spouse abuse or as the victim of child abuse, but numerous men who grew up in violent homes do not abuse their wives, and many men who do abuse their partners did not experience violence in their families of origin. Fear of abandonment is an important aspect of abusive men's behaviour (Dutton et al, 1994). A threat that a partner might leave the relationship is dangerous. Leaving or attempting to leave was found to provoke potentially lethal violence on the part of the husband (Aldridge and Browne, 2003) in many violent relationships.

While domestic violence occurs in all demographic groups, several demographic characteristics have been related to the perpetration of partner abuse. For example, youth has been found to be predictive of violence. Rates of domestic violence tend to decrease somewhat as the age of the couples increases (Straus et al, 1980). Lower socio-economic status has also been identified as a predictor of violence in the general population as well as unemployment. However, it should be noted that batterers come from all social backgrounds.

Prior arrest for violent crime is one frequently mentioned risk factor for domestic violence re-assault. Generally, it was found that people with criminal records are more likely to be violent. Also, substance (drugs and alcohol) abuse has consistently been linked with domestic violence (Cattaneo and Goodman, 2003). It has been reported that women who are pregnant are at increased risk of being assaulted by their abusive partners (Riggs D.S. et al, 2000) as well as those who are unmarried and cohabiting. The presence of children in the household is associated with the risk of domestic violence.

Concerning psychological characteristics, spouse abusers tend to be generally more angry and hostile than non-violent men. Their personality exhibits characteristics of emotional dependence, insecurity, low self-esteem, low empathy, low impulse control, poor communication and social skills, antisocial personality, narcissism, anxiety, depression, and aggressive and hostile personality styles. In terms of psychopathology, mood disorders, depression, post-traumatic stress disorder (PTSD) and borderline personality disorder have been identified as markers for domestic violence.

It should be noted that in these studies the differences between abusers and non-abusers are relatively small and there is no single factor that can be used to identify men at risk. Violence may occur even in the absence of identified risk markers.

Risk assessment

Risk assessment in cases of domestic violence can be defined as trying to identify those victims who are most at risk of experiencing violence in the future. The assessment of risk for marital violence perpetration or victimization is not a simple process. The variety of risk markers and the general lack of information regarding risk markers for specific incidents of spouse abuse make it quite difficult for professionals to confidently evaluate the dangerousness of a particular person or situation.

Recently, attempts have been made to develop instruments to assess the risk of domestic violence. These measures include items that evaluate a subgroup of the risk markers described above, including characteristics of the perpetrators, victims and/or abusive relationships. Accurate risk assessments are very important as they provide a structured way for responding officers to gather detailed and relevant information from victims. This information when shared with other agencies can help provide better services to victims and perpetrators because their specific needs are identified.

The Spousal Assault Risk Assessment (SARA; Kropp et al, 1995; Kropp and Hart, 2000), a 20-item clinician administered rating form, was designed to assess risk of re-offending in the criminal justice system. A complete evaluation with the SARA requires psychological assessment of the perpetrator and clinical judgement. Other risk assessment instruments include:

- The Danger Assessment (DA): a measure designed to assist battered women in the assessment of their own risk of femicide (Campbell, 1986).
- The Domestic Violence Screening Instrument (DVSI): designed not only to assess risk of re-assault but also to assess treatment needs. Unlike the SARA, the DVSI is a structured questionnaire to be completed by the perpetrator.
- The Kingston Screening Instrument for Domestic Violence (K-SID) was developed from the extensive programme of research of Richard Gelles (Straus and Gelles, 1990) as a screening instrument. The K-SID consists of 10 risk markers for re-assault.
- The DV-MOSAIC is a computer-assisted method of threat assessment developed by Gavin de Becker and Associates (de Becker, 2000). DV-MOSAIC is not a predictive instrument. It is an overall method used to aid police officers in their assessments and investigations of domestic violence situations.
- The Conflict Tactics Scale (CTS; Straus, 1979) is used to measure intrafamily conflict.
- The Index of Spouse Abuse (ISA; Hudson and McIntosh, 1981) was designed to measure the severity of abuse, as was
- The Danger Assessment Instrument (Campbell, 1995).

Various police forces and related agencies have also developed their own procedures for assessing the risk associated with reports of violence within the home. Unfortunately these procedures are not developed using any established psychometric principles and are not published in scholarly outlets where they can be openly and independently evaluated. They thus tend to operate as checklists of what needs to be considered with little indication that their use actually reduces risk (see Focus box 6.2).

Focus 6.2

Cases of women who were killed despite reporting domestic violence incidents

Hayley Richards, 23, from Trowbridge, Wiltshire, was murdered by ex-boyfriend Hugo Quintas in June 2005. A week before, police were told that the Portuguese factory worker had threatened to kill her and attacked her so violently she needed hospital treatment. Officers judged that the risk of Quintas attacking again was low. Less than a week after her phone call, Quintas cut her throat in her flat. She was pregnant. Hayley told police where they could find Quintas, but officers who could have responded were already dealing with a report of a dog locked in a car. The Independent Police Complaints Commission blamed 'institutional failings'. Quintas was jailed for a minimum of 18 years. (Source: *The Observer*, 31 December, 2006)

Julia Pemberton, 47, from Hermitage, Berkshire, was shot four times by her estranged husband in November 2003. Before the killing, she reported three incidents of serious abuse to Thames Valley Police, but insufficient action was taken. Julia had suffered years of emotional abuse by her husband. Alan Pemberton killed their 17-year-old son outside their home while Julia hid inside and called 999. An operator heard her scream: 'Oh my God, I'm going to die', before gunshots were heard. Thames Valley Police were criticized for taking almost seven hours to enter the property. Pemberton shot himself. (Source: *The Observer*, 31 December, 2006)

Vicky Horgan, 27, from Oxfordshire was shot dead, along with her 25-year-old sister, Emma Walton, by estranged husband Stuart Horgan at a family barbecue in June 2004. She had contacted Thames Valley Police's domestic violence team about him on several occasions. He committed suicide while on remand in prison. (Source: *The Observer*, 11 March, 2007)

Interventions

A wide range of interventions exists for reducing domestic violence re-victimization. Intervention means trying to eliminate or improve an existing problem and trying to stop future occurrences or relapses. In cases of partner violence this means helping people lead non-violent and safe lives. Since the problem of violence against women in the home was 'discovered', thousands of projects, programmes, policies and practices have been developed worldwide to respond to those who suffer abuse and intervene with respect to its perpetrators.

Many of these approaches consist of providing some form of safe haven or shelter for the victims. Some of these try to enable the victims to understand the processes that give rise to violence by teaching safety planning. This involves preparing in advance the possibility of leaving when the victim recognizes that the violence is likely to become even more severe or life-threatening.

There has also been a growing move to improve the responses of the justice system, particularly of the police, by providing support for those who have been abused and responding more effectively to the perpetrators of abuse. Domestic Violence Units were first established in London in 1987; more than half the police forces in England and Wales have a DVU. The units have staff who offer advice and help to victims of domestic violence. They have links with other specialist organizations and agencies in their local areas such as local solicitors and Women's Aid groups. Protection orders, injunctions, restraining orders, sanction through fines, probation and prison are some forms of legal intervention, but these often do not deal directly with the central psychological issues involved in the perpetuation of domestic violence. They may even make matters worse by treating a psychological problem as a legal one.

A more psychological approach is the development of treatment programmes for the people who are violent. Although the primary goals of virtually all programmes/groups are to ensure the partners' safety, they do put emphasis also on altering attitudes towards violence. There are attempts to increase perpetrators' sense of personal responsibility and learn non-violent alternatives to past behaviours. Other treatments include couple therapy where both partners are helped to take responsibility for their actions and their own behaviour, and mental health treatments such as individual psychotherapy or group therapy.

Activity 6.1

Below is an example of a domestic violence case. Based on what you have read so far, assess the risk of future violence to Emma.

Emma has been with 32-year-old James for 12 years and they have three children, aged nine, seven and three. James is unemployed and has a long criminal history including violence and property offences. He often drinks alcohol to excess. There have already been a number of instances of domestic violence between the couple. In the past Emma decided no longer to put up with his abusive behaviour and asked him to leave the house. James hung around outside her house and slept at night in his car parked across the street. He began calling her on the telephone, begging her to let him return, and promising not to drink alcohol any more. On one occasion he entered her home, struck her on the back of the head with a hammer, hit her in the face and sexually assaulted her. After living apart for a month, James is now back at home living with Emma.

Conclusions

Domestic violence is a widespread problem, the full extent of which is not fully known due to under-reporting by both victims and official agencies. Many theories of domestic violence have been offered but none of them has been adequate in thoroughly explaining domestic violence. A number of risk factors for domestic violence perpetration have been identified and many programmes for abusers and their victims exist, with mixed results. More recently professionals have taken a more responsible and informed attitude to domestic violence but resources available to the health, social and law enforcement services are still too limited to deal appropriately with the issue.

The underlying psychological mechanisms are still only poorly understood. It is likely that social processes such as those highlighted by the feminist perspective as well as individual psychological problems, probably having roots in the violent person's own upbringing, combine together to give rise to this pressing problem. This means that a variety of different strategies at the individual and public level will be needed to reduce the incidence of domestic violence.

Key concepts and terms

Domestic violence	Risk assessment
Intimate partner violence	Stalking

Sample essay titles

- Critically discuss the different ways of classifying domestic violence.

- Discuss how stalking can be a form of domestic violence.

- Describe and evaluate the risk factors that have been associated with domestic violence.

- What psychological processes do you think give rise to domestic violence?

Further reading

Books

Browne, K., and Herbert, M. (1997). *Preventing Family Violence*. Chichester: Wiley.

Dobash, E.R., Dobash, R.P., Cavanagh, K., and Lewis, R. (1999). *Changing Violent Men*. Thousand Oaks, CA: Sage.

Journal articles

Aldridge, M.L., and Browne, K.D. (2003). Perpetrators of spousal homicide: A review. *Trauma, Violence and Abuse*, 4, 265–276.

Cattaneo, L.B., and Goodman, L.A. (2003). Victim-reported risk factors for continued abusive behaviour: Assessing the dangerousness of arrested batterers. *Journal of Community Psychology*, 31(4), 349–369.

Douglas, K.S., and Dutton, D.G. (2001). Assessing the link between stalking and domestic violence. *Aggression and Violent Behavior*, 6, 519–546.

Kropp, R., and Hart, S.D. (2000). The Spousal Assault Risk Assessment Guide (SARA): Reliability and validity in adult male offenders. *Law and Human Behavior*, 24, 101–118.

Riggs, D.S., Caulfield, M.B., and Street, A.E. (2000). Risk for domestic violence: Factors associated with perpetration and victimisation. *Journal of Clinical Psychology*, 56, 1289–1316.

7 Rape

Freya Newman

This chapter presents key concepts and research into the psychological study of rape. The legal definition of rape is given alongside incidence rates and a discussion of the problem of **attrition** in rape cases. A summary of empirical research into rape is outlined as well as the advantages and disadvantages of using certain methodologies. Various theories of why rape occurs are then explored, highlighting the main differences between **biological models** and **environmental models of rape**. Typologies seeking to classify rapists are presented with an examination of motivational and **behavioural classification** systems of rapists and rape offences.

Learning outcomes

When you have completed this chapter you should be able to:

1. Know the legal definition of rape.
2. Appreciate incidence rates and the problem of attrition.
3. Understand the empirical research into rape.
4. Know the biological and environmental explanations of rape.
5. Appreciate the key classifications of rapists and rape offences.
6. Appreciate the value of the application of the thematic approach of rape classification in rape investigations.

The legal definition of rape

The UK Sexual Offences Act 2003 states that the crime of rape is committed when a person 'intentionally penetrates the vagina, anus or mouth of another person' when that other person 'does not consent to the penetration' or that the offender 'does not reasonably believe' that the other person consents (p. 42). The Act ensures that the laws are equally applied to both male and female victims, as well as clarifying issues surrounding consent. The Act also outlines the crime of 'assault by penetration' treating the penetration by other objects, other than the penis, just as seriously. In the UK, both rape and assault by penetration hold the maximum sentence of life in prison.

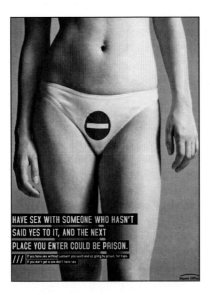

Figure 7.1 The Home Office recently launched an advertisement campaign in men's magazines, highlighting the consent issue. They advise that gaining consent means more than an assumption and men should actively seek a 'yes' before intercourse. Home Office Consent Campaign – Campaign poster 2007 taken from the Home Office Website © copyright material is reproduced with the permission of the Controller of HMSO and Queen's Printer for Scotland.
Source: © Home Office.

Incidence rates

Home Office statistics show that there were over 14,000 recorded rapes in England and Wales between 2004 and 2005 (Nicholas et al, 2005). This accounts for less than 0.5 per cent of all recorded crime. However, this may not be the complete picture; it is estimated that only 15 per cent of rapes are reported to the police (Walby and Allen, 2002). Over recent years, the incidence rate of rape seems to be increasing; however, conviction rates have been steadily decreasing. Now, one in 18 cases of rape ends with a successful conviction (Kelly et al, 2005). Recent government research has sought to discover the reasons behind this.

Attrition rate in rape cases

The withdrawal of rape cases from the Criminal Justice System (CJS) is known as the *attrition rate*. Kelly et al (2005) identify four key stages in the CJS where cases are likely to be withdrawn.

1. *Decision to report*. A victim of rape may not report a rape to the police for a number of reasons, including fears about the investigation and trial process, the traumatic nature of having to relive the rape again, feelings of shame, embarrassment, guilt or fear of retribution.
2. *Investigative stage*. Victims may decide to withdraw a complaint of rape or refuse to prosecute the accused after they are detained. This may be

attributable to the perceived negative psychological effects they may associate with a trial (as described in Stage 1). At this stage in the process, it may also be the case that the police cannot detect the suspect and, therefore, the case is dropped.

3. *Discontinuance by prosecutors.* If an offender has been apprehended, the Crown Prosecution Service (CPS) may make the decision not to take the case to trial. This could be if they believe there is not enough evidence to secure a prosecution, perhaps because of the perceived credibility of the victim or any witnesses or the difficulty of determining if consent was withheld.

4. *Trial.* If the case goes to trial, the jury may decide the suspect is not guilty of the crime and, therefore, will acquit. Alternatively, the offender may be convicted for a lesser crime or have the conviction overturned on appeal.

Factors that influence the attrition process

There are several factors that may influence the attrition process, especially at the early stages of the investigation. For example, Kelly et al (2005) found that younger victims are more likely to report rape to the police while 16–25-year-olds are more likely to withdraw their statements at the investigation stage. The relationship the victim has with the offender may also be a factor. Cases where the victim knows the offender are least likely to be reported (Kelly et al, 2005). Also, if the alleged perpetrator is a partner, ex-partner or friend rather than a stranger or family member, victims are more likely to withdraw their statements (Feist et al, 2007). Finally, if a rape is part of a linked series, the case is more likely to continue to prosecution and to end with a successful conviction (Feist et al, 2007).

Studies of rape

The following section summarizes key findings in the descriptive studies of rape, rapists and their victims.

Gender of victims and offenders

Rape victims are more frequently female, while their attackers are male (*female-male* rape). Studies estimate that male rape perpetrated by male offenders occurs in approximately 5–10 per cent of reported cases of rape (Hodge and Canter, 1998). Victim and medical surveys in the UK and USA echo these figures (for example, Riggs N. et al, 2000; Kerr et al, 2003; McLean and Balding, 2003; Finney, 2006). However, because of popular beliefs in the causes of male-male rape it may be greatly under-reported.

Age of victims and offenders

Victim age and offender age are typically positively correlated (for example, Lea et al, 2003; Feist et al, 2007). As the age of the victim increases, so does the age of the offender. Therefore, offenders seem to be targeting victims of the same age. Studies based on recorded crime such as Amir (1971) suggest that the average age of offenders is 23 with the highest frequency of offenders being aged between 15–19 and 20–24. More recent studies, however, suggest that the average ages of offenders could be slightly higher. Ruperal (2004) records an average age of detected rapists in London as 30, where most offenders were falling into the 26–30 age group. It is important to note that offender age is only really known when the offender has been apprehended. Therefore, it would be incorrect to assume that these findings can be generalized to those offenders who remain undetected.

Studies of reported rapes seem to suggest that younger people are more at risk from sexual victimization than older people. Amir (1971), for example, found that victims were more likely to be 15–19 or 10–14, with an average age of 19.6. Studies from the UK support this trend. Ruperal (2004) found that the mean age of victims was 26, and that a third of victims were aged less than 21. Other victim surveys report that those who are within the 16–19 age group are more at risk from sexual assault (Myhill and Allen, 2002). Younger females may be being raped more than older females because they are more likely to be interacting socially with younger males, who are more likely than older males to be offenders.

Victim–offender relationship

Rape by an unknown offender

This kind of rape, also known as stranger rape, is carried out by a perpetrator unknown to the victim. It is not quite as easy to define as may be first thought because the offender may be a casual acquaintance of a few minutes, hours or days in duration. The crucial point is that the victim does not have any clear knowledge of the identity of the assailant.

A recent study in the UK, using levels of rape recorded by the police, indicates that 14 per cent of recorded rapes are committed by strangers (Feist et al, 2007). Results from the 2004/05 British Crime Survey indicate that levels of rape perpetrated by strangers are low compared to other forms of rape, at a level of 11 per cent. These findings seem to indicate that attacks by strangers are rarer than the media would have us believe. Clinical studies report higher levels of offending. Kerr et al (2003) found that just over a half of victims had been raped by a stranger; McLean and Balding (2003) indicate that over a third of their clients had been raped by someone that was unknown to them. These differences may well be due to differences in the sample of victims who seek clinical help.

Rape by a known offender

Rapes committed by a known perpetrator are those that consist of a wider range of victim–offender relationships. The offender could be a partner (intimate), an ex-partner, a colleague, a friend, a family member or could know the victim in another way (Kerr et al, 2003). Intimates seem to commit the most rapes against victims, as reported in studies from different data sources (Finney, 2006; Feist et al, 2007), although the percentages are lower within research using police records. These figures suggest that rapes occur most frequently in a domestic situation.

Additional physical and verbal violence

Although the rape itself is violent, studies show that additional physical and verbal violence is often used by offenders. Studies using both police records and medical notes suggest that additional violence and physical assault occurs in 25–82 per cent of cases (Riggs et al, 2000; Myhill and Allen, 2002; Kerr et al, 2003; McLean and Balding, 2003; Ruperal, 2004; Sugar et al, 2004; Feist et al, 2007). In the UK, weapons (knives or firearms) have been found to be used in a small percentage of cases (4–11 per cent), either to harm or coerce the victim (Kerr et al, 2003; McLean and Balding, 2003; Ruperal, 2004; Feist et al, 2007). In the USA, the percentage of rapes where weapons were used is higher. Sugar et al (2004), for example, found that knives, guns, ropes and blunt objects were used in 24 per cent of rape cases, derived from medical notes over a 34-month period. Verbal violence is also used within rape attacks. Feist et al (2007) found that specific threats were made in 29 per cent of cases studied, while emotional threats were used in 19 per cent of the cases. These threats included not only threats for the welfare of the victim but also for the victim's family or friends.

There is some evidence to suggest that stranger rapes are significantly more likely to be physically violent, and cause more injury, than rapes where the victim knows the offender (Jones et al, 2004). Research also suggests that strangers are more likely to use weapons to harm or threaten than acquaintances (Riggs et al, 2000). When studies explore the different types of rapes where an offender is known and compares these with stranger rapes, the results differ slightly. In fact, rapes committed by an intimate (partner or ex-partner) seem to demonstrate similar levels of violence and physical harm as stranger rapes, when compared to other forms of acquaintance rape (Ruperal, 2004; Ullman et al, 2006; Feist et al, 2007). Instead, there is some evidence to suggest that acquaintances more often use verbal violence within attacks (Jones et al, 2004).

Spatial patterns

Studies examining the spatial patterns of rape offences tend to measure the distance travelled from the offender's base to offence location (as reviewed in Canter and Youngs, 2008b) or aspects of the location of the offence.

Distance travelled to offend

Amir (1971) found that in 82 per cent of solved rapes, the offender and victim lived in the same neighbourhood. Other empirical studies, examining distance travelled to crime, generally find that rapists, like other offenders, do not travel very far to commit crimes. Studies carried out within the UK produce findings consistent with these US results. Canter and Larkin (1993) found that a sample of serial rapists within the UK travelled an average of 1.53 miles to commit their crimes, while in the USA serial and non-serial offenders have been recorded as travelling mean distances of between 1.15 miles (Rhodes and Conly, 1981) and 3.5 miles (LeBeau, 1987). In comparison to offenders who commit property offences, rapists, on average, do seem to travel shorter distances.

Location of offence

The location of the initial approach and the location of the attack are often measured researching the spatial patterning of rape. A recent study (Feist et al, 2007) found that in the 558 cases they examined, the location of the *initial approach* of the offender to the victim was a public place in 23 per cent of cases, but that in 18 per cent of cases it was the offender and the victim's shared home. The attack was only instigated by forced entry into the victim's home in 4 per cent of the cases.

Studies suggest that the *location of the attack* is more likely to be the home of the suspect, the victim's own home or their shared home (Feist et al, 2007). Age of victim seems to be a factor that is related to the location of the attack. Feist et al (2007) relate how victims over the age of 16 are more likely to be attacked in their own homes (around 30 per cent), while victims under 16 tend to be attacked in the offender's home or where they both live. This would make sense as victims under the age of 16 are thought to be more likely to be raped by a relative or an acquaintance.

Ruperal (2004) found that within stranger rapes in London, in more than half of the rapes the approach occurred outdoors, while 17 per cent occurred in a licensed premises (for example, a bar, pub or club). Conversely, she found that 64 per cent of the victims of intimate rape were approached within their own home, while a lesser percentage of victims were approached outside (17 per cent).

However, when a comparison is made between stranger and non-stranger attacks, a different pattern emerges. Stranger rapes do tend to occur more often in the victim's own home than outdoors (Jones et al, 2004), while rapes committed by a known offender tend to be committed more often in the offender's home (Jones et al, 2004).

Theories of rape

Biological models

As discussed in Chapter 2, biological models of rape follow the nature side of the nature-nurture debate and assert that perpetrators commit the act of rape due to their biological makeup and not environmental factors. In the context of rape these often merge into explanations that draw heavily on particular psychological characteristics of the individual perpetrator. One of the most widely cited of these is that put forward by Groth (1979). He asserts that individuals who seek to rape others suffer subconscious, uncontrollable sexual urges and exist on the edge of society. This model, therefore, takes some of the responsibility away from the rapist by suggesting that rapists are 'ill' and that they can not help themselves.

Critics of this approach refute its main assumptions. First, research suggests that only a small proportion of men who rape have a psychological disorder or mental illness, few being referred for psychiatric help. The model is also refuted by the evidence that rape is committed frequently in our society, a fact that would not be the case if rapists were a few disturbed individuals. Finally, many rapes are not impulsive events. Amir (1971) found that 80 per cent of rapes in his sample of rapes in the USA were planned.

Evolutionary models

Evolutionary theorists, or socio-biologists, believe that males who rape females do so in order to pass on their genes to future generations as they are unable to do so by consensual intercourse (Thornhill and Palmer, 2000). Such theories are based on observations of behaviour, seeming to be rape, in the animal kingdom. Female animals often seem to be penetrated by force, often by a dominant male. This behaviour is thought to ensure that the strongest, fittest genes are passed on to offspring and thus is considered as 'adaptation'. Evolutionary theorists have thus extended these observations in an attempt to explain rape in humans.

Criticism for evolutionary models is widespread. Those opposed to the idea that rape is a form of adaptation believe it is difficult to extend theories of animal behaviour to draw conclusions about human actions. Also, evolutionary theorists only seek to explain why males rape females and not why some males rape other males, or why females rape. These latter forms of behaviour can not be explained by a need for gene transmission. Furthermore, if the genetic driver were due to the inability of the rapist to have consensual intercourse then it would not be expected that any rapists had established sexual relationships outside of their rapes or any offspring. However, this is manifestly not the case as some rapists have had long-standing sexual partners and children.

Environmental models

Environmental models of rape behaviour reject the biological arguments and follow the nurture side of the debate. Therefore, these theories assert that individuals will rape others as a result of their interpretation of environmental cues and influences.

Feminist models

Feminists believe that males rape as a result of the need to punish and control women. They dismiss biological theories of rape and claim that it is a result of male domination in our society, rather than uncontrollable sexual urges. At an individual level, some feminists believe that males rape because their masculinity is at risk. At a societal level, others argue that rape exists to ensure that there remains an unequal balance of power between men and women and that women should, therefore, be subjugated. The feminist Brownmiller (1975: 5) insists 'it is nothing more or less than a conscious process of intimidation by which all *men* keep all *women* in a state of fear'. These arguments are, of course, very similar to those put forward to explain domestic violence in the previous chapter. At their heart they assume that all men are potential rapists.

Feminists and others believe that male rapists, and men in general, hold a set of inter-correlated beliefs and stereotypical ideas that seemingly justify or excuse rape behaviours. These *rape myths*, evidence for which is found in studies such as Scully and Marolla (1985) and Burt (1980), can be summarized as the following:

- Certain women deserve to be raped (for example prostitutes, victims with a prolific sexual history, anyone who invites a man into their home on a first date, a woman who wears the 'wrong' clothes or hitchhikers).

- Women unconsciously wish to be raped.

- Women often make false rape allegations because they have become pregnant from having consensual sexual intercourse, they are angry about being jilted by a partner, or they seek attention or financial recompense.

- Healthy women can resist rape.

- Rapists are unable to control their sexual urges and are pathologically disturbed.

Research has found that these rape myths are present both within the belief systems of offenders (Scully and Marolla, 1985) and in non-offending populations (for a summary, see Ryan, 2004).

The feminist perspective has come into criticism, especially for Brownmiller's assumption that all men are potential rapists. Evidence does not support this notion – the majority of men do not rape women. The feminist approach has also been criticized for not seeking to explain other types of rape, such as those perpetrated by females.

Activity 7.1

Discuss the following situation in a mixed group of men and women and consider the variations in their views:

A young man and a young woman have recently met at a nightclub and had enough to drink to make them feel too drunk to drive home but sober enough to go back to her house for a coffee. When they are alone in her house she allows the man to undress her, but when she tells him she is too drunk to have sex he says she will enjoy it once it gets started. She struggles a little but not enough to prevent him penetrating her vagina. The next morning she reports him to the police for rape.

- Was she right to do this?
- What further information should the police collect to proceed to a court case?
- What reasons might there be for the man not being convicted?

Developmental models

Developmental models assert that rape occurs as a result of inadequate bonding within childhood. As discussed in Chapter 2, these are strongly influenced by Bowlby's (1952) ideas of maternal deprivation and attachment. This suggests that rape occurs because, as a child, offenders do not form a close, 'healthy' bond with their mothers at a crucial point in their development. Therefore, as an adult, the offender is unable to form normal relationships with peers and potential partners and thus has to rape in order to gain intimacy and to satisfy a desire for social contact (Marshall, 1989). This theory is supported by evidence that some rapists do score highly on measures of intimacy and loneliness (Seidman et al, 1994). However, there is no evidence to suggest that lack of a parental bond will have a causal relationship with lack of intimacy in adulthood and it is likely that other mediating factors are involved. Not all people who do not have a parental influence within childhood go on to be criminals, let alone become rapists.

Typologies of rape and rapists

Motivational classification systems

Early classification systems categorized *rapists* by their motivations to rape. These systems were based primarily on interviews and observations of convicted rapists within clinical settings and were closely linked to the psychopathological model of rape. One of the first such **clinical classification** systems differentiated male rapists in terms of whether they were motivated by *sexual urges* or *aggression*.

Cohen, Seghorn and Calmas (1969) proposed a four-fold classification system, categorizing rapists as Compensatory, Displaced-Aggressive, Sex-Aggression Diffusion or Impulsive. Compensatory rapists were thought to be those who are primarily motivated by the need to act out rape fantasies and to alleviate feelings of sexual inadequacy. Displaced-Aggressive rapists were those who rape in order to vent their anger against a significant other female. Sex-Aggression Diffusion are offenders who rape in order to gain sadistic pleasure. Lastly, Impulsive rapists were those who are not motivated by sexual needs or aggression. Instead, these are offenders who seize the opportunity to rape if it arises, perhaps while committing another crime.

A shift in thinking came about in the mid 1970s, when Groth asserted that rape was not just about fulfilling sexual needs or releasing aggression. Instead, he believed that rapists were more likely to express their need for power through rape and hostility (Groth et al, 1977). Groth (1979), therefore, proposed a four-way typology that emphasizes the sexual act of rape as a way in which to express inner aggression and the need to control. The Power-Assertive rapist is one who feels the need to assert power to lessen feelings of general inadequacy. The Power-Reassurance rapist feels more specific feelings of sexual inadequacy and rapes in order to redeem his masculinity. The Anger-Retaliation offender feels aggression towards women in general and therefore will rape in order to seek revenge. The Anger-Excitation rapist will gain sadistic pleasure from acting aggressively to and by raping the victim.

Empirical clinical classification systems

As earlier motivational typologies of rapists were based on clinical observations, later models were adapted from more detailed empirical observations and statistical analysis in an attempt to improve their validity and reliability. The Massachusetts Treatment Center Taxonomic Program (MTCTP) in the USA was the first programme to empirically test these typologies. The MTC classification system (now in its third revision) was put forward by Knight (1999), based on empirical testing of large clinical samples. The MTC: R3 classifies rapists based on the four primary motivations of Opportunistic, Pervasive Anger, Sexual and Vindictiveness.

Echoing earlier systems, those within the Opportunistic category were impulsive and predatory. The Pervasive Anger category described those who were primarily motivated by highly generalized aggressive feelings. The Sexual category was thought to include those who were either sadistic (driven by a fusion of sexual urges and aggression) or non-sadistic (enthused by feelings of sexual inadequacy and the need to dominate). The Vindictive category included those who hold deep resentment towards women. In addition to these four primary motivations, Knight (1999) proposed that additional dimensions could be used to discriminate between nine subtypes of rapists, depending on whether they were thought to score highly on a set of eight dimensions. These are:

1. juvenile and adult antisocial behaviour;
2. social competence;
3. expressive aggression;
4. offence planning;
5. global or pervasive anger;
6. overt and muted sadism;
7. sexualization (sexual thoughts and fantasies);
8. hostility towards women.

New cases can then be assigned to one of the nine subtypes depending on how they score on each of the dimensions.

Motivational classification systems for use in police investigations

At around the same time as the MTC were trying to validate Groth's (1979) typology for use in clinical investigations, the Federal Bureau of Investigation (FBI)'s National Center for the Analysis of Violent Crime (NCAVC) was modifying the categories for use in criminal investigations. The model was adapted in an attempt to describe the sorts of behaviours indicative of these motivations so that offenders could be classified from their actions at the crime scene. Hazelwood and Burgess (1987) proposed a four-fold typology of rapists, the analysis of the physical, verbal and sexual actions of the offender being used to assign unknown offenders to one of these four categories.

Focus 7.1

Utility of motivational classification systems

Academic utility

- These models help to build theory around the motivations behind rapists' behaviour.

- Interviews using clinical samples may help to identify the causes of rape.

Practical utility

- These models can be used to design specific treatment programmes for rapists.

- Clinical typologies may also be used to make decisions around forensic issues such as sentencing and risk assessment.

Limitations of motivational models of rapists

- Early clinical classification systems were based on observations using clinical populations. Therefore the validity and generalizability of the models have been called into question.

- The sample sizes of these clinical populations were small. Therefore the reliability of the models is limited.

- It is difficult to objectively measure motivation from crime scene behaviour, even though certain models attempt to do so. Therefore, the utility for these models within investigations is limited.

- Models are based on clinical interviews with the offender present. Thus, it is tenuous to classify an unknown, absent offender based on their crime scene behaviours (Canter and Heritage, 1990).

Behaviourally-based classification systems

In contrast to motivationally-based typologies, there has been a drive to produce more empirically sound classification systems. Thus, instead of attempting to classify rapists on the basis of what may motivate them, investigative psychologists have developed models of rape based on the systematic analysis of the offence behaviours themselves. These models were developed with the aim of complementing findings from motivational studies (Canter et al, 2003a).

Canter and Heritage (1990) developed the first behaviourally-based classification of rape by analysing 66 stranger sex offences from UK police records. They hypothesized that the analysis of the co-occurrence of offence behaviours would reveal certain ways in which the offender would interact with their victim. They found that certain offence behaviours did seem to occur

Theme	Examples of offence behaviours
Sexuality	Vaginal intercourse Other types of sexual behaviours
Violence and aggression	Violence used as a means of controlling the victim Violence used but not as a means to control Aggressive verbal behaviour
Impersonal, sexual gratification	Impersonal language Surprise attack No response to the victim's reaction
Criminality	The use of bindings The use of gagging Blindfolding the victim
Interpersonal intimacy	The offender requires the victim to participate physically in the attack The offender compliments the victim The offender apologizes to the victim

Table 7.1 Themes identified in Canter and Heritage's (1990) model of rape alongside the behaviours that characterize these themes

together within and across crimes and these behaviours seemed to share similarities. Indeed, Canter and Heritage (1990) identified five themes from this analysis which are shown in Table 7.1.

These themes seem to reflect the various psychological themes as identified within the rape literature. All seem to have roots in theoretical models, from an arena of different perspectives and reflect the type of interaction that the offender will have within the rape situation.

Not only did Canter and Heritage (1990) highlight qualitative differences in the way in which offenders were interacting with their victims, the model suggested that there were certain focal aspects of the rape. They suggested that core offence behaviours, such as vaginal intercourse, can be seen as aspects of the rape that are often found in the majority of rapes and perpetrated by the majority of offenders. However, they were able to show, using sophisticated analytical techniques, that there were certain offence behaviours that rarely seem to co-exist with other behaviours and were performed by offenders in a minority of cases. These behaviours included when the offender apologized to or complimented the victim. Such actions, it was argued, were those which would more readily distinguish between offences.

Subsequently, Canter et al (2003a) continued to examine the behavioural structure of rape in this way and developed a similar model using victim statements from 112 British rapes. They identified a four-themed model of rape behaviour where the offences could be differentiated into Hostile, Involvement, Controlling and Stealing types of behaviour. Canter et al (2003a) also used statistical techniques to examine the levels of violation within rapes; they found that these themes could vary in the types of sexual, physical and personal violation used in the offence. Sexual violation was used in a majority of the cases, then physical violation, whereas personal violation was rarer and thus could be used to more readily differentiate between offences.

Focus 7.2

A behaviourally-based model of rape

Another example of a behavioural model of rapists was presented by Canter (1994) and considered how rapists could be differentiated in terms of the role they assign to a victim. Violent behaviours were differentiated three ways, depending how the offender sees his victim, either as a 'vehicle', an 'object' or a 'person'.

Vehicle

Within this theme, the offender uses the victim as a medium for their own benefit. For example, an offender may act violently towards a victim in pursuit of sexual gratification or monetary gain. Typical behaviours that could be seen within this theme would include robbery and sexual assault. Behaviours defined within this theme are also thought of as being more excessively violent than those seen within the other two themes.

Object

Here, the offender treats the victim as a depersonalized object to be manipulated and controlled. Typical behaviours seen within this style of offending would therefore include such items as gagging, binding, threatening and being verbally derogatory towards the victim.

Person

Here, the offender will treat the victim as a human being rather than an object and may show behaviours that indicate some kind of pseudo-intimacy. The offender will therefore be interested in his or her victim's life and may request that the victim participate verbally or physically in any sexual contact as if they were having a relationship.

Focus 7.3

Utility of behavioural classification systems

Academic utility

- The statistical methods used to establish styles of offending from the analysis of behaviours empirically validate the theory or perspective linked to themes within which they occur.

- Although these classification systems are built on the analysis of offence behaviours, protagonists of this approach do not assert that the behaviours occur in a social vacuum. Indeed, Canter and Heritage's early model emphasizes that rape is a form of social interaction and that the themes identified are ways in which the offender interacts with his victim.

- These models provide frameworks that can be tested for replicability or used as a basis for further hypothesis testing.

Practical utility

- The behavioural models describe the actions occurring at the crime scene, rather than rapists' motivations. Therefore when new cases are presented to criminal investigations, police officers and analysts have an objective framework within which to note the absence or presence of behaviours.

- Using a thematic approach to classifying offences may be more robust than adding meaning to behaviours on an individual basis. Thus, the themes are not dependent on certain behaviours being present.

- Crime scene behaviours are often used to link crimes, where there is a lack of evidence or eye witness testimony (comparative case analysis, or CCA). Thus crimes are considered to be linked or unlinked in terms of how behaviourally similar the crimes were. Thematic analysis of rapes could be a practical way of carrying out CCA instead of comparing crimes on a point-by-point basis.

Limitations of behavioural classification systems

- These models, like all the others, rely on crimes that have been reported. Therefore, given the high attrition rate, it seems very probable that they only represent a subset of rapes. Further research is needed to establish whether other rapes can be differentiated in the same way.

- Without incorporating information from the offenders themselves these models reveal little of the thought processes of offenders. They may thus be a useful starting point for therapeutic interventions with rapists, but will need to be taken much further in terms of the offenders' cognitions and attitudes if they are to be really powerful.

Conclusions

Rapists vary considerably in terms of the nature of their relationship to their victim and the underlying psychological processes that give rise to rape. Overall the general view of most theorists is that sexual gratification is only one aspect of the reasons why rape is carried out. Some people argue that it is almost irrelevant and that power and control of the victim is much more significant. However, the behaviourally based models that show the sexual act to be such a prevalent and focal part of the assault do give a rather different picture.

Key concepts and terms

Attrition
Behavioural classification of
  rape offences

Biological models of rape
Clinical classification of rapists
Environmental models of rape

Sample essay titles

- Discuss the issues that may account for the high levels of attrition in rape cases.

- 'Rapists are born and not made.' Discuss.

- Compare and contrast two typologies of rapists.

- Why do men rape?

Further reading

Books

Amir, M. (1971). *Patterns in Forcible Rape*. Chicago: University of Chicago Press.

Brownmiller, S. (1975). *Against our Will: Men, Women and Rape*. New York: Simon and Schuster.

Canter, D.V. (1994). *Criminal Shadows*. London: Harper Collins.

Groth, A.N. (1979). *Men Who Rape: The Psychology of the Offender*. New York: Plenum.

Journal articles

Canter, D., Bennell, C., Alison, L., and Reddy, S. (2003a). Differentiating sex offences: A behaviourally based thematic classification of stranger rapes. *Behavioral Sciences and the Law*, 21, 157–174.

Hodge, S., and Canter, D. (1998). Victims and perpetrators of male sexual assault. *Journal of Interpersonal Violence*, 13, 222–239.

Scully, D., and Marolla, J. (1985). 'Riding the Bull at Gilley's': Convicted rapists describe the rewards of rape. *Social Problems*, 32(3), 251–263.

8 Homicide and serial killing

Natalia Wentink Martin

This chapter provides an overview of **homicide** and serial killing and relevant research within a forensic and criminological framework. Various offender and offence classifications are discussed and evaluated. The advantages and disadvantages of such classifications in an investigative setting are discussed. This chapter also highlights the role cultural context may have on the manner in which people behave and interact with one another, which can play a role in single and multiple homicide. It is anticipated that this chapter will encourage the reader to seek out and critically evaluate additional literature in this important area which greatly affects not only victims and their family and friends, but also the general public and individual feelings of safety and security in society.

Learning outcomes

When you have completed this chapter you should be able to:

1. Identify the different types of single and multiple homicide.
2. Describe offender, victim and offence characteristics of single and serial homicide.
3. Appreciate offender typologies and research supporting and refuting these.
4. Identify alternative ways of understanding homicide and serial murder.
5. Understand the possible role culture may play in single and multiple homicides.

Homicide and serial murder

Public fascination with murder, particularly **serial murder**, is evident in the quantity of films, books and television programmes on this topic (Bartol, 1991; Egger, 1998). Public fear and curiosity are often aroused by these portrayals, and sensationalistic approaches in the public domain run the danger of incorrectly outweighing more careful, scientific and systematic analyses of offenders and their offences. However, there is a growing body of knowledge which is providing a more scientifically grounded account of single and serial murder.

Homicide

Definition of homicide

Criminal homicide is defined as causing death to an individual without legal justification (Bartol, 1991: 205), whereas lawful homicide is justified legally under particular circumstances. An example of a lawful homicide is a soldier killing the enemy in combat. The focus of this chapter is criminal homicide. Key features of criminal homicide are issues of responsibility, mental capacity, intent and pre-planning by the offender (Mitchell, 1997).

Homicides vary in nature and type (Wolfgang, 1958):

Manslaughter

Homicides not classified as murder are considered a form of manslaughter. Consequently, this category ranges from accidental death to events very similar to murder. In some cases, the line between manslaughter and murder is difficult to determine because of this broad definition (Brookman, 2005).

Voluntary manslaughter

This describes a homicide which was unplanned, but the offender wilfully killed another individual. One example is someone killing in the midst of an argument, where the original intent was not to kill, but the reaction to the situation escalated to a deadly response (Bartol, 1991: 206). Legal circumstances lessen the severity of the offence. The Homicide Act (1957: ss 2–4) defines these circumstances as the offender being provoked to kill, the offender suffering mental incapacity, or the offender being part of a suicide pact.

Involuntary manslaughter

There are cases in which there was no intent to kill but the law finds the individual responsible. Such instances include accidents (such as a car accident or work-related accidents) and suicide pacts. This chapter will focus only on intentional killing.

Prevalence rates

Homicide rates vary greatly around the globe. In the years 1997/99, South Africa had one of the highest homicide rates at 564.9 victims per million people. It is believed the country's violent history of apartheid created a culture in which violence is a way of life for some (Brookman, 2005). Comparatively, Switzerland has a homicide rate of 11.8 victims per million people, and England and Wales have a rate of 14.5 per million people (Scottish Executive, 2001: 30). However, the accuracy of prevalence rates should be assessed with awareness of those who are not included in the statistics. There may be a hidden population of homicide victims among those who are reported as 'missing' each year. The National Missing Persons Helpline (NMPH) reports that in the UK more than 250,000 are reported missing each year. While most of these individuals return within three days, some do not and remain 'missing'. It is possible that some have become victims of homicide (Brookman, 2005).

Comparison of homicide rates between countries can be a challenge. For example, a study into homicide rates in Europe over the past 50 years would have to take into account that country borders have changed, that statistics are collected in different ways, and that legal systems and legal classifications vary (Salfati, 2001). Even within the UK, homicide victim definition categories vary between countries, making categories difficult to compare to one another. Brookman (2005: 40) notes that in Scotland 'acquaintance' homicide includes friends, business and criminal associates, gang members and individuals known to the victim, whereas the English definition is more limited. Brookman also highlights lack of clarity in definitions such as 'son/daughter' when there is no indication of if and how to classify stepchildren. This lack of definitional precision makes it difficult for researchers interested in this area to know precisely what they are examining and attempting to compare between countries.

Possible role of situational and cultural factors in homicide

The identified differences in homicide rates between countries are believed to be due to socio-cultural environments in which violence is an accepted and learned behaviour (Beeghley, 2003). Wolfgang and Ferracutti (1967) call this the 'subculture theory of violence'. In such a context, individuals justify the use of force in threatening or insulting situations. This justification is explained in a cultural context of shared norms and values. Huesman and Eron (1989) argue that social behaviour is a learned habitual response – the manner in which one approaches solving social problems, or reacts in social situations, is deeply embedded and resistant to change. The culture surrounding the individual provides that person with a lens through which situations are interpreted and a variety of possible actions and reactions are provided. Leyton (1995: 161) argues that it is not the presence of guns, knives or fists which ignites homicidal behaviour, but rather 'the will to use that technology that is culturally coded, the decision that is half-consciously culturally applauded [that] shapes the number of homicidal assaults in a nation'. In some cultures, conflict is dealt with through compromise, in other cultures it may be dealt with through violence or displays of power and influence.

Types of homicide

Most homicides in the UK occur between people who are acquaintances, current or former spouses, or relatives (Brookman, 2005). In a study of 75 Canadian homicides, the victim knew the offender in 87 per cent of cases, a number which reflected national statistics as well (Salfati and Dupont, 2001).

Of the offender–victim possibilities, male-on-male homicides frequently occur between strangers or acquaintances, arising from arguments over relatively minor issues or related to honour or reputation. Male-on-female homicides most frequently occur between current or former romantic partners when the relationship is failing or has failed (Brookman, 2005). The Homicide Index from 1995 to 2000 reports that roughly 30 per cent of homicides in England and Wales and 26 per cent of homicides in Scotland were of this type. Female-on-male homicides predominantly occur in a domestic setting with a partner or child as the victim. Such offences comprise about 11 per cent of homicides per year in the UK. Female-on-female homicides are the least common type of homicide, constituting less than 3 per cent of homicides per year in the UK from 1997 to 2001 (Homicide Index).

Offender, victim, offence characteristics

Concerning race, data from England and Wales indicate that blacks and Asians, compared to Caucasians, are over-represented as homicide victims as well as offenders (Brookman, 2005). Studies in the USA have found that blacks have a higher rate of victimization (Bartol, 1991). In fact, in the US, black males have the highest rate of victimization. It is suggested that this over-representation of ethnic minorities reflects social inequalities and that these groups may reside where homicide rates are higher (Bartol, 1991; Richards, 1999). Males comprise the majority of both offenders and victims[1]. In 2001 in England and Wales, 90 per cent of homicide offenders were male and 70 per cent of homicide victims were male. Similar findings were found in Scotland and in Ireland (Brookman, 2005).

Alcohol is often a factor in homicide. Brookman's (2005) research found that over half of all homicides committed by males involved alcohol, often in excessive quantities. These findings are echoed in studies in the USA and Australia. In a Dutch study of 202 homicides, alcohol was involved either before or during the offence or was a part of the offender's lifestyle (Bijleveld and Smit, 2006). According to the Scottish Executive, in 2000 over half of all individuals arrested for homicide were intoxicated and 13 per cent were under the influence of illegal drugs. Roughly 25 per cent of those arrested were not under the influence of alcohol or drugs.

The most common weapon used in American homicides is a firearm. In the UK it is a sharp object, such as a knife. The availability of certain weapons and access to medical care influences the likelihood that a violent confrontation will result in death. The use of a firearm is more likely to be deadly than a knife. The availability of firearms in the USA and South Africa is evident in the number of firearm-related homicides. Access to medical care may also determine whether a violent confrontation results in wounding or death (Brookman, 2005). For example, a gunshot wound in a large US city is likely to receive immediate medical attention whereas an ambulance may not even enter into some South African townships, leaving the victim without the treatment which may have prevented death.

Models for understanding homicide: Evidence for and against

Offender and offence typologies are a first step towards understanding the variety of offenders and as a result are useful in indicating the possibilities of different aetiologies (Megargee, 1982). Typologies can also identify offender

---

[1] The male pronoun will be used throughout this chapter given that the majority of single and multiple homicide offenders are male.

motives or victim–offender relationships (Arrigo and Purcell, 2001). The identification of different **offender typologies** can also have legal implications and implications for offender sentencing and management.

Issues concerning typologies

Some researchers mix offender motivation with victim–offender relationship. For example, Harlan (1950: 746) proposed a classification of 'ostensible' motive for homicide with the following types:

- Killing a family member.

- Sex triangle/quarrel over wife or lover.

- Quarrel over cards, dice, money, etc.

- Quarrel of relatively trivial origin – insult, curse.

In this typology there is possible overlap of categories (offender belongs to more than one category) and functions on a descriptive level which reveals little to nothing about the offender's motive. However, it is important to identify problems with the use of motive in a typology for investigative purposes. Wolfgang (1958: 185) emphasizes that the only way to identify motive would be to be in the suspect's head at the time of the offence. The use of motive runs a clear danger of subjectivity (Gibson, 1975: 21). There is no objective way to determine the offender's thoughts at the time of the offence. This challenging issue has led some researchers to focus on more concrete aspects of the offence, particularly victim–offender interaction and behaviour.

Behavioural classification: Understanding homicide as an interpersonal event

Behaviour is a useful focus for classification and investigative purposes because it is present at the crime scene and objective. Furthermore, the use of crime scene evidence for the development of models is of greater practical use for investigators because crime scene evidence is what they readily encounter as a routine part of their job (Salfati and Harastis, 2001). The interpersonal nature of the homicide event is an integral part in understanding how the homicide unfolds. For this reason, the victim–offender interaction is a useful unit of analysis in the study of these offences (Canter, 1994; Silverman and Mukherjee, 1997; Salfati and Canter, 1999).

Functional use of violence to differentiate between homicides

Fesbach (1964) identified aggression as the key feature of violent crime. His proposal of two types of aggression – expressive and instrumental, which are each characterized by the rewards they provide to the offender – has been very influential. Expressive aggression occurs in response to anger-inducing conditions such as insults, physical attack or personal failures. Instrumental aggression arises from the desire for material goods (money, car) or status (power, prestige).

Another example of research into the functional use of violence in single and multiple homicide examines the role of the victim to the offender. Canter (1994) proposed that there were three distinct roles:

1. The victim is an *object* for whom the offender has no sympathy, yet desires control over. He murders and mutilates without feeling as these victims are objects to do with as he desires.
2. The victim is a *vehicle* upon whom the offender expresses anger and frustration. These offences are described as taking on a more controlled form than when the victim is an object. The victim will bear the brunt of the offender's emotions to indirectly suffer his pain.
3. The victim is a *person* with whom the offender tries to establish some kind of rapport.

When studying 247 British single offender–single victim homicides, Salfati (2000) proposed that the role of the victim as discussed by Canter (1994) related closely to the way in which homicides could be differentiated in terms of being either expressive or instrumental. In addition, offender background characteristics had a discernable theme of being predominantly expressive or instrumental. However, when offender and offence characteristics were analyzed together, Salfati was unable to indicate any clear or simple connections.

The use of such models takes into account unpredictable variables such as victim response, which varies from one situation to the next. It is hypothesized that the offenders' behaviour will be varied, but that the style of interaction and the types of behaviour exhibited will be representative of one of these themes. Furthermore, these styles of victim–offender interaction are hypothesized to reflect the offender's overall mode of interaction in his everyday life with other individuals. This can ultimately aid investigators in making decisions concerning the characteristics of a particular offender (Canter and Heritage, 1990).

Focus 8.1

Harold Shipman: Serial murderer

BBC News, 31 January, 2000

Family GP Harold Shipman has been jailed for life for murdering 15 patients, as he goes down in history as the UK's biggest convicted serial killer.

He was also found guilty of forging the will of Kathleen Grundy, one of his patients.

The 54-year-old GP, from Hyde, Greater Manchester, was given 15 life sentences to run concurrently for the murders, and four years for the forgery. The jury reached its verdict after six days' deliberation.

Figure 8.1 Harold Shipman.
Source: © epa/Corbis.

Dr Harold Frederick Shipman (1946–2004) deliberately killed 150–250 of his patients between 1970 and 1998. He is known as the most prolific serial killer in the UK. His victims were most often elderly women in good health who lived alone. He eventually came to the attention of police in 1998 when a colleague reported the high death rate of his patients and an investigation was launched. The initial investigation was dropped due to lack of evidence. However, the daughter of one of his victims suspected foul play when she discovered a large sum of money had been left to Shipman, rather than to her, in her mother's will. The victim's body was exhumed and traces of diamorphine (a pain medication) were found to be present. In addition, Shipman's typewriter was identified as being that which was used to create the will. Consequently, there was an investigation of the other deaths Shipman had certified. He was convicted in January, 2000, of murdering 15 others by lethal injections of diamorphine. He was sentenced to life imprisonment. In 2004, Shipman was found hanging in his prison cell. The cause of death was suicide.

Prior to his suicide, Shipman refused to comment on why he committed these murders. Some believe he had the desire to murder older women to alleviate future suffering; others claim it was his personal desire to be in control of the life and death of others.

Article source: http://news.bbc.co.uk/1/hi/uk/616692.stm

Serial murder and multiple murder

Definitions and examples: Distinguished on time and spatial features

Multiple murder is categorized into serial murder, mass murder and spree murder. The differences between these categories are based on time between killings and the geographic distances over which the murders occur (Douglas et al, 1992; Hickey, 2002; Delisi and Sherer, 2006). There is debate over the number of murders which must occur before an offender is considered a serial murderer: three victims is frequently utilized, but definitions range from two to four victims (Jenkins, 1988; Rappaport, 1988).

Typically, the term 'serial murder' is applied to killings that occur when three or more victims are killed over a period of time spanning from days to years. Between each murder there is a 'cooling off' period in which the offender does not kill (Gresswill and Hollin, 1994; Holmes and Holmes, 1998a,b). Serial sexual murder involves evidence of sexual activity before, during and/or after death (Meloy, 2000). Not all serial murderers are sexual murderers. Examples of serial murderers are Jack the Ripper and Juan Vallejo Corona.

Jack the Ripper murdered five prostitutes in the Whitechapel area of London in 1888. He is infamous not only for the murders but for the way in which he mutilated the victims' bodies. Today, Jack the Ripper's identity is still debated in many circles. Juan Vallejo Corona was found guilty of murdering 25 farm workers in the USA in 1971. Vallejo was well liked by neighbours, attended church regularly and was married with four children. He was diagnosed with schizophrenia and ultimately confessed to the murders.

Mass murder is defined as an offence in which there are at least four victims killed in the same general location at one time (Fox and Levin, 2003; Delisi and Sherer, 2006).

Spree murder occurs when multiple victims are killed over period of time in two or more locations and often occurs in conjunction with other criminal behaviour (Holmes and Holmes, 1998a; Delisi and Sherer, 2006).

Serial murder prevalence rates

The number of serial murderers and victims at any given time is difficult to determine. Challenges in determining this figure may be due to policing but predominantly have to do with offenders themselves. Undetected offenders are likely to be adept at concealing their identity and crimes. This, in turn, allows them to continue offending, so yielding a greater number of victims over time. Offenders who do not take precautions to remain undetected are more likely to be apprehended by police (before killing enough victims to be considered a serial killer, in some cases).

A widely cited, though doubtful, estimate by Holmes and DeBurger (1998) for the USA suggests there are 3500–5000 serial murder victims each year. This shocking number is based on their calculation that serial murderers were responsible for up to two-thirds of the nation's unsolved homicides as well as a portion of undetected victims, or 'missing persons'. This prevalence rate has been heavily criticized (Egger, 1990:10; Gresswell and Hollin, 1994; Coleman and Norris, 2000), specifically for its attribution of unsolved murders to serial killers (Fox and Levin, 1998) as well as for its contribution to propagating serial murder sensationalism (Jenkins, 1988). More conservative estimates propose that the number of multiple murderers (serial, mass and spree murders) active in the USA is between 30 and over 100 at any given time.

Serial murder is more frequent in some countries than in others and fluctuates over time. For example, periods in the UK devoid of serial murder activity have been followed by several cases. In the UK in the 1970s it was reported that there were four or five active serial murderers at once (Jenkins, 1988: 5). This accords well with Canter et al's (1996) estimate a decade later, of about five serial killers active, on average, each year in the UK. Jenkins (1988) estimates that in England serial murder accounted for 1.7 per cent of murderers between 1940 and 1985, increasing to a rate of 3.2 per cent between 1970 and 1993. US serial murderers are estimated to account for 1–2 per cent of murders annually.

International comparisons of serial murder

Given the geographical variations in homicide rates discussed earlier in this chapter, a brief survey of serial murder cases in different countries merits exploration. Although there have been fewer cases of serial murder in England and Wales than in the USA, the nature of the cases is very similar (Nettler, 1982). Jenkins' (1988) examination of multiple murder offender and offence characteristics from the USA and the UK reveals two noteworthy differences. First, the use of firearms in cases of American mass and spree murderers is evident. This is believed to be due to the availability of such weapons in American society. Second, the spacious geography of the USA allows for more successful concealment of bodies. If a body is not found, the offender is far more likely to remain undetected and to continue offending. However, in his detailed examination of South African serial murder, Hodgskiss (2003) found a higher rate of cross-ethnic offending and a lack of sexually violent offending, a feature more frequently described in American cases. In addition, offender behaviours were found more similar to non-European serial murderers than to American serial murderers, a finding which Hodgskiss correctly asserts needs further investigation concerning the ways in which offence behaviours are affected by the social environment in which offending occurs.

Offender and victim characteristics

Offender characteristics

Despite public perception, serial murderers come from a variety of different ethnic backgrounds (Egger, 1998; Fox and Levin, 1998; Hickey, 2002), though in his study of over 200 serial murderers, Hickey (2002) found most to be roughly 30 years old, Caucasian and male. They had killed between eight and 14 people in four to six years. The offenders generally start killing in adulthood, between the ages of 24 and 40 (Jenkins, 1988; Bartol, 1991), though most kill their first victim before the age of 30 (Meloy, 2000). A history of violence is often absent from their police records, though offences such as fraud and theft are not uncommon, and serial offending is said to exist within the offender's broader criminal lifestyle (Delisi and Scherer, 2006: 273). In a study comparing single and serial homicide offenders, a greater percentage of serial murderers had prior convictions (79 per cent) than single homicide offenders (51 per cent). In a study of 217 American serial murderers, Canter et al (1996) found that 75 per cent had prior convictions and nearly half had been arrested as juveniles.

Certain background characteristics are highlighted in serial murderers. The 'MacDonald triad' (MacDonald, 1963) is considered a precursor; it is a constellation of enuresis (bed-wetting), cruelty to animals and deliberate fire-setting in childhood. The case of Patrick Mackay is an example of this triad. By the age of 15 Patrick had set fire to a church, was habitually cruel to animals, had attacked his family and neighbours, and had already attempted murder. Other background characteristics involve family violence, substance misuse and parenting issues. A study of 20 serial murderers by McKenzie (1995) found that 80 per cent of serial offenders had experienced family violence in childhood, 93 per cent had experienced chaotic parenting, and 75 per cent had at least one alcoholic parent.

Mental health

The public perception of serial murderers is that they are mad, insane or psychotic. Gresswell's (1991: 216) study of English and Welsh multiple murderers found evidence of psychiatric history in 45 per cent of cases and only 24 per cent of offenders had a history of mental illness. In cases of serial sexual murder there is often a DSM IV dual diagnosis of sexual sadism and antisocial personality disorder (Gerberth and Turco, 1997).

Serial murderers are often labelled as a 'psychopath' without accurate clinical diagnosis using the revised psychopathy checklist, or PCL-R (Hare, 1991), discussed in Chapter 4. Psychopathy and serial murder should not be considered synonymous. They are not inevitably linked. Of course there have been serial murderers who display the characteristic traits of superficial charm, intelligence, lack of remorse, impulsivity and associated psychopathic traits. However, there are those diagnosed as psychopathic who are not serial murderers. One danger of the use of this term, or any other psychiatric diagnosis, is that it is used as the sole explanation for the behaviours rather than being understood as an important feature in a series of unfolding events (Mitchell, 1997).

Victim

Most serial murder victims are women, particularly prostitutes and those living on the edges of society (Jenkins, 1988; Ressler and Schachtman, 1992; Egger, 1997: 79). These individuals are more vulnerable and are also less likely to go unnoticed if they are missing. In cases of sexual homicide the victims may be both strangers or acquaintances and are often of the same race as the offender (Ressler et al, 1988; Dietz et al, 1990; Meloy, 2000).

Activity 8.1

The internet contains many accounts of serial killers, their crimes and lives. Review those you can find to determine whether accounts from totally different sources agree with each other about the details. Then determine what are the typical background characteristics of the killers described.

Serial murder typologies

There have been a handful of attempts to classify serial murder. Such classifications provide a first step towards understanding the variety of such killers and therefore have value in indicating the possibilities of different aetiologies (Megargee, 1982). They can also elucidate different offenders' motives or offender–victim relationships (Arrigo and Purcell, 2001), which can have legal implications as well as implications for the sentencing and management of offenders. Some classification schemes have been developed to directly aid investigations (Egger, 1984). Many typologies classify offenders on the basis of a mixture of features including inferred motives, crime scene evidence and offender background characteristics. This is problematic for the development of systematic tests of these typologies because they mix objectively based definitions, such as the gender of victims, with subjective interpretations such as psychological motivations. Such classification schemes are also of limited practical use, especially to investigators, because the only objective data are those drawn from crime scenes (Canter and Wentink, 2004).

Among violent individuals, Megargee (1966) identified two personality types, *under-controlled* and *over-controlled*, informed by an offender's ability to control the desire to be aggressive. Under-controlled offenders have little control over their aggressive urges and consequently react quickly and hastily. Over-controlled offenders repeatedly suppress their anger; the anger builds up to an eventual explosion of violence in response to an event.

The organized/disorganized classification is the most frequently cited offender classification. It was constructed by a number of special agents of the Federal Bureau of Investigation (Ressler et al, 1986). This dichotomy rests on the assumption that the offender's behaviour and personality characteristics can be determined from crime scene information. It is claimed that the organized offender leads a planned and orderly life which is reflected in the way he commits his crimes. The organized offender is described as having average to high intelligence, likely to be employed, and confident. The organized crime scene shows evidence of planning, use of restraints, and use of a weapon brought by the killer and subsequently removed from the crime scene. The disorganized offender, it is proposed, has low intelligence, lacks social confidence, and is less likely to be employed. The crime scenes reflect features such as little to no planning, a sense of disorder, and careless leaving of blood, semen and/or the murder weapon at the scene.

This typology has weaknesses concerning the data from which the classification was developed (Turco, 1990; Rossmo, 1997) and the principles upon which the distinction between offenders was made (Canter et al, 2004). Significantly, research using data from 100 serial murders examining the co-occurrence of characteristics purported for each type of offender did not support this dichotomy and did not distinguish between offenders. Rather, the research revealed that a subset of organized features are typical of most serial murders, thereby facilitating offenders to successfully complete the crime and remain undetected. Disorganized features were not found to be a distinct type (Canter et al, 2004). This study is one of many examples of the ways in which offender and offence typologies can be empirically examined and evaluated as a first step towards developing more precise investigative tools and ways to understand a constellation of offending behaviour.

Visionary, mission, lust, power

Another example of a serial murder typology is a four-fold classification by Holmes and Holmes (1998a) who describe *visionary, mission, lust/thrill, and power/control killers*. Canter and Wentink (2004) found only limited support for this model and highlight the difficulty in trying to operationalize a model using a mix of motive and crime scene evidence in its typology. Canter and Wentink (2004) suggest that a thematic classification focusing on the manner in which the offender interacts with the victim may prove to be of greater value

Concerns with models

Through the discussion above of the typologies, several issues emerge which students and researchers need to identify and address when working within this area. These are the assumptions on which the typology is based, the difficulty of working with fantasy and motive, their utility for investigative purposes, and the issues of generalization.

First, as Canter et al (2004) discuss in detail, certain assumptions underlie any typology:

1. Each type is distinguished by certain characteristics; the characteristics within each type co-occur with regularity.
2. Characteristics used to define a type do not occur with characteristics of another type. To be useful, each type must have characteristics that are distinct from other types. Essentially, each type must be mutually exclusive and the set of types should be exhaustive (Fox and Levin, 1998).
3. If types are assumed to contain a mix of characteristics from other types there needs to be a clear set of criteria in place to determine how an individual is categorized. If these criteria are not in place the utility and validity of the typology are in doubt.

Second, motivation is difficult to establish. A typology based on motivation is dependent upon establishing a motive. This is a difficult task at best. An offence may have several motives. An offender may not be entirely clear as to why he committed an offence. A motive recorded by police may not recognize other important behaviours which occurred. For example, a crime recorded as having a financial motive may have also featured torture, overkill and additional features which may contribute significantly to the overall nature of the offence (Keppel and Walter 1999: 418).

Offender profiling

This chapter has identified some of the issues surrounding offender typologies and the challenges facing investigators who may come across such classification schemes. Offender profiling is the process of linking offence behaviours to characteristics of the offender (Canter, 1994). This process can be applied to any type of crime. A number of FBI special agents (cf. Ressler et al, 1986) were some of the first to report consideration of the behaviours of offenders from the crime scene and to propose ways of deducing the different types of offenders responsible, although detectives have done this ever since people have investigated crimes. Systematic research followed the early proposals from these FBI special agents.

A major criticism of profiles is that they are not scientific and are too vague for investigative use (Levin and Fox, 1985; Egger, 1998). The field of investigative psychology addresses this valid criticism through the use of psychological principles and empirical approaches to profile construction and analysis (Canter, 1994). While the area of profiling merits far greater discussion, it is important to highlight the link between profiling and offender typologies which hold great potential benefit to offender profiling, provided such typologies are constructed in a systematic, scientific manner with robust sets of relevant data. Ideally, the results of such work allow the investigator to identify, prioritize and interview suspects in an effort to correctly identify an offender from crime scene evidence (Warren et al, 1996).

Current challenges

There are current challenges and respective opportunities for research in the area of homicide and serial offending. At present, detailed studies which include structured interviews with offenders are limited. The existing interview studies have utilized small, non-random samples which make it difficult to make generalizations (Fox and Levin, 1998). The low base rate for serial murder heightens this problem of generalization. Larger scale serial murder studies have had to utilize information from public sources which has both advantages and disadvantages (see Canter, 1995).

Offender typologies have had little success linking offence characteristics to offender characteristics; only broad trends have been found thus far. Such a link would be of significant benefit to investigators constructing a profile of a suspect. Davis (2006) proposes that future research meets this challenge through investigation into which offence behaviours are least affected by situational factors to determine which behaviours are more likely to remain constant across a variety of situational factors and victim reactions. He believes these behaviours may be more clearly linked to offender personality traits.

Western research and literature dominates our knowledge and understanding of homicide and serial murder. Additional research in other countries by native researchers could be of great benefit to our understanding of these offences and offenders. More thorough integration of the socio-cultural framework within which these offences occur would serve to strengthen our understanding of not only the actual events, but the larger social context in which they happen and why.

Conclusions

While the science of DNA (and crime scene analysis techniques) provides valuable scientific and technological advances, it is important to emphasize the empirical and verifiable advances in the study of homicide and serial murder introduced in this chapter which reach beyond sensationalist newspaper headlines and cinema box office sales. This chapter has discussed various offender and offence classifications for homicide and serial killing. Issues concerning offender classifications have been highlighted. This chapter has also noted the role that situational and cultural factors may play in the manner in which victim–offender interaction unfolds in a homicide event.

Key concepts and terms

Homicide	Serial murder
Offender typology	Subculture theory of violence

Sample essay titles

- Describe and compare three different serial murder typologies.

- What are the advantages and disadvantages of using behaviours, rather than motive or a mixture of motive and behaviour, as the focus for analyzing homicide?

- What potential utility do homicide typologies have for investigative purposes?

- What are the challenges faced when comparing homicide studies from different countries or contexts?

Further reading

Books

Bartol, C.R. (1991). *Criminal Behaviour: A Psychosocial Approach.* Englewood Cliffs, NJ: Prentice Hall.

Brookman, F. (2005). *Understanding Homicide.* Portland, OR: Sage.

Canter, D. (1994). *Criminal Shadows.* London: HarperCollins.

Hickey, E. (2002). *Serial Murderers and their Victims,* (3rd Ed.). Belmont, CA: Wadsworth.

Lester, D. (1995). *Serial Killers: The Insatiable Passion.* Philadelphia, PA: The Charles Press.

Ressler, R.R., Burgess, A.W., and Douglas, J.E. (1988). *Sexual Homicide.* Lexington, KY: Lexington Books.

Journal articles

Canter, D.V., Alison, L.J., Alison, E., and Wentink, N. (2004). The Organized/Disorganized typology of serial murder: myth or model? *Psychology, Public Policy, and Law,* 10, 293–320.

Delisi, M., and Sherer, A.M. (2006). Multiple homicide offenders: Offence characteristics, social correlates, and criminal careers. *Criminal Justice and Behaviour,* 33, 367–391.

Gresswell, D.M., and Hollin, C.R. (1994). Multiple murder: A review. *British Journal of Criminology*, 34, 1–14.

Keppel, R.D., and Walter, R. (1999). Profiling killers: A revised classification model for understanding sexual murder. *International Journal of Offender Therapy and Comparative Criminology*, 43, 417–437.

Meloy, J.R. (2000). The nature and dynamics of sexual homicide: an integrative review. *Aggression and Violent Behaviour*, 5, 1–22.

9 Criminal groups and networks

Sam Mullins

Most psychological approaches to understanding criminal behaviour tend to offer individual-orientated explanations, focusing for example upon possible biological or psychological abnormalities or else upon individual decision-making processes. The aim of this chapter is to draw attention to the fact that criminal behaviour, like all human behaviour, is rooted in social interaction, and without an appreciation of this, including the fundamental normality of many of the social psychological processes involved, we cannot fully understand or combat crime.

Learning outcomes

When you have completed this chapter you should be able to:

1. Understand how crime is much more than just a lone activity or simply the result of rational or pathological processes.
2. Discuss the key social psychological processes involved in criminality.
3. Demonstrate awareness of methodologies used to study the social psychology of crime.
4. Generate ideas for future research.
5. Appreciate different levels of social analysis, from individuals to co-offending groups and teams, to organizations and networks and above.
6. Understand the importance of social psychology for understanding the Criminal Justice System.
7. Integrate social psychological theory and research with other accounts of crime.

Many familiar concepts from 'ordinary' social and organizational psychology are relevant and often complement one another as well as more traditional theories of crime. In particular, social learning theories (e.g. Akers, 1977) help explain origins of criminal behaviour as well as learning of new criminal skills over the course of offenders' lifespans. Social identity theories (Tajfel, 1982; Turner et al, 1987) are especially amenable for interpreting group-based offending behaviour but are also an indispensable tool for expanding comprehension of all aspects of crime. Both qualitative and quantitative research methods are of utility, although social network analysis (SNA) is highlighted as a somewhat underused technique which provides insight into the importance of social structure to individual and group psychology. Finally the relevance of social psychology to the criminal justice system (CJS) is considered, as the same principles of organization and interaction that affect criminals may impact decisions made by police and courts.

Learning to commit crime

As discussed in Chapter 3, rather than simply committing antisocial or criminal behaviour as the result of biological abnormality or by weighing the costs and benefits, offending behaviour is learned from others. Socialization in the formative years acclimatizes children to their native culture and teaches prevailing standards, morals and norms. However, socialization is not the same for everyone; counter-cultural values may be learned and majority values can be rejected.

The acquisition of criminal tendencies involves a process of **social learning**, whereby differential association, mutual reinforcement and imitation among peers have been found to be important to moral reasoning (Walker et al, 2000), drug use (Akers et al, 1979), non-violent and violent delinquent behaviour (Henry et al, 2001) and 'serious' offending (Chung and Steinberg, 2006). By combining social learning theory with social control theory, Hawkins and Weis (1985) concluded that the impact of association with different groups depends upon skills and available opportunities. Association with delinquent peers is more likely when conventional skills or opportunities are lacking. Thus offending behaviour is more likely when benevolent and authoritative units of socialization, (family, schools, etc.) are dysfunctional or unavailable.

Furthermore, given that a large proportion of all crime goes undetected, criminal behaviour that is rewarded within the group will only rarely be directly punished. When this does occur it may serve to further the psychological distance between the individual and conventional social groups by increasing the salience of social identity and related in- versus out-group attitudes. Finally, when delinquent group values are internalized it will increase the likelihood of lone offending.

Social facilitation

Learning continues throughout the lifespan and although the significance of one's peers may not be constant, social processes remain influential (see Chapter 3), so that social contact can facilitate criminal behaviour. Values, attitudes and behaviour are likely to be influenced by individuals' regular social interactions with others at work, recreationally and in the family. Generally speaking, work and family values often discourage crime. Sampson and Laub (1990) used longitudinal data to study change and continuity in a group of delinquents and controls into adulthood. They found that while childhood delinquency predicted adult crime, alcohol abuse, financial difficulties and divorce, job continuity and strong marital attachment in adulthood related to significantly less criminal behaviour. From a social learning perspective this reflects differential association and **conformity** to the norms of significant social groups.

However, family and work can also present opportunities for crime and involve social norms that legitimize it. Likewise people's various friendships and acquaintances can serve as protective factors against criminal behaviour or else may expose individuals to criminal ideologies and opportunities and serve as pools of human resource for such activities. Morselli, Tremblay and McCarthy (2006) suggest that a key factor in continued delinquent and criminal behaviour may be the presence of influential criminal 'mentors' who convey **social capital** within certain groups, teach specific skills and promote a value system that neutralizes conventional beliefs.

Routine criminal behaviour also often relies on social interaction, illustrated by Shover (1973) who, from interviews of convicted burglars, highlights the importance of social settings for informal recruitment, making 'contacts', sharing technical information and planning. Such opportunities afforded by the gathering of criminals are also cited as criticism of prison systems. Offenders themselves have agreed that prisons serve as 'criminal universities', acting to reaffirm belief systems and increase criminal knowledge (Kolstad, 1996).

Criminal identity

A major determinant of people's behaviour is their **identity** or self-concept, and major determinants of self-concepts are the social groups to which people belong (Tajfel, 1982; Turner et al, 1987). A person who associates with criminals and successfully learns the norms and skills of that group is likely to develop a related sense of belonging the more they participate; group membership becomes a defining element of self-perceived identity and compels congruent behaviour. Thus peers are particularly influential sources of learning because their perceived similarity means they are classed as part of our *in*-group. Furthermore, when other group memberships are lacking, (e.g. family), the significance of one's specific peer group to identity is amplified, thereby increasing pressure to conform.

The 'crisis' of identity in adolescence (Erikson, 1994) means that alternative value systems are more likely to be explored as part of the process of discovering a satisfactory sense of self during this period of people's lives. Many people participate in various offending behaviours as adolescents but settle on a conventional identity as they experience negative consequences or become members of law-abiding groups. Hence desistence (the fact that most young offenders do not continue to offend into adulthood) can be understood in terms of changing social groups because the majority of people enter the world of legitimate work and their sense of self becomes more stable.

For those that do choose a life of crime, it may often be the result of continued importance of deviant peer groups. Membership of legitimate groups may be precluded via externally applied criminal labels, which may then create self-fulfilling prophecies (e.g. Becker, 1963). Accordingly the deviant social group and identity becomes more important as the only source of social acceptance and support. This is even more likely given the disparity between external negative labels and individual positive definitions of criminal activity. As an example consider *The Times* headline 'Yobs want an ASBO[1] as a badge of honour' (Ford, 2006).

Focus 9.1

Hooligans, crowds and identity

Figure 9.1 German police confront crowds of supporters in Frankfurt at the 2006 World Cup.
Source: © Cliff Stott.

One of the most explicit applications of social psychology in contemporary crime research looks at violent crowd behaviour and attempts to control it. By applying social identity theory (Tajfel, 1982; Turner et al, 1987), using questionnaires, interviews and observations, understanding of why peaceful crowd events such as football matches can erupt into riots has been greatly advanced, with practical implications for public order policing of major events (see Reicher et al, 2004).

The traditional explanation of crowd violence has been that within crowds '**deindividuation**' occurs, causing people to forget their sense of identity and values. Accordingly when a minority behaves violently (such as football hooligans), this violence 'infects' the normally docile

---

[1] Antisocial behaviour order.

masses who follow suit, prompting and justifying an indiscriminate forceful response from police. However, there is growing evidence that this is not the case and crowd behaviour can be understood in terms of the identities and interactions within the crowd and between them and the police.

Rather than people losing their identities within a crowd, they experience **depersonalization**, a shift in emphasis from their individual to their collective identity, with related norms and expectations. Within this larger collective there are subgroups, most of whom have no interest in violence, and in the context of football only a small minority of 'hooligans' seek to incite conflict. If the police as a controlling out-group act to punish or suppress a crowd indiscriminately (e.g. all England fans) they act to threaten the overall sense of collective identity and the crowd will unite in opposition. Alternatively crowds often police themselves and disparage minority malcontents when they can see that the rights of the many are not being withdrawn for the actions of a few. Key to the processes of interaction between football crowds and police are perceptions of legitimacy – each group's ideas about what they are entitled to do and what constitutes appropriate or unjustified behaviour.

Careers, roles and narratives

The term **criminal 'career'** is most often used to refer to offending over the life course (see Chapter 3). Alternatively it may be used to imply some semblance of legitimate working careers with various **roles** and status levels, from apprentice to recognized **leadership** (Canter and Youngs, 2003). The levels at which criminals operate and the roles they perform are likely to affect their sense of identity.

Sporadic low-level petty crime may involve role flexibility, limited status and a wide range of offence behaviours and so can be dabbled in without becoming self-defining. As a person engages in more regular criminal activity, especially when it becomes their main activity in life, they are more likely to fulfil a particular role, often within a wider criminal network involving awareness of relative statuses. What a person *does* becomes who they *are*. This implies a degree of specialization as an offender's criminal career advances, and this is supported by Youngs, Canter and Cooper (2004), who found evidence for core, very common offences but also thematic specialization in terms of dishonest, violent or antisocial offending. Of course specialization does not necessarily imply career advancement, which will depend on opportunities and offender learning and ability – higher status roles may require more complex skills as well as social support and appropriate 'vacancies'.

Additionally different crimes may involve more or less well defined social systems to varying extents. Thus Glaeser, Sacerdote and Scheinkman (1996) reported social interaction levels being highest surrounding more petty crimes, moderate but still large for assault, robbery and burglary, and negligible for arson, murder and rape. This may reflect likelihood of **co-offending** as well as the extent to which these crimes are embedded in a system of social support and thereby involve role differentiation, statuses and career-like opportunities. These differences between crimes in terms of 'social embeddedness' are a useful way of distinguishing between them for purposes of determining which aspects of social psychological theory are most appropriate.

More socially embedded crimes may be understood in terms of a person learning from and embracing a criminal fraternity and role-related identity as part of a career. Lone and secretive crimes may involve less reference to a criminal career and a greater reliance on comprehension of interactive style and personal narrative identity. Narrative identity refers to the way in which individuals interpret coherence into their lives, i.e. the way they construct a consistent sense of self, based upon their life history and experience (see Kirkman, 2002). It is the story people tell themselves to explain their actions and social standing. Broadly speaking, then, lone or more social crimes may involve greater reference to individual or social identity respectively, although both represent guides for interaction with others.

Having considered the relevance of the career analogy, it is important to reiterate that desistence is common and offending careers are often intermittent and lacking discernible structure. The fact that most people belong to various groups in life – family, work, recreational – means they have multiple roles and multiple selves (Kunda, 1999), allowing for contradictions in people's apparent values and behaviour, therefore dysfunctional or lacking families or communities are not essential for a person to engage in criminal offences. Moreover, the concept of multiple selves means many criminal careers barely get off the ground, for most criminal behaviour may remain relatively unimportant to individual or social identity. Nevertheless even temporarily adopted roles may affect a sense of identity for the duration the role is performed and carry with them a **script** or **schema** for how to behave.

Activity 9.1

Armed robbery role-play

First split up into groups of different sizes. Now imagine that you are going to commit a robbery of a mini-mart or convenience store with your group! Spend 10 minutes together planning how you would do it – in particular who will do what and what sort of experience of crimes or other background do you imagine each person might have? Once you have returned to being law-abiding psychology students, discuss your different plans:

- What were the different roles that each group used?
- Did you have a leader?
- What behaviour was expected of each role?
- What sorts of background were expected for different roles?
- Do you think your group had too few or too many people in it?
- What might be an optimum number of people for an armed robbery?

Group processes

Having considered broad social processes surrounding criminal activities, it is equally important to consider **group processes** involved within the actual commission of offences, most notably in co-offending situations, which account for about a quarter of all crime in England and Wales (Budd et al, 2005). Co-offending can occur for a variety of reasons including instrumental, strategic and/or social. That is to say it involves social exchange of both material and immaterial goods (Weerman, 2003). Factors affecting how a group is formed may include the complexity of the crime, the level of planning, perceived or desired outcomes and pre-existing relationships as well as available candidates. The way a group is formed will also influence its organization and behaviour.

A useful distinction in terms of studying group processes may be between transient *groups* and established *teams*. The former involve less role certainty even when roles are formally assigned, while the latter involve regular roles and shared mental models (see Cannon-Bowers et al, 1993). Role composition and clarity are likely to affect behavioural schemas held and definitions of group identity. Clearly defined, complementary roles are likely to promote cohesion and a coherent sense of group-self. In turn, mechanisms of control and processes of social influence including conformity and leadership are likely to be clarified and routine.

In the case of armed robbery most groups/teams consist of three members: a leader who grabs the money, a 'heavy' and a driver. Their criminal records often reflect crimes consistent with their roles, and even when there are more members the number of roles is fairly consistent[2] (Einstadter, 1969; McCluskey and Wardle, 2000). This reflects considerable role differentiation and division of labour, creating behavioural norms for each member and giving the group structure. Roles arise from the demands of the task and so different crimes will involve more or less role differentiation, while individual expertise and interactions determine role allocation, and the experience of offending together gives role clarity (the transition from group to team). Situational demands also affect role expression in terms of representing different challenges to criminals' goals and eliciting particular behavioural strategies. Hence commercial robberies involve more cooperative behaviour between offenders and victims because victims are needed to perform certain tasks and the robbers are chiefly motivated to gain money rather than inflict harm (Porter and Alison, 2006a).

However, even in more complex crimes, well-organized teams may be less common since many co-offenders operate as transient groups (Reiss, 1988) making co-offending behaviour somewhat unpredictable and more prone to escalation beyond individual and group norms. More commonly, groups of individuals often act as a function of each other's presence and behaviour – one influential member may instigate events while others act as facilitators and supporters, conforming and imitating in order that their group membership is not withdrawn. Such leading by example has been documented in delinquent

---

[2] How does this compare with your discussion from the Activity box role-play above?

groups and also adult gang rapes and robberies (Warr, 1996; Porter and Alison, 2001, 2006b). Thus co-offending behaviour is the product of mutual influence and interaction between group members, which is in part determined by their goals and their degree of organization, as well as situational demands including task complexity and victim reactions.

Levels of analysis

Social processes are at work in all forms of crime, not just within the commission of offences where more than one offender is present. Lone offenders must often still interact with victims, or else they might operate as part of a larger criminal network. Even lone speeding drivers may offer social justifications (because 'everybody' does it). The same crimes can be examined at different levels of social analysis, from individuals to groups and sometimes teams, to organizations and networks, and even societies. The level of analysis chosen will depend upon the questions being asked of the available data, although it is also likely to be a function of the number of people and the roles directly involved in an offence. If we consider cases of murder where a single offender kills a single victim, the focus in this instance is very likely to be upon the interactions between these two social actors. However, it is not uncommon for other people to be present when murders are committed and their very presence can contribute to the violent interaction that occurs (Deibert and Miethe, 2003). In recognition of the contribution of social contexts to offending behaviour, it may be beneficial for researchers to expand their level of analysis when possible to include indirect sources of facilitation.

Just as social embeddedness and context may suggest appropriate theoretical explanation, concomitantly different research methodologies may be implicated. Individual narratives are likely to require in-depth qualitative methods such as interviews. Small groups and teams might still be interviewed or else members might fill out questionnaires relating to role differentiation and the presence of leaders/instigators. Analysis of networks and more clearly defined organizations may include a mixture of qualitative and quantitative methods and involves effort to identify each member, their roles and their relationships with each other, strategies of **communication** and control, and various subgroups and norms. Finally, when analyzing crime at the most general level, widespread surveys and nationwide statistics are most useful in discovering societal attitudes and trends.

Of course, methods employed also rely enormously on availability of data, which is constantly a challenge in investigative psychology. A lot can be gleaned from relatively sparse information about the number of offenders directly and indirectly involved in an offence and the particular crime scene actions that occurred, but even this can be problematic. Self-reports have their limitations and in addition will often be unavailable. Police records are very useful provided access to them is granted, and even publicly available journalistic accounts of crime can be used as the basis for analysis, but neither are constructed for purposes of research and so information will frequently be missing. Whatever the methods used, it is vital that researchers recognize the application and limitations of those methods and of the data with which they must work.

Research methods 9.1

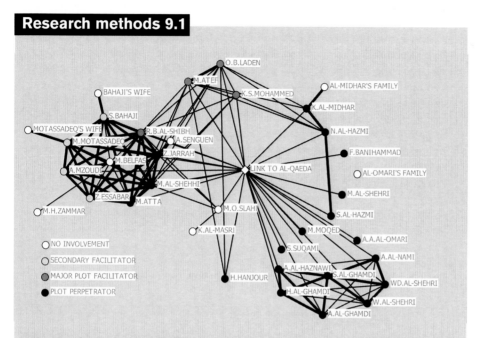

Figure 9.2 Spring 2000 in the development of the September 11th terrorist network. Key members of the network are represented as nodes. The ties connecting them signify different kinds of relationship between members with thicker ties representing stronger psychological and emotional bonds[3].

Social network analysis

A particularly useful research method for discovering social structures and thereby understanding inherent roles and relationships is **social network analysis** (SNA). SNA is increasingly being recognized as having great potential within the field of criminal investigation and has been utilized in research into crimes ranging from adolescent drug use (Pearson and West, 2003) to terrorist activities (e.g. Krebs, 2002).

SNA is based upon the principle that relationships between people result in social structure, which in turn affects social processes and opportunities for, or constraints upon, behaviour. SNA represents networks as multiple nodes connected by lines. It can be applied at any level of analysis so nodes might signify individuals, groups, organizations or societies, and can even include inanimate objects or locations of interest.

At its simplest SNA involves no more than identifying the presence or absence of a link between nodes such as whether two people know each other or not. This results in a binary matrix of zeros and ones, which is converted into a diagram depicting the overall social structure of who knows who. Figure 9.2 demonstrates this but uses a third level of association to

Continued ...

... Continued

indicate 'stronger' bonds between certain network members, and is part of a sequence of network diagrams.

It is extremely important to remember that networks are ever-changing fluid structures as relationships between people constantly change. Network visualizations, combined with quantitative network measures, help identify central or peripheral members, overall cohesion, subgroups, roles and channels of communication and resource flow. SNA can also be used to identify structural weak points that in the context of law enforcement may be targeted in efforts to disrupt or destroy networks, and this makes it a potentially very powerful tool for developing 'destructive organizational psychology' (see Canter, 2000) as a means to fight crime. By understanding the social structure within which people operate we gain insight into the psychology of those individuals as well as the functioning of social entities to which they belong. This in turn aids understanding of how to manipulate and disrupt that functioning.

To learn more about SNA there is freely available software such as UCINET (Borgatti et al, 2002), available online. See also Further reading.

---

[3] Figure 9.2 is one of a sequence of SNA diagrams used to model the dynamic development of this network over time. An in-depth account of this development is given by Mullins (2008).

Social psychology and the criminal justice system

Just as criminal behaviour is subject to forces of social interaction, the processing of offenders through the criminal justice system (CJS) is equally a product of such forces. From the moment the type of crime is known, judgements are made about the nature of the crime and who might be responsible, involving reference to social values. For example, murder investigations are a higher priority than fraud because society deems loss of life more distressing than loss of capital.

The way investigations are organized is likely to influence how they proceed. The organization of the police service as a militaristic hierarchy is as an encompassing framework within which investigative teams of varying size operate. This affects command, communication and accountability, with important implications for decision-making processes (Mullins and Alison, 2008). Police interactions with members of the public, communities and other agencies are also steeped in social psychology as social identities may foster in-group/out-group attitudes and relationships between different roles dictate the nature of social exchange. Similarly, interviews of suspects, witnesses and victims involve a process of collaboration between different parties with both shared and competing goals.

Court proceedings and trials are also not detached from social psychological processes. Judges, defendants, witnesses, lawyers and juries all interact in accordance with their assigned roles and the values and expectations of the social group to which they belong. Juries in particular have been the subject of psychological research and are a fascinating stage for the playing out of group processes including emergence of informal dynamics and leadership, conformity, dissension and construction of meaning. Likewise, as discussed in Chapter 10, eyewitness testimony has been the subject of much interest, being reliant on memory, which is an imaginative reconstruction (Bartlett, 1932) guided by schemas, stereotypes and information after the event. Hence social values and interactions act as builders working within the scaffolding provided by objective knowledge of the past.

It is clear that social psychology can be drawn upon to expand our understanding of the CJS from start to finish, in investigations, courts, prisons and probation, and as reliable research accumulates, so too will our ability to inform standards of best practice.

Conclusions

This chapter has served to highlight the importance of a social psychological perspective for comprehending the antecedents and functioning of criminal behaviour. The surface has barely been scratched in terms of the theory and research presented here, however the reader is encouraged to delve deeper into these introductory topics and also to reflect upon how *any* piece of social psychological research might apply to the criminal world and how it may 'fit' with existing theory. Currently a good deal of extrapolation is involved from studies of 'legitimate' social interactions but with increasing recognition of this relevance the social psychology of crime will be more directly explored.

Key concepts and terms

Communication	Leadership
Conformity	Roles
Co-offending	Schemas
Criminal careers	Scripts
Deindividuation	Social capital
Depersonalization	Social facilitation
Group processes	Social learning
Identity (social/collective, individual, narrative)	Social network analysis

Sample essay titles

- Outline the relevance of social psychology for understanding the criminal behaviour involved in one of the following types of crime: rape, burglary, armed robbery, drug dealing.

- How might group size affect offending behaviour?

- If the roots of crime lie in social interaction, what might work as social 'solutions'?

- What social psychological processes are relevant to court proceedings?

- What relevance does our understanding of crowd behaviour have for public order policing?

Further reading

Books

Canter, D. (2000). 'Destructive organisational psychology.' In: D. Canter and L. Alison (Eds), *The Social Psychology Of Crime: Groups, Teams and Networks*. Aldershot: Ashgate.

Canter, D., and Alison, L. (Eds) (2000b). *The Social Psychology of Crime: Groups, Teams and Networks*. Dartmouth: Ashgate.

Stott, C., and Pearson, G. (2007). *Football Hooliganism: Policing and the War on the English Disease*. London: Pennant.

Tajfel, H. (1982). *Social Identity and Intergroup Relations*. Cambridge: Cambridge University Press.

Wasserman, S., and Faust, K. (1997). *Social Network Analysis: Structural Analysis in the Social Sciences*. Cambridge: Cambridge University Press.

Journal articles

Einstadter, W. (1969). The social organisation of armed robbery. *Social Problems*, 17, 64–83.

Hanneman, R., and Riddle, M. (2005). Introduction to Social Network Methods. Riverside, CA: University of California, Riverside. Published online, available at http://faculty.ucr.edu/~hanneman/nettext/

Reicher, S., Stott, C., Cronin, P., and Adang, O. (2004). An integrated approach to crowd psychology and public order policing. *Policing: An International Journal of Police Strategies and Management*, 27, 558–572.

Weerman, F. (2003). Co-offending as social exchange: Explaining characteristics of co-offending. *British Journal of Criminology*, 43, 398–416.

3 | Dealing with crime

10 Interviewing and testimony

Laura Hammond and Katie Thole

This chapter addresses some of the key issues relating to suspect, witness and victim interviewing, and the 'cognitive interview' is critically evaluated. Issues in eyewitness testimony/identification are addressed, with discussion of the factors impacting on eyewitness accuracy/reliability.

Learning outcomes

When you have completed this chapter you should be able to:

1. Understand the key issues relating to interviewing and eyewitness testimony.
2. Understand the relevance of each throughout the legal process.
3. Understand what strategies and techniques make for an effective interview.
4. Recognize the impact of various factors and processes on the accuracy and reliability of eyewitness testimony.

Interviewing

What is an interview?

In everyday life, we encounter interviews in a wide range of settings, from job interviews to market researchers on the street. Whatever the reason for the interview, the basic objective remains the same: to gain information. The same is true in the investigative domain. The interview is an opportunity to gain information, whether that be from suspects or witnesses, in the court room or in the police custody suite.

The process of gaining information varies greatly depending upon the type of interview being conducted, by whom it is being carried out and for what purposes. The first section of this chapter will explore the main issues associated with both suspect and witness interviews.

Interview styles

In psychological terms there are three main styles of interview: the structured interview, semi-structured interview and unstructured interview. In investigative terms, structured styles are favoured, such as the structured interview or cognitive interview.

Interviewing suspects

Many police officers view suspect interrogations as being the single most important stage in the investigative process (Baldwin, 1993). Almost all suspects are interviewed at some stage in the judicial process, regardless of the offence type, and it is often at this point that a suspect's fate is sealed. Yet, there has been continued debate as to what the central purposes of conducting a suspect interview are: is the aim to induce a confession, or to get to the truth at the heart of the investigation? Research has found that the majority of police officers view securing a confession as the principal purpose of an interview. Baldwin (1993) shows that many officers approach interviews anticipating a confession. Confessions are highly desirable since securing a confession reduces the need for further enquiries.

So what might make a suspect confess? Research has identified three broad reasons (Gudjonsson, 1992):

1. The suspect perceives the *evidence* against them to be very strong, and sees denial as futile.
2. The suspect is *sorry* for their crime and wants to explain what happened.
3. The subject is reacting to *pressure*, for example from the police or the stress of confinement.

Of these, the first is by far the most important.

There are a number of methods that police officers reportedly employ to increase the likelihood of an offender confessing. These include tactics such as:

- *'Intimidation'*, e.g. emphasizing the seriousness of the offence; maximizing a suspect's anxiety about their predicament, and the officer's position.

- *'Manipulation'*, e.g. minimizing the seriousness of the offence, the suspect's role within it, and suggestions of scenarios for the offence.

- *'Appeal'* – appealing to the suspect to make a confession, telling them it is in their best interests to do so.

However, the use of such tactics is not conducive to encouraging suspects to put forward their side of the story, and in this sense it is arguable that interviewing using these methods cannot be an objective search for truth. As a suspect interview will inevitably involve the discussion of details of the case and the allegations made within a framework of the points or issues that might later need to be proven, Baldwin (1993: 327) suggests that it may be "more realistic to see interviews as mechanisms directed towards the 'construction of proof'". In other words, suspect interviews are perhaps best thought of as a search for evidence.

Police and Criminal Evidence (PACE) Act 1984

To protect suspects, police officers and criminal trials in England and Wales, the Police and Criminal Evidence (PACE) Act was introduced in 1984. This provides a full and detailed account of what is, and is not, acceptable during police interviews.

Interviewing victims and eyewitnesses

The interviewing of victims and eyewitnesses often requires a very different approach to that of interviewing suspects. Victims and eyewitnesses may have feelings of fear or intimidation, or have problems remembering what has occurred. There are thus a variety of methodologies that an interviewer can employ when interviewing victims and eyewitnesses. Perhaps the most well known of these are the structured interview and the cognitive interview.

The structured interview follows three main phases – free report, questioning and second retrieval phase. This interview technique has some merit, but has been superseded by methods such as the 'cognitive interview' which tend to yield more satisfactory results (Memon and Stevenage, 1996; Colwell, Hiscock and Memon, 2002).

Question style can have a substantial effect on the kinds of information produced during a witness interview:

- *Open questions*, such as "What happened?" produce fuller accounts by the witness.

- *Closed questions*, such as "Were you scared?" will produce accounts laden with 'yes' and 'no' answers.

- *Leading questions*, such as "Was the car red?" will produce accounts that suffer greatly from misinformation effects.

Interviewing vulnerable or intimidated victims/eyewitnesses

The overwhelming majority of research into interviewing victims and eyewitnesses has focused on vulnerable or intimidated witnesses, and research has aimed to increase the quality of information being produced during the interviews with such people. This has been reflected in public policy with Home Office research focusing on *Achieving Best Evidence* (Home Office, 2006b) from such witnesses.

Vulnerable/intimidated witnesses include:

- those under 17 years old;

- those with learning/physical disabilities;

- those with mental disorders/illness;

- those suffering from fear or distress.

It is noteworthy that with the exception of children and some people with physical/learning disabilities, it is not possible to reliably establish exactly who else is likely to be a 'vulnerable' witness. These days the police in the UK therefore tend to err on the side of caution, especially for serious crimes such as murder, and will thus treat anyone they think may be 'vulnerable' in the same way they treat a child or person with learning disabilities.

Interviewing children

The use of children in criminal proceedings is uncommon and usually reserved for serious offences, such as sexual assault. Children rarely appear in an actual court and it is far more likely that they will be interviewed in a separate room and the interview video-recorded. This provides a less intimidating atmosphere and is therefore more likely to be successful.

It may be necessary to use an interview supporter, interpreter or intermediary in an interview to ensure that a child can understand what is being asked of them. Such a person, who is drawn on in any interview with vulnerable people, is referred to as an 'appropriate adult'. It may also be useful to use props, such as dolls, in the interview.

The Home Office suggests that, when interviewing children, four main phases should be followed:

1. *Establishing rapport* with the child.
2. Asking the child to provide a *free narrative account* of what happened.
3. Asking *specific questions* based on the free narrative provided in phase 2.
4. *Closure* (e.g. post-interview counselling).

Interviewer effects

One often overlooked aspect of the interview process is the impact of the interviewer, who should be aware of the following when conducting an interview:

- The extent to which an interviewer's *knowledge* of the event can impact on the interview. Memon and Stevenage (1996) highlight that this can lead to an increase in the number of closed questions, which can have a detrimental effect on the interview process.

- The perceived *status* of the interviewer can also affect the outcome of the interview.

Focus 10.1

Enhancing eyewitness memory: The cognitive interview

The 'cognitive interview' (CI) was developed by Geiselman, Fisher and colleagues in the early 1980s. They examined real-life forensic interviewing conditions and drew heavily from research into the effectiveness of standard and hypnotic interviewing procedures. They proposed four principles ('mnemonics') that should be used in instructions given to witnesses during an interview to enhance both the quantity and quality of the information they provide (Geiselman et al, 1985):

1. *Reinstate the context*; mentally visualize the context of the original event.
2. *Report everything*; even if it seems trivial or irrelevant.
3. *Recall the events in different orders*; for example, in reverse order as well as in chronological order.
4. *Change perspectives*; when you recall the incident, try and adopt the perspectives of others who were there.

These principles formed the earliest version of the cognitive interview.

The cognitive interview was later revised to include 13 basic skills for an interviewer to use. These consisted of steps taken by the interviewer to optimize the performance of the witness in the interview, as well as instructions to be given to the witnesses themselves, including:

- Establishing rapport.

- Actively listening.

- Encouraging spontaneous recall.

- Asking open-ended questions.

- Pausing after responses.

- Avoiding interrupting.

- Requesting detailed descriptions.

- Recreating the original context.

The cognitive interview has been found to be an effective means of enhancing eyewitness recall both in laboratory and field studies. These days it is used by police forces and law enforcement agencies around the world.

Although the cognitive interview has been shown to be an effective memory enhancement technique, producing more detailed and accurate information than a standard interview (see Geiselman et al, 1985, for a detailed discussion), there are still a number of problems with the approach (Hammond et al, 2006):

- The CI, if used inaccurately or by untrained interviewers, can produce a notable amount of errors and incorrect information.

Continued ...

... Continued

- Police officers frequently encounter difficulties using the CI, and sometimes fail to adhere to the correct procedures.

- Using a CI can be time-consuming, both in terms of time taken to train interviewers and the time that conducting an interview takes.

However, all in all, the cognitive interview has proven a valuable and useful means of enhancing eyewitness memory, and continues to be endorsed by police forces, academics and forensic practitioners alike.

Figure 10.1 A police 'identification parade'. What weaknesses can you see in using this line-up to help a witness recognise the offender?
Source: © Fat Chance Productions/Corbis.

Testimony

What is testimony?

Testimony refers to evidence produced by a witness or suspect in a criminal case. In adversarial proceedings testimony is most often given in person in a court of law, but can be given by interview or video conferencing with the court, or in some jurisdictions by a written account. Testimony is predominantly an act of memory retrieval and as such is subject to misremembering. Bartlett (1932: 205) sums up memory as 'far more decisively an affair of reconstruction than one of mere reproduction'. As such, it is important that the impact of misremembering is taken into account as much as possible when using testimony in criminal proceedings.

However, it is well documented that when testimony by a witness is given in a criminal trial, the chances of a suspect being convicted of an offence are very high. This was found to be true by Loftus (1979), who found that judges would be likely to convict a suspect based on the eyewitness testimony given even by a legally blind witness.

Research methods 10.1

Field versus laboratory research

A critical issue when conducting research into any aspect of applied psychology is the applicability of empirical findings from the laboratory to real-world phenomena. This is particularly important with eyewitness testimony research because, as we have seen, it is often a vital part of the investigative process.

There are essentially two main types of research into eyewitness testimony:

1. Empirical repeated-measures studies conducted in a laboratory.
2. Field studies or archival case analyses.

The benefits and drawbacks of each are discussed below.

Eyewitnesses in the laboratory

A typical laboratory experiment into eyewitness testimony involves large numbers of mock eyewitnesses being shown a staged crime, either actually happening or via video-recording, and later being asked to answer questions on what happened or to identify key characters from the event. Usually different experimental conditions will be used, for example half will be shown a violent crime, the other half a non-violent crime, and differences between the groups compared.

Laboratory studies allow manipulations that would be impossible to achieve in a real-world setting. Such experiments are tidy and easy to control, but for obvious reasons may not be ecologically valid.

Students are typically used as participants, a population that is readily available to academic researchers but which has been repeatedly shown not to be representative of the general population.

Laboratory experiments also generate various 'expectancy effects'.

Until recently the majority of published studies into eyewitness testimony took this format, and the main findings on influences on witness accuracy are the result of laboratory-based research.

Eyewitness research in the field

An increasing number of researchers have used field studies or case analyses to assess eyewitness testimony. Such methods allow less control and are usually more complex than laboratory studies, although they have the advantage of being more realistic and therefore more reliably applicable to real-world phenomena.

Continued ...

... Continued

Typically, this type of research involves the experiment being conducted in a real-life setting and the accuracy of eyewitnesses being explored within this context. For example, an individual may purchase an item from a store clerk in the clerk's natural retail environment, and the clerk may later be asked to identify them from a photographic line-up.

There are influences on eyewitnesses' accounts that can only be measured using field or case studies, such as fear or stress – aspects of the witness experience that are difficult, and unethical, to recreate in the laboratory. Field studies also often involve more realistic, less abstract tasks for the eyewitnesses to complete than those employed in laboratory research.

Motivation is also a key difference between the two formats – in the laboratory witnesses know that their responses will have little consequence, whereas in the field (and in real life), the pressure to perform and the desire to be correct will be much greater.

Factors affecting eyewitness performance

Research has identified factors that influence how accurate an eyewitness is, not only in terms of their account of what happened during the event and their description of the perpetrator, but also in terms of their identification accuracy (eyewitness identifications are discussed in more detail later).

Loftus (1979) suggests that these factors fall into four main groups, each of which relate to one of the three main stages of remembering: *acquisition* – factors relating to the event and factors relating to the witness or person; *retention* – factors influencing how well the information is retained; and *retrieval* – factors governing how the information is retrieved (Loftus, 1981).

Factors relating to the event

Many of the key factors relating to the nature of the event or incident that influence an eyewitness's ability to remember it were identified in what is known as the 'Turnbull ruling' (*R. v Turnbull and Others, 1977*), and can be remembered using the mnemonic '*ADVOKATE*' (Kebbell and Wagstaff, 1999):

- *Amount of time under observation* – the longer a witness observes an event, the better they remember it.

- *Distance of the witness from the person or event* – the closer they are, the better they are likely to be at encoding and remembering details.

- *Visibility* – the more visible the event, the better the witness is likely to recall it.

- *Obstruction* – the fewer obstructions to the witnesses view, the better they will remember the event.

- *Known or seen before* – if a witness has seen an offender before, they will be more likely to remember that person when they see them again in different situations.

- *Any reason to remember* – if something is salient or novel, then it is more likely to be 'memorable' for the witness.

- *Time lapse* – the greater the amount of time between an event and a witness's attempts to recall it, the worse their memory for that event is likely to be.

- *Errors or material discrepancies* – if parts of a witness's testimony are inaccurate, then other aspects of their testimony are also likely to be inaccurate.

Other major event factors influencing eyewitness performance are *stress* or *fear*, and *violence/the presence of a weapon* – the more stressful or intense something is for a witness, the greater the impact that it is likely to have on them and the more likely they are to remember it, for example, violent events tend to be remembered better than non-violent events. However, stress (e.g. caused by the presence of a weapon) can also cause a witness to narrow their focus, and so other information relating to the event may not be remembered as well, as it is not encoded so effectively.

Factors relating to the person (witness)

- *Age* – children are usually less able to effectively recall information as their memory is generally poorer than that of adults and they are less articulate. Older adults also tend to make worse witnesses than younger people; perceptual abilities and visual acuity may become impaired with age, and they may have more difficulty in storing and retrieving information.

- *Race* – people are better able to recall and identify people who belong to the same racial group as themselves.

- *Expectations* – witnesses may reconstruct an event according to what they expect to have happened, or what they feel is most likely to have occurred, rather than what they genuinely remember. Expectancy effects, in terms of what the witness feels they should be remembering or saying, may also come into play.

- *Pressure to perform* – witnesses will tend to want to be helpful, and keen to be as accurate as possible. Pressure to perform, and the desire to avoid seeming foolish or useless, may impact upon a witness's recollection and their reporting of the memory that they have of an event.

Factors influencing retention of information

- Length of *retention interval* (see 'Time lapse', above).

- *Post-event suggestions* – information that is made available to a witness between the original event and subsequent attempts to recall it (e.g. through feedback provided by interviewers/investigators or discussions with other witnesses, or information that is reported in the media) may impact upon an eyewitness's testimony and alter their memory for an event.

- *Confabulations and distortions* – as memory for an event decreases over time, a witness may fill in gaps or ambiguities in their memory, causing 'confabulations' in their account. This may or may not be conscious, and witnesses' recollections will often be distorted. Confabulations and discrepancies are frequently produced by exposure to additional or conflicting information presented to the witness between the event and their attempts to remember it (see 'Post-event suggestions', above).

Retrieval factors

- *Actions vs. descriptions* – generally, witnesses are good at describing what happened during an event but encounter more problems in describing the physical characteristics of the perpetrator.

- *Confidence and accuracy* – research has shown that the confidence of an eyewitness in their testimony and recall is not necessarily related to their accuracy. However, the confidence–accuracy relationship is complex (Kebbell and Wagstaff, 1999) and tends to be malleable – it is easily influenced by, for example, comments or feedback from interviewers.

Other factors influencing the retrieval of information include those relating to the questioning of the witness, such as method of questioning and the influence of the person asking the questions, which have been discussed earlier in this chapter.

Factors influencing eyewitness identification performance

Eyewitness identification is notoriously problematic, and there has been considerable research examining the influence of different factors, in addition to those detailed above, on the accuracy and reliability of the identification evidence of eyewitnesses. These include:

- The *format* of the line-up from which the witness is asked to make their selection and the people that compose the line-up.

- The *instructions* given to the witness prior to the line-up.

- The *influence* of line-up administrators.

- *Exposure* to suspects or people featuring in the line-ups through previous identifications.

Mistaken identifications by eyewitnesses are one of the leading causes of wrongful convictions within the criminal justice system (www. innocenceproject.org and Wells et al, 1998). A number of steps have been proposed that should be taken when conducting identification line-ups to enhance eyewitness identification accuracy and reduce the risks of mistaken identifications:

- Line-ups should be presented sequentially.

- The individual conducting the line-up should not know the identity of the actual suspect.

- Witnesses should be warned that the suspect may or may not be in the line-up.

- Additional line-up members should be selected based on the eyewitness's description of the perpetrator.

- No feedback should be given during or after a line-up.

- Witnesses should provide confidence ratings at the time of making their identification.

Focus 10.2

False memory

False memories occur when a person remembers something that has not actually occurred. The most famous example of false memories can be found in the Loftus and Palmer (1974) study where participants were asked to watch a video of an automobile accident then asked questions about the footage. Participants reported aspects of the accident they could not possibly have seen with confidence. This occurred through a process known as 'misinformation' where participants are led to believe they have a memory through the way in which a question is phrased. Misinformation effects are an element of the criminal process that require considerable attention, since many witnesses are questioned in the court room.

Since psychologists are rarely involved in the questioning of witnesses, especially those being questioned in the court room, misinformation is an aspect of remembering and false memories that remains a central problem in eyewitness testimony.

Another aspect of false memories that deserves some consideration is that of 'recovered memories'. These particular forms of false memory came to the fore with a number of well-publicized accounts of people suddenly remembering that they had been abused as children. Accusations were often made about innocent people and the effect on their lives was devastating. Of note, however, is that these memories felt real to the person experiencing them. It has been suggested that recovered memories are brought about by questioning methods that have many parallels to a person being hypnotized. See Loftus (2003) for review.

Activity 10.1

Inducing false memories

Spend 30 seconds memorizing the 15 words below. After this 30 seconds cover the list and then write down as many of the words as you can remember.

Table	Desk	Swivel
Sit	Recliner	Stool
Legs	Sofa	Sitting
Seat	Wood	Rocking
Couch	Cushion	Bench

(Roediger and McDermott, 1995.)

How many did you remember? Check the words you wrote down against the list of words here. Are there any 'odd' words in your list?

The Deese–Roediger–McDermott (Roediger and McDermott, 1995) list learning paradigm is a reliable way of inducing false memories in the laboratory. The basic idea behind the list learning paradigm is that each of the words in the list is semantically related to a common associate. When recalling the words from the list, the semantic associate of these words is likely to be recalled as well. In the list above, the common associate is 'chair' and many of you will have recalled chair in your list of remembered words although it is not in the list at all.

Conclusions

This very brief overview of the psychology of interviewing has outlined the central significance of memory in the interviewing processes. This has led to the recognition that reliable testimony is more likely to be produced if procedures that enhance memory are utilized. However, these do need to take account of the risks of distorting memory by intrusive processes. The challenges of achieving effective testimony are especially important in relation to eyewitness identification in which the pressures on the witness to give the answer the investigators want may be very strong. This area is consequently noteworthy for the impact that psychological research can have in the improvement of criminal justice processes.

Key concepts and terms

Cognitive interview
Eyewitness identification
Investigative interviewing

Testimony
Vulnerable/intimidated witness

Sample essay titles

- Discuss the 'cognitive interview' as a memory enhancement method.

- What similarities and differences would you recommend for the methods used by police to interview suspects as opposed to victims?'

- What influences how reliable eyewitnesses are likely to be?

- What is a 'vulnerable' witness and what are the implications for such a person being interviewed?

- What conditions are likely to give rise to 'false memories'?

- Why do you think it is useful to have laws about how police officers should carry out interviews?

Further reading

Books

Bartlett, F.C. (1932). *Remembering: A Study in Experimental and Social Psychology*. London: Cambridge University Press.

Canter, D., and Alison, L. (Eds) (1999). *Interviewing and Deception*. Aldershot: Ashgate/Dartmouth.

Gudjonsson, G. (1992). *The Psychology of Interrogations, Confessions and Testimony*. Chichester: Wiley.

Loftus, E.F. (1979). *Eyewitness Testimony*. Cambridge: Harvard University Press.

Police and Criminal Evidence Act (1984). London: Home Office. Available online: www.homeoffice.gov.uk/documents/PACE-cover

Journal articles

Baldwin, J. (1993). Police interview techniques: Establishing truth or proof? *British Journal of Criminology*, 33(3), 325–352.

Geiselman, R.E., Fisher, R.P., MacKinnon, D.P., and Holland, H.L. (1985). Eyewitness memory enhancement in the police interview: Cognitive retrieval mnemonics versus hypnosis. *Journal of Applied Psychology*, 70(2), 401–412.

Hammond, L., Wagstaff, G.F., and Cole, J. (2006). Facilitating eyewitness memory in adults and children with context reinstatement and focused meditation. *Journal of Investigative Psychology and Offender Profiling*, 3, 117–130.

Roediger, H.L. III, and McDermott, K.B. (1995). Creating false memories: Remembering words that were not presented in lists. *Journal of Experimental Psychology: Learning, Memory and Cognition*, 21, 803–814.

11 Detecting deception

Mary Santarcangelo

This chapter provides a review of the theories behind deception detection and the methods. It summarizes what people think are the verbal and **non-verbal cues** to lying and how these relate to findings from research. The technology used for lie detection is also discussed together with its strengths and weaknesses.

Learning outcomes

When you have completed this chapter you should be able to:

1. Discuss the strengths and weaknesses of the theories of deception.
2. Understand the non-verbal and verbal cues of deception detection.
3. Evaluate the ability to detect verbal and non-verbal cues to deception.
4. Understand the principles underlying physiological techniques for detecting lies (known as 'lie detectors').
5. Consider possibilities for improving the detection of deception.

Deception theory

Over 30 years of deception research has produced different theories explaining deceptive behaviour (see DePaulo et al, 2003, for an overview). The most popular theory referred to in the literature is Zuckerman, DePaulo and Rosenthal's (1981) three-factor model that was developed to explain the behavioural differences that emerged between truth-tellers and liars in their meta-analysis.

The three-factor model assumes that liars display deceptive behaviours as a result of experiencing emotions, cognitive load or behavioural control. Liars might experience emotions such as guilt for telling a lie, fear of not being believed or excitement at fooling someone. Liars might have to think hard to come up with a story that is plausible and convincing, especially if they do not have time to plan or rehearse what to say. Liars might also try to control their behaviours, trying not to look nervous in order to make a convincing impression.

However, not all people experience these processes when telling a lie. Individual differences and situational differences such as personality, motivation to succeed, consequences of getting caught and planning what to say in advance play a role in the deceptive processes (Vrij, 2000). Further, truth-tellers may experience these processes if they are highly motivated to be believed, such as during a police interrogation. This makes it difficult to distinguish truth-tellers from deceivers.

Activity 11.1

Are you a good liar/detector?

Demonstrating lie detection

Here is an activity you can try in your class or with a group of people. Randomly select half your group to be 'senders' and the other half 'detectors'.

Senders will tell a truth or lie, and detectors will judge whether the sender is telling a truth or a lie.

Instructions for the senders

1. Please take a moment to decide if you will be a truth-teller or a lie-teller. Write this down on a piece of paper and keep it hidden, do not discuss.
2. You will be telling the detectors a story about a significant event in your life. This can be any event that was meaningful to you; however, please avoid telling a distressing event or an event that the receiver may know about.
3. If you are a truth-teller, you will tell a true story (i.e. one that you remember very clearly and actually happened to you). If you are a lie-teller, you will tell a false story (i.e. one that you made up and did not actually happen to you).
4. The senders will now stand before the detectors and tell their story one at a time. The detectors will judge each sender on whether they are a truth-teller or a lie-teller so give them a moment to make their decision before you begin telling your story.

Instructions for the detectors

1. You will be testing your lie detection ability. The senders will each stand before the detectors and tell a story about a significant event in their life. Some of the senders are truth-tellers and some are lie-tellers (i.e. telling a true story about a significant event or a false story about a significant event).
2. After each sender tells their story, you will write down on a piece of paper a) your judgement of whether this person is telling a truth or a lie, b) what cues you paid attention to when making your judgement, and c) how confident you are in your judgement on a nine-point scale where 1 is not at all confident and 9 is absolutely certain. (Note: you are not allowed to ask the senders any questions.)

Once all the senders have told their stories and the detectors have made their judgements it is time to reveal the lie-tellers!

- How many truths did you accurately detect? How many lies did you accurately detect?
- What cues did you rely on the most in making your judgement?
- How confident were you in your judgements?
- Ask the lie-tellers what strategies they used to deceive you.

Recommended reading: DePaulo et al (2003).

Ability to detect deception

Lab-based research on the ability to detect deception usually consists of showing videotaped clips of liars and truth-tellers to observers (undergraduate students) who have to indicate after each clip whether it contained a truth or a lie. These studies are common in the literature and the observers base their judgements on limited information (i.e. lack of factual evidence, statements of third parties, etc.). Results of these lab-based studies demonstrate a 50 per cent accuracy rate, the chance of flipping a coin. Bond and DePaulo (2006) reviewed the results of 186 studies, including 22,282 observers. On average, observers achieved a 54 per cent accuracy rate, correctly classifying 47 per cent of the lies as deceptive and 61 per cent of truths as truthful. The ability to correctly identify more truthful than deceptive messages is explained by the truth bias. We tend to assume people are being truthful. Studies conducted on prisoners found that they correctly identified more lies than truths, i.e. a lie bias. This could be explained by the nature of their environment (they tend to assume people are being deceptive) (see Hartwig et al, 2004).

A few studies have examined the ability of professional lie-catchers, such as police officers, rather than undergraduates, to detect deception. Granhag and Vrij (2005) in a review of 10 studies found these professionals performed similarly to the undergraduates with an overall accuracy rate of 55 per cent (55 per cent lie accuracy rate and 55 per cent truth accuracy rate). However, Ekman, O'Sullivan and Frank (1999) found that some groups of professionals are better than others: members of the Secret Service (64 per cent accuracy rate), Central Intelligence Agency (73 per cent accuracy rates), and sheriffs (67 per cent accuracy rates). These professional lie detectors were equally good at detecting truth and lies, i.e. they did not show a truth bias. This could be explained by the nature of their work, they are more suspicious of being lied to.

The poor ability to detect deception in lab-based studies has raised criticism regarding the **ecological validity** of these studies. Both undergraduates and professionals in these studies lie for the sake of the experiment in university laboratories. The lack of motivation to get away with the lie and lack of consequences if the lie is found out may not elicit the deceptive behaviours that are needed to base judgements upon (Miller and Stiff, 1993). Lie detectors can only make their best guess.

Research methods 11.1

Designing a deception detection study

When designing a lab-based or field-based deception detection study, it is important to consider the reliability and validity of the study. Deception detection literature consists of studies varying in ecological validity, deception scenario and behavioural scoring. In order to interpret the results of these studies you must be aware of how these design differences may elicit different responses from the liars and lie detectors.

Frank (2005) recommends that you ask yourself the following questions when designing a deception detection study.

1. Will the study involve lies sanctioned by the experimenter for research purposes or will the senders decide on their own whether to lie or tell the truth (e.g. lie to gain reward or avoid punishment)?

   – Feeley and deTurck (1998) found behavioural differences between sanctioned and unsanctioned liars. One explanation is that unsanctioned liars are more motivated to lie than sanctioned liars and may therefore display more behaviours related to emotion, cognitive load and behavioural control.

2. Who will be the liars or lie detectors?

   – Subjects from different cultures may exhibit different behavioural cues and may have different beliefs regarding the social acceptability of lying. Further, undergraduates may display different behaviours compared to the general population or more vulnerable subjects such as imprisoned offenders.

3. Will the subjects be interviewed by the experimenter or a third party (i.e. student or police officer)? Is the interviewer in an oppositional, confrontational or informational relationship with the subject?

   – The relationship between interviewer and subject can affect the motivation of the subjects and the intensity of emotions experienced. This may elicit different behavioural responses from the subjects.

4. What type of lie will the subjects tell?

   – It is important to consider what the subjects lie about as each situation may produce a different response. For example, if the subject simply has to deny an action they committed in a certain scenario, this may produce fewer words and may be less cognitively challenging than a lie about why the subject has a certain opinion.

5. Will subjects be assigned to conditions or will they choose whether to lie?

– Knowing what issues you wish to address will help you to decide. If you want to infer causality then you must randomly assign. Ecological validity would dictate that you allow subjects to choose, since we choose whether to lie or not in everyday life.

6. How long will subjects have to concoct their lie, or how long will they have to maintain it?

– Cognitive load is affected by whether or not the lie is planned and the length of the lie, and these differences would therefore elicit different responses.

7. How many lies should a subject tell and in what order?

– Most studies have subjects tell a single lie about a single event. Deciding whether to alternate lies and truths, or randomly assign the location of the lies, or allow the subject to choose when or whether to lie or how often depends on what it is you want to examine. Frank (2005) offers suggestions for different scenarios.

8. What stakes are involved in successful or unsuccessful lies?

– Ethically, lab-based studies cannot replicate the stakes faced by a murderer if caught in a lie. But stakes can be manipulated by offering subjects incentives to tell a successful lie (i.e. get away with the lie). High-stakes scenarios would elicit different behavioural responses as the subject would be more motivated to get away with the lie. Low-stakes situations such as telling white lies tend to go unnoticed in everyday life as they tend not to elicit deceptive behaviour and are therefore likely to be more difficult to detect.

■ Based on this information, how do you now interpret the results of the demonstrating lie detection activity, above?
■ How would you design your own demonstrating lie detection activity?

Recommended reading: Frank (2005).

Non-verbal and verbal cues to deception

Despite weak ecological validity in lab-based studies, our poor ability to detect deception is also related to the fact that people have incorrect beliefs about lying behaviour. Studies investigating how people think liars respond have revealed that both laypersons and professional lie-catchers expect liars to behave nervously, with 'liars look away' and 'liars make grooming gestures' being the most popular beliefs.

People also believe that they show nervous behaviour when lying. Studies have shown that people have poor insight into their own behaviour (see Vrij, Edward, and Bull, 2001). Results indicated that people did not behave nervously when lying even though they thought they had. In fact participants showed a decrease in behaviours. This is explained by the cognitive load and behavioural control approach where liars control their behaviours in order to make an honest impression.

Research on the verbal cues to deception is limited. The belief is that, since verbal behaviour is controlled by the speaker, it is less likely to provide deceptive cues. For the most part laypersons' beliefs about verbal cues to deception are accurate (see Vrij, 2000).

Focus 11.1

The most common *subjective* cues to deception

Expressed by laypersons	Expressed by practitioners
Non-verbal	*Non-verbal*
■ Liars are more gaze aversive.	■ Liars are more gaze aversive.
■ Liars shift position more often.	■ Liars make more self-manipulations.
■ Liars make more illustrators.	■ Liars make more head movements/nods.
■ Liars make more self-manipulations.	■ Liars' speech is less fluent.
■ Liars make more arm/hand movements.	■ Liars make more arm/hand movements.
■ Liars make more leg/feet movements.	■ Liars make more leg/feet movements.
■ Liars blink more often.	■ Lairs fidget more.
■ Liars have a higher-pitched voice.	■ Liars shift position more.
■ Liars make more speech disturbances.	■ Liars make more body movements in general.
■ Liars have a slower speech rate.	
■ Liars have a longer latency period.	
■ Liars take more and longer pauses.	
Verbal	*Verbal*
■ Lies seem less plausible.	■ Lies are less consistent.
■ Lies are less consistent.	■ Liars' stories are less plausible.
■ Liars give more indirect answers.	■ Lies contain fewer details.
■ Lies make fewer self-references.	
■ Lies are less detailed.	
■ Lies are shorter.	
■ Lies contain more negative statements.	
■ Lies contain more irrelevant information.	

The most reliable *objective* cues to deception

Non-verbal	*Verbal*
■ Liars speak in a higher pitch. ■ Liars make fewer movements with arms/hand/fingers. ■ Liars make fewer illustrators. ■ Liars take longer pauses. ■ Liars make fewer movements with legs/feet.	■ Liars' answers are less plausible and convincing. ■ Liars' stories contain fewer details. ■ Liars give more indirect answers. ■ Liars provide shorter answers. ■ Liars make fewer self-references. ■ Liars tell the story more chronologically correct. ■ Lies contain more negative statements. ■ Lies contain less temporal information. ■ Lies contain less spatial information. ■ Lies contain less perceptual information.

Refer to the following article for full definitions and discussion: Stromwall et al (2004).

Applications 11.1

Deception guidelines

Why do liars get caught? (Vrij, 2000):

... because it is cognitively too difficult to continue lying, or because the way in which they deal with their emotions gives away their lies.

Guidelines for detecting deception
- Be suspicious.
- Ask questions.
- Do not reveal important information.
- Be informed (context and personalities).
- Ask liars to repeat what they have said before.
- Avoid and abandon stereotypes.
- Compare liars' behaviour with their natural behaviour – baseline.

Guidelines for deceiving
- Be well prepared.
- Be original.
- Be able to think quickly.
- Be eloquent.

Continued ...

Deception detection technology

The ability to detect deception is a skill that is necessary within various occupations from the military to crime investigators, customs agents and insurance agents. Money is invested to develop reliable lie detectors for use against terrorism and in the judicial system. These technologies all assume that telling lies produces a physiological response. The limitation of these technologies is that they can accurately measure physiological response but not accurately detect deception. These are only a few of the current technologies being used to detect deception.

Polygraph: The arousal detector

What is the polygraph?

The **polygraph** gets its name from the Greek *poly* (many) and *graph* (to write). It is a general purpose piece of equipment used in many areas of physiology that records a number of different measures of physiological response together. The polygraph is based on the age-old assumption that liars will be more aroused than truth-tellers due to feelings of guilt and fear and as a result display changes in physiological activity. It is not a lie detector but rather an arousal detector; an indirect measure of lie telling.

The polygraph is an instrument that accurately measures and records changes in physiological activity related to arousal. An examinee would be attached to a blood pressure cuff to measure heart rate and blood pressure, pneumographs to measure respiration, and galvanometers to measure the skin resistance produced by palmar sweating. As the examinee answers questions relating to an incident or event, the examiner looks for changes in physiological activity as displayed on to chart paper or a computer screen that records all the measures together.

Lie detection procedures

There are several types of polygraph test procedures used by examiners. The two most commonly used procedures in the field are the **control question technique** and the **guilty knowledge test**.

The control question technique (CQT) is a four-phased procedure. First the examiner becomes familiar with the facts of the crime by reading the case file and by speaking with the investigating officer and develops the appropriate questions. The examiner then conducts an extensive pre-test with the examinee in order to establish rapport, allow the examinee to give their version of the crime and for the examiner to explain the test procedure to the examinee. Once the examinee understands the procedure and the examiner has developed their questions into 'yes' or 'no' answer format, the examinee is attached to the polygraph.

The third phase is the actual test phase. The examinee is asked three types of questions:

1. Relevant questions (R) relate to the crime under investigation. It is assumed that both guilty and innocent examinees will answer 'no' to these questions otherwise they would be admitting to the crime.
2. Control questions (C) are general, non-specific misconducts that are used to establish a baseline lie. Both guilty and innocent examinees are expected to lie about these questions by answering 'no' because the examiner will tell the examinee that admitting to such a misconduct would cause the examiner to conclude that the examinee is the type of person who would commit the crime in question and is therefore considered guilty.
3. Irrelevant questions (I) relate to neutral issues and both guilty and innocent examinees are expected to tell the truth about these questions by answering 'yes'. These questions are intended to allow rest periods between the more important relevant and control questions.

Generally, a series of 10–12 questions are asked which are repeated three or four times.

For example, the polygraph examiner's questions could run as follows:

Respond 'yes' or 'no' to the following questions:

I: 'Is your name James?' 'Yes'

C: 'Have you hit anyone?' 'No'

R: 'Did you slap Liam?' No'

I: 'Is today Wednesday?' 'Yes'

C: 'Have you ever told a lie to stay out of trouble?' 'No'

R: 'Did you threaten Liam?' 'No'

I: 'Are you sitting in a chair?' 'Yes'

C: 'Have you ever threatened anyone?' 'No'

R: 'Did you punch Liam?' 'No'

The CQT is based on the assumption that guilty examinees will be more concerned with the *relevant* questions and become aroused while answering these questions than while answering the *control* questions. Innocent examinees are assumed to be more concerned with the control questions and will become more aroused while answering these questions than while answering the relevant questions.

The final phase is where the examiner compares the responses of the control questions to the relevant questions. This phase may also be used to obtain a confession from the examinee.

The limitation of the CQT is that the specific relevant questions are not comparable to the general control questions and may lead to a high false positive rate, where the innocent are mistakenly deemed as guilty. Studies have found that 40–50 per cent of innocent examinees 'fail' the CQT polygraph test (National Research Council, 2003). To pass the test you have to lie. If an innocent person is honest on the control questions they will provide a higher physiological response to the relevant question than to the control question, eliciting a response of a guilty examinee. The polygraph can be beaten by intentionally eliciting stronger responses on the control questions than on the relevant questions. The way to do this is by changing your blood pressure and heart rate by doing maths in your head, thinking of something frightening or squeezing your buttocks during the control questions.

The guilty knowledge test (GKT) does not attempt to determine whether the person is lying but whether the person possesses guilty knowledge. It is based on a series of multiple-choice questions, each having only one correct alternative, a critical crime-relevant detail that only a guilty examinee would know, and several control alternatives, not related to the crime. The examinees are instructed to respond 'no' to each response alternative. It is assumed that the guilty examinee will be more aroused by the correct alternative than the control alternatives. Only if responses to the correct alternative are consistently larger is the examinee deemed guilty. This controls against false positives. A selection from a GKT interview may therefore be as follows:

Regarding the abduction location, do you know for sure it was ...

1. '... *at a toy shop?*' '*No*'

2. '... *at a shopping mall?*' '*No*' *(correct alternative)*

3. '... *at a city park?*' '*No*'

4. '... *at a friend's house?*' '*No*'

5. '... *at school?*' '*No*'

The GKT is limited by the difficulty in certain cases of designing questions to which only the suspect would know the answers. In cases where details are highly publicized (i.e. the O.J. Simpson case) or if memory is affected (e.g. suspect under the influence of drink or drugs, or long period between time of crime and polygraph test) there would be no guilty knowledge to detect. (*Recommended reading*: National Research Council, 2003.)

Voice stress analysis: The stress detector

Voice stress analysis (VSA) assumes that liars will be more aroused than truth-tellers due to feelings of guilt and fear and as a result display stress in their voice. The VSA measures and displays inaudible fluctuations in the human voice known as 'micro-tremor' patterns on a computer screen which indicate when a speaker delivers words under stress. It is not a lie detector but rather a stress detector, an indirect measure of lie telling.

The appeal of VSA is its ease of use in the field. The computer voice stress analyser (CVSA) can be easily brought to the crime scene to interview suspects and results are instant. The CVSA is also being used by insurance companies to identify false insurance claim calls.

The National Research Council (2003) has examined the reliability of the VSA and concluded that 'The practical performance of voice stress analysis for detecting deception has not been impressive' (p. 168) and that the relevant research offers 'little or no scientific basis for the use of ... voice measurement instruments as an alternative to the polygraph ...' (p. 168).

Despite the lack of scientific basis for its use it continues to be used in the field. [C]VSA has been found to be effective in eliciting confessions from suspects and also in eliciting false confessions, as in the case of Michael Crowe who was accused of the murder of his sister in 1998.

Focus 11.2

'Innocent until proved guilty?'

ABC News Primetime, 30 March, 2006

Confesses to Murder Based on Machine

After Michael Crowe's 12-year-old sister, Stephanie, was found stabbed to death in her bedroom, the Escondido, Calif., police department brought him into the station for questioning and hooked him up to the CVSA in the middle of the night.

From tapes recorded during his questioning, Crowe answered "Yes" when the detective asked, "Is today Thursday?" But when Crowe replied "No" when asked whether he took Stephanie's life, the detective told him that he had failed the test.

"I started to think that, you know, maybe the machine's right, especially when they added on top of it that the machine was getting my subconscious feelings on it, that I could be lying and not even know it," Crowe, now 21, told "Primetime." "They said the machine is more accurate than the polygraph and is the best device for telling the truth, for finding the truth."

Once the detective told him that he had failed the test, Crowe said he began to doubt his own memory and wonder whether he might have killed his sister.

Continued ...

... Continued

"I didn't want to go to prison, and I just wanted to be out of that room," Crowe recalled. "So my only option was to say, 'Yeah, I guess I did it,' and then hope for the best."

Crowe said the police used the machine to persuade him to confess and then to implicate two of his classmates.

"So I got a knife, and I went into her room, and I stabbed her," Crowe can be heard saying on tapes from his questioning.

But one week before the start of his trial, the police found DNA evidence that led to the real killer, a transient who is now in prison for killing Crowe's sister.

Focus 11.3

Brain fingerprinting – the P300 detector

Jimmie Ray Slaughter was convicted and sentenced to death for the 2 July, 1991, murders of his girlfriend and their 11-month-old daughter. Slaughter underwent brain fingerprinting in an attempt to overturn his conviction. Test results indicated that he did not commit the crime. Slaughter was executed by the state of Oklahoma on 15 March, 2005.

Figure 11.1 Brain fingerprinting.

Source: Courtesy of Dr. Larry Farwell.

Recommended reading: Rosenfeld, 2005.

Ethics 11.1

fMRI – The brain activity detector

Below is an extract from an article that can be found on the Times Online website. Since 9/11 the American Department of Defense agencies and the Department of Homeland Security have invested tens of millions to hundreds of millions of dollars in the development of new lie detection technologies that can identify a liar with 100 per cent accuracy. This new technology has been tested within the lab and is already being used in the real world. What are some of the ethical implications of these new brain scan technologies?

Brain lie detection
David Rowan, Times Online, 21 October, 2006

... As advances in neuroscience have mapped out the brain in unprecedented detail in recent years, businesses have been clamouring to commercialise the emerging research. The newest trend is for companies to offer magnetic resonance imaging (MRI) scans that they claim identify brain activity associated with deception. Already this year, new companies such as No Lie MRI and Cephos have been pitching defence lawyers, counter-intelligence agencies and suspicious spouses with their promises to reveal the cold truth. Plenty of sceptics see the claims as overhyped, and there are serious worries about ethics and civil liberties. But with billions of pounds to be made if lie detection can be reliably merchandised, the sector is about to take off.

The industry's premise is that brain activity, measured by blood flow in specific regions associated with dishonesty, can be mapped while a subject stretches inside an MRI scanner. So if, as you are being scanned, a computer screen asks questions to which you know the true answer, the patterns revealed by your brain can supposedly determine whether your responses are accurate. The claims are backed up by academic research which set out to find the truth about lying: a now famous 2001 study by psychiatrist Daniel Langleben, for instance, peered inside the heads of 18 volunteers who were told that they could keep $20 if they lied about the playing cards they were holding in a game, something that prompted lively activity in parts of the prefrontal cortex. Dr Langleben is now an adviser to No Lie MRI, which charges out its lie-detection service at around £1,000 an hour.

The company is ambitious about its potential market: immigration agencies, airport security, the CIA, accounting firms and avowedly innocent prisoners. The rival Cephos Corporation, which is claiming 90 per cent accuracy in clinical tests of its brain lie detectors, is pitching primarily at government security-clearance agencies and at "the legal marketplace". "There is enormous potential for Cephos's deception detection services to change the world of litigation," according to Robert Shapiro, an American defence lawyer who advises the company. "I'd use it tomorrow in virtually every criminal and civil case on my desk."

Recommended reading: Wolpe, Foster and Langleben (2005).

Conclusions

Lie detection is not as easy as many people think. In general people are very poor at detecting deceit. This may be because 'white lies' are a natural part of human interactions, so we must all be able to lie convincingly at some time or other. However, detecting deceit is a crucial part of the criminal justice system and so there is a great deal of interest in developing procedures to help discover lies. The physiologically based 'lie detectors' have rather less utility than is often believed and may be of more value in encouraging confessions than detecting lies. No system does a great deal better than chance across all situations, but the cognitive and emotional load sustained that lying requires is a reasonable basis for exploring the psychology of deceit which may, in limited circumstances, with some people, provide a productive basis for understanding how lying occurs and so how it may be detected.

Key concepts and terms

Control question technique
Ecological validity
Guilty knowledge test

Non-verbal cues
Polygraph

Sample essay titles

- What are the main challenges to producing ecologically valid studies of lie detection?

- What are lie detectors? Do they work?

- Are any groups of people better at detecting liars than others? Why might that be?

- What are the main psychological processes involved in sustaining a lie?

Further reading

Books

Canter, D., and Alison, L. (Eds) (1999). *Interviewing and Deception*. Aldershot: Ashgate/Dartmouth.

Ekman, P. (2001). *Telling Lies: Clues to Deceit in the Marketplace, Politics and Marriage*. New York: W.W. Norton.

Ford, C.V. (1996). *Lies! Lies!! Lies!!: The Psychology of Deceit*. London: American Psychiatric Press.

Granhag, P.A., and Stromwall, L.A. (2004) (Eds). *Deception Detection in Forensic Contexts*. Cambridge: Cambridge University Press, 229–250.

National Research Council (2003). *The Polygraph and Lie Detection*. Committee to Review the Scientific Evidence on the Polygraph. Washington, DC: The National Academic Press.

Vrij, A. (2008). *Detecting Lies and Deceit: Pitfalls and Opportunities*, (2nd Ed.). Chichester: Wiley.

Journal articles

DePaulo, B.M., Lindsay, J.J., Malone, B.E., Muhlenbruck, L., Charlton, K., and Cooper, H. (2003). Cues to deception. *Psychological Bulletin*, 129, 74–118.

Rosenfeld, J.P. (2005). "Brain fingerprinting:" A critical analysis. *Scientific Review of Mental Health Practice*, 4, 20–37.

Vrij, A. (2004). Why professionals fail to catch liars and how they can improve. *Legal and Criminological Psychology*, 9, 151–181.

Wolpe, P.R., Foster, K.R., and Langleben, D.D. (2005). Emerging neurotechnologies for lie-detection: promises and perils. *The American Journal for Bioethics*, 5, 39–49.

12 Psychology and investigations

Donna Youngs

This chapter outlines the ways in which psychology can interact with and contribute to the investigative process. The contributions psychologists can make to investigations fall within three broad areas. The first of these is the examination of the styles and patterns of criminal action within offenders' behaviour and the unravelling of how these relate to psychological and social characteristics, sometimes referred to as 'offender profiling'. The work of psychologists can be used here to help in the identification of the sorts of individuals that may be responsible for a crime that is under investigation. Although sometimes assumed only to be relevant to serious, serial or sexual crimes, in fact these 'investigative inferences' can be derived for all forms of criminality from burglary or fraud or arson through to serial killing, kidnapping and terrorism.

The second contribution psychologists can make is to the analysis of the investigation process itself. Psychology may be drawn on to improve the effectiveness and appropriateness of the way in which detectives make decisions during an investigation. The focus is on the consideration of the activities, systems and approaches used by investigators to detect crime, rather than their selection and training, which is discussed in Chapter 13.

Learning outcomes

When you have completed this chapter you should be able to:

1. Identify the three broad types of contribution psychologists can make to investigations.
2. Identify the operational questions where investigators can use psychology to help them answer.
3. Explain the concept of 'profiling equations', and how these are used to make inferences about crimes.
4. Distinguish the three common roles that a perpetrator assigns to his or her victim.
5. Discuss the role decision-making plays in investigation.
6. Outline the issues that psychologists might think about when assessing investigative information.

Third, psychologists contribute to investigations through the assessment and improvement of the material and information that is the basis of the investigation or the case in court. This may be, for example, through techniques that help to identify when an allegation – or even a confession – may be false. It may be the development of interviewing approaches to help witnesses remember more to inform an investigation or, in the court context, it may be the psychological evaluation of eyewitness testimony (discussed in Chapter 10).

How can psychologists contribute to investigations?

The three classes of contribution by psychologists to investigations (source www.ia-ip.org)

Focus 12.1

1. **Investigative inferences** (e.g. actions– characteristics equations, offender profiling, geographical profiling, modelling offence styles, psychological correlates of offence style).
2. **Investigative and legal process** (e.g. investigative strategy, interviewing, prediction of violence, detective decision-making).
3. **Assessment of investigative and legal information** (e.g. false allegations, eyewitness testimony, detecting deception, psycholinguistic authorship attribution).

Recognition of the potential contributions of scientific psychology (Canter 1989, 1993) has led to the development of the science of **investigative psychology** (for a full account of this discipline, see Canter and Youngs, 2008a).

A brief definition of investigative psychology is:

The scientific discipline concerned with . . . the psychological principles, theories and empirical findings that may be applied to investigations and the legal process, with the aim of improving the effectiveness of criminal detection and the appropriateness of the work of the courts.

Investigative psychology is an overall approach to thinking about criminals and criminal action that captures David Canter's perspective on the psychology of human action and how it should be studied, outlined in his laws of criminality (Canter and Youngs, 2008a). It has generated studies of topics as diverse as the nature of the criminal emotional experience, the social networks of offenders, the identification of lying in insurance claims or false rape allegations, burglary *modus operandi* or the spatial behaviour of serial killers. But all of these studies proceed from an attempt to inform one of the three points of connection between psychology and investigations as mapped out here.

Investigative inferences: The Canter 'profiling' equations

The contributions that psychologists can make to police investigations are most widely known and understood in terms of 'offender profiles'. **Offender profiling**, as typically practised, is the process by which individuals, drawing on their clinical or other professional experience, make judgements about the personality traits or psychodynamics of the perpetrators of crimes. From the perspective of scientific psychology, such a process is flawed in its reliance on personal judgement rather than actuarial (based on empirical analysis) assessment. These flaws have been shown in a wide range of professional applications through extensive studies first reviewed by Meehl in 1954 (republished in 1996). The theories about criminals and their behaviour upon which much 'offender profiling' has been based are also open to question. The lack of scientific rigour evident in the profiling process has for two decades driven proponents of investigative psychology research to map out a more scientific approach to underpin and systematize this almost mystical 'profiling' process.

At the heart of this are what have become known as the 'profiling equations' (after Canter, 1994). These are hypothetical equations that capture the scientific perspective for inferring associations between the actions that occur during the offence – including when and where they happen and to whom – and the characteristics of the offender, including the offender's criminal history, background, base location, and relationships to others. They are also known as the actions > characteristics or A > C equations, where A are the actions in the crime and C are the characteristics of typical offenders for such crimes, and > is the theory or argument and the evidence for inferring one from the other.

Investigative psychologists conduct a wide range of empirical studies of different types of offences and the offenders who committed them with the purpose of establishing solutions to these equations, in the hope of providing objective bases for the inferences that detectives make in an investigation about the perpetrator's likely characteristics. A number of ideas about the processes that may underlie A > C links can be drawn from general social and psychological theory. These include personality and interpersonal behaviour theories, as well as frameworks drawing on interpersonal narratives and on socio-economic factors. Any or all of these theories could provide a valid basis for investigative inferences if the differences in individuals that they posit correspond to real variations in criminal behaviour.

Starting principles: The consistency hypothesis

In the first instance, the feasibility of profiling depends on the extent to which two fundamental hypotheses about offenders and their offending behaviour hold. As Canter and Youngs (2008a) explain, in order to generate some form of A > C equation, it is essential that offenders show some consistency between the nature of their crimes and characteristics they exhibit in other situations. This is rather different from psychological models that attempt to explain criminality as a displacement or compensatory activity, whereby the way the individual behaves in committing the crime differs from the way they would behave in 'normal' situations. Canter and Youngs favour this general consistency model, suggesting that processes relating to the offender's characteristic interpersonal style may be particularly useful in linking actions and characteristics (Youngs, 2004).

Starting principles: The differentiation hypothesis

As well as being consistent, different sets of offenders need to be different from one another if drawing investigative inferences is to be useful to police. If every offender offended in the same way then the A > C equations would provide characteristics that were the same for every offender.

In *Criminal Shadows*, Canter (1994) advanced a general framework of psychological differences in offending style. Arguing that 'the inner narratives that violent men write for themselves cast their victims in less than human roles', he proposed that differences in the way offenders carried out their crimes would relate to the role assigned to the victim or the 'mode of interpersonal transaction' adopted by the offender. Canter (1994) proposed three types of role to which a victim may be assigned:

1. *Victim as object*. The offender treats the victim as an object, i.e. as something to be used and controlled through restraint and threat, often involving alternative gains in the form of other crimes such as theft. Offenders have a complete lack of empathy. Victims are chosen opportunistically so tend to be vulnerable individuals.
2. *Victim as vehicle*. The offender sees the victim as a vehicle for the offender's own emotional state, e.g. anger and frustration. There is some awareness of the victim as human but this recognition facilitates the offender using the victim to express his feelings and desires. The victim is typically subjected to extreme violence and abuse. The victim may have symbolic importance, e.g. women of particular appearance.
3. *Victim as person*. The offender sees the victim as a person. These offenders nurture the confused belief that through the assault they achieve some sort of personal intimacy with the victim, so offending actions will include attempts to create a degree of rapport or relationship. Offenders think they are heroes – in *Criminal Shadows* one offender is quoted as saying to his victim 'be more careful, next time someone nasty may attack you'.

Studies have shown that this general model does help to understand the specific empirical differences in offending behaviour found within rape (Canter, 1994) and paedophilia (Canter et al, 1998) as well as stranger homicide (Salfati and Canter, 1999).

Is profiling possible?

Youngs (2008) points out that it was in the 1970s and 1980s that the Federal Bureau of Investigation (FBI) first drew attention to what investigators had long known: deductions about the likely perpetrator can be drawn from a consideration, in detail, of the crime itself (Douglas et al, 1986). However, it was the FBI that drew particular attention to this process and gave prominence to the label 'offender profiling'. Coming from a scientifically grounded psychological perspective, David Canter argued that the profiling process was a rather more profound one, requiring formal specification. He proposed, as a first step in unravelling this process, that the relationship between actions and characteristics was one that, in mathematical terms, could be represented as

$$F_1A_1 +\text{........} + F_nA_n = F_1C_1 + \text{.........}+ F_mC_m$$

where the As represent the actions in the crimes, the Cs the characteristics of the perpetrator, and the Fs the functions that relate the two, i.e. the degree, level or amount of the action/characteristic.

What this equation means is that the A > C mapping does not take the form of a number of one-to-one relationships that can simply be collected together to provide the description of an offender, like 'clues' in a typical crime fiction. Rather the relationship between the offending actions and the offender's characteristics takes the form of a combination of interacting action variables that map on to a combination of interacting characteristic variables.

Technically this type of relationship is known as a canonical equation. What it tells us is that particular actions do not map on to particular characteristics in any simple or direct way. As Youngs (2008) points out, this may be because the same action can, on a consistent basis, indicate more than one characteristic, and equally, the same characteristic can be inferred from different actions. She cites the example of extreme violence that may be threatened in a robbery carried out by an inexperienced or a highly experienced offender. Conversely both rapists and robbers will tend to have criminal histories that include burglary convictions.

The actions–characteristics relationship is further complex in that the same action can indicate different characteristics in different contexts or at different points in an offender's criminal progression. So, for example, using a weapon against a weak or elderly victim who was being totally compliant may indicate a rather different individual than the use of a weapon against a victim who was fighting back. Similarly, forensic awareness may indicate an above average intellect in a young rapist but less so in one that was more experienced (Canter, 1993; Youngs, 2004).

Further complexities in the profiling process

The second thing that became clear in specifying the potential relationships between the offending and the offender in these formal terms was that there were many reasons why 'offender profiling' just was not going to be possible (see Canter and Youngs, 2008a). One of the reasons for this is the problem of 'contingency destabilization' (Youngs, 2008). This effect is most readily understood through consideration of the example she provides (Focus box 12.2).

Focus 12.2

The contingency destabilization effect (adapted from Youngs, 2008)

Crime description A

One Monday afternoon in November, a suburban house in Manchester is burgled. The offender disabled the alarm then entered by smashing a downstairs window. He stole cash and jewellery without making any mess but leaving fingerprints. The larger electronic goods in the house were not stolen. Just as he was about to leave, the offender encountered the occupant and reacted violently, punching her in the face several times before running off.

Crime description B

At 2 a.m. one Saturday morning, a suburban house in Manchester is burgled. The offender disabled the alarm then entered by smashing a downstairs window. He stole cash and jewellery without making any mess but leaving fingerprints. The larger electronic goods in the house were not stolen. Just as he was about to leave, the offender encountered the occupant and reacted violently, punching her in the face several times before running off.

Crime B differs from the previous one (A) on just one action – when the offender chose to carry out the offence. Yet this change in one behavioural detail puts the entire offence in a different perspective, casting a whole new light on many of the other components of the offence. For example, the smashing of the window is a rather different behaviour in the middle of the night than in the middle of the day. Similarly, the offender's violent reaction to encountering the occupant is less readily construed as a panic-based reaction given that he must have expected someone to be in at that time. So, a change in one action component within a crime description can change the meaning of exactly the same actions, indicating an entirely different style of offending and suggesting a very different type of offender.

Despite these complexities in relating actions to characteristics, there are now a number of studies that show these links between offending style and offender characteristics do exist and can be established (e.g. Canter and Fritzon, 1998; Lobato, 2004; Youngs, 2004; Santtila et al, 2005). The results from one such study are shown in Table 12.1. Clearly, the identification of such relationships must point to the general feasibility of the inferential process. The challenge for the future is the development of theoretical and conceptual approaches to the complexities that allow full solutions to the original **Canter profiling equations** that were mapped out at the birth of investigative psychology.

Study	n	Offending style	Offender characteristic	Correlation (Pearson's r)
Canter and Fritzon (1998)	175	Expressive object (EO)	Repeat arsonist (RA)	0.56
		Expressive person (EP)	Psychiatric history (PH)	0.38
		Instrumental object (IO)	Young offender (YO)	0.44
		Instrumental person (IP)	Failed relationship (FR)	0.49

Table 12.1 Actions and characteristic relationships for arsonists

Figure 12.1 Police officers meeting to plan the investigation of a crime.
Source: © Jeff Greenberg/Alamy.

The investigation process

A second major area of contribution psychologists can make to investigations relates to improving the investigation process itself and in particular the way in which decisions are made about which lines of enquiry to pursue and what actions to take during that process. The main challenge to investigators is to make the right decisions under highly pressurized conditions. Where the crime under investigation is a serious one or an ongoing series of offences, there will be intense media attention, political and organizational stresses that make objective judgement very difficult. Alongside these pressures the investigators must handle a vast amount of information, much of which may be of unknown reliability or simply irrelevant, that needs to be amassed, organized and interpreted.

Within investigative psychology, the investigative process is conceptualized as a series of decisions that detectives must make, so can be represented as in Figure 12.2 (Canter and Youngs, 2003). In this diagram, the lines represent investigative actions by the police while the nodes are the results of that action, i.e. new pieces of information or facts. In the period immediately after a crime occurs, investigators will often have very little information. Rapidly, however, the investigation will uncover further pieces of information that, in turn, will produce more information, suggesting further directions for investigative action. After a typically fairly short period of time the options will typically narrow down as the police actions (the lines) show more and more of the information to be irrelevant to the case and detectives establish facts that close off all but one of the lines of enquiry.

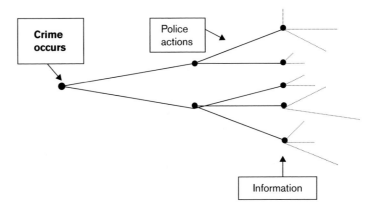

Figure 12.2 An unfolding investigation.
Source: Adapted from Canter and Youngs, 2003.

Understanding the investigation process in these terms draws attention to two possible points at which detectives may be particularly prone to making erroneous decisions and therefore at which psychological contributions could be most useful.

The first potential problem point occurs early on in the process. In investigations decisions about the actions to be undertaken or the leads to follow up must rely upon the information that comes in, information which has come to light as a result of previous actions. In other words, the range of options about what actions to take at each point is contingent upon the previous decisions that have been made. This opens up the potential for investigations to proceed along entirely wrong lines if the early information is wrong or even just incomplete. It is in the early stages then that investigative psychological findings about the features of the crime to focus on or the geographical area to explore or the suspect pool to consider could be most instructive.

The second problem point is the result of the way in which information builds rapidly in the early stages of an investigation. Each lead can give rise to numerous others that, in turn, generate multiple follow-on leads. As Canter and Youngs (2003) argue, this will give rise to exponential increases in the cognitive load on detectives, reaching some maximum weight typically after a few days. The weight of this cognitive load on those involved in the investigation can distort the decisions that are made at this point of the investigation. Detectives labouring under huge quantities of information and time pressures may rely on heuristics or 'rules of thumb' rather than more systematic approaches to make decisions. Yet as seminal psychological research has shown, decisions made in this way are often inappropriate ones (Kahneman and Tversky, 1979). As the investigation progresses, they will eventually be able to start to narrow down their lines of enquiry, reducing the general demands upon them and the probability of distorted decisions. The general diamond shape in Figure 12.3 shows the possible build-up of conditions under which various biases in investigators' thought processes are likely to occur, with consequent inadequacies in the decisions made and the subsequent actions.

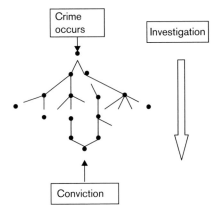

Figure 12.3 A schematic representation of the investigation process.
Source: Adapted from Canter and Youngs, 2003.

Recognition of the potential for these problems is leading to the development of decision-support tools that reduce the complexity of the information that needs to be understood and facilitate empirical analyses that can inform the decisions investigators face. One such decision-support tool is iOPS, an interactive offender profiling system developed by Canter and colleagues. This is one of the next generation of software tools for police and law enforcement analysts that integrates large police databases at speed, drawing on the very latest research findings to improve and systematize the investigation process through its ability to (Canter and Youngs, 2008a):

- Link crimes.

- Prioritize suspects.

- Build catalogues of offenders' geo-behavioural profiles.

- Generate potential TICs (further offences 'taken into consideration').

- Explore co-offending networks.

- Indicate locations for intelligence gathering.

- Map crimes and perform hotspot analysis.

Assessment and improvement of investigative information

A further broad class of contribution psychologists can make to investigations concerns the evaluation and enhancement of the information detectives are relying upon to advance their enquiries. This information can be evaluated against the same scientific principles that psychologists would use to evaluate their data in a study. More particularly, psychological research on distortions in recall, whether from normal psychological memory deficiencies or deliberate attempts at deception, can be applied to assess and offer ways to improve the material the police have (as discussed in Chapter 10). In relation to **investigative information**, psychologists will be concerned with improvements on two components of the scientific data assessment approach. One of these is the usefulness and detail of the material. The second is its accuracy or validity.

The usefulness and detail of the data

Psychologists can help to increase the amount of relevant information that can be drawn out in an investigation. It is important to the progress of an investigation that the information obtained has as much detail as is possible. Psychologists have therefore helped to develop processes, especially for police interviews with witnesses or victims, which maximize the information obtained. A number of guidelines for interviews have been developed. The best known of these is the 'cognitive interview' developed by Fisher and Geiselman (1992).

The cognitive interview is based on the scientific psychological, rather than lay, perspective on memory as an active reconstructive process, not a simple passive act of recall over which the individual has no control. As part of the way in which memory works, the recognition of information will be much easier than its recall. As such, it is argued that more information can be obtained from witnesses to a crime if they are helped to recreate actively the events in their own mind (as detailed in Focus box 10.1). This is encouraged by reinstating the context of the offence whenever possible, by returning to the scene or revisiting details like sounds and smells. One particularly innovative component of the cognitive interview is its advice to witnesses to consider the events from a variety of different perspectives, for example as other witnesses or as the victim or even the offender. This approach generates more and more useful, detailed information than the more traditional approach in which witnesses simply answer particular questions in a given sequence. Investigative hypnosis has also been used to improve recall of information. However, rather than being a 'special' technique, many experts argue that hypnosis is simply a more intensive form of cognitive interview in which the respondent is helped to relax and concentrate (Wagstaff, 1984).

In an investigation, it is important that the information is operationally useful. Canter (1993) notes that this is a criterion against which 'offender profilers' have often neglected to evaluate the advice they have given to police. An indication of the broad location where an offender could be living is a clear example of useful information to an investigator, but more subtle material such as how others may regard the offender or their likely skills and domestic circumstances may also be of value. On the other hand, intensive psychodynamic interpretations of the offender's motivations, that might only become available during in-depth therapeutic interviews, are less likely to be of direct assistance to police investigators.

The accuracy and validity of the information

There are many contributions psychologists can make to the improvement of the accuracy and validity of the information available in an investigation. The nature of contributions depends on whether we are dealing with a witness, suspect or victim.

Witnesses

With witnesses, the threat to the accuracy and validity of the information they generate comes from weaknesses and distortions in memory which are exacerbated by the widespread belief among witnesses in the certainty of their memories. The large amount of psychological research into the accuracy of eyewitness evidence has revealed a range of specific effects: for example, estimations of age and height vary in accuracy according to the age and height of the witness, such that the more closely they map on to the witness' own characteristics the more accurate will the description be (Wells and Olson, 2003). Importantly for the police and the courts, this research has shown little relationship between the eyewitnesses' confidence and their accuracy.

The particular challenge within this, of eyewitness identification of a perpetrator from within some form of line-up, has been shown to be open to a number of particular biases and psychological distortions (Stuesser, 2005). These include the particularly interesting 'unconscious transference' effect where people falsely identify individuals as the perpetrators they believe they saw at the scene of a crime, completely unaware that their familiarity with the individual comes from a different, innocent context. Numerous procedural recommendations for carrying out 'identity parades' or line-up identifications have emerged out of these studies and have been adopted by many police forces around the world.

Suspects

Of course, when the suspect is the source, it is likely that he or she will deliberately provide invalid information. There are many objective, conventional police strategies for detecting deception, most obviously determining if the known facts contradict the suspect's claims, but behavioural and psycholinguistic cues to deception can also be helpful (as discussed in Chapter 11).

As Canter and Youngs (2003) outline, a number of researchers, most notably Paul Ekman, have claimed that deception can be detected through consideration of these sorts of cues, which include self-manipulatory gestures, such as scratching, hesitancy of speech, as well as repetition and other account dysfluencies. However, other researchers are more sceptical as to the possibility of any generally available indexes of deception from the actions or words of the suspect during a police interview.

There is some evidence to indicate that for some people, psycho-physiological reactions rather than more overt cues may be indicators of lying. The procedure for examining these responses is often referred to as a polygraph or 'lie detector' test which records changes in the autonomic arousal system. Physiological responses occur whenever a person perceives an emotionally significant stimulus. It has been well established that these responses do occur when an offender is asked about aspects of the crime that only the perpetrator would be aware of (the so-called 'guilty knowledge' test). In general 'lie detection' is more productive in supporting a claim of innocence than in providing proof of guilt. For this reason many jurisdictions do not allow 'lie detector' results to be presented as evidence in court. However, because of its apparent usefulness in establishing innocence, it is used as a technique for eliminating possible suspects by some police forces around the world.

Victims

Sometimes the concern will be not with the veracity of the suspect's account but with that of an alleged victim. False allegations are typically most possible in relation to interpersonal crimes so can be an issue in cases of sexual or other abuse. Anecdotal evidence suggests that false allegations may be surprisingly prevalent among certain subgroups of the population. In such cases the complainant is not a suspect, of course, and may well be a victim, so the more intrusive processes of lie detection are rarely used.

Rather, a number of formal psychological validity assessment techniques have been developed to assess the truthfulness of victim accounts when no objective means of doing this are available. Most of these techniques are based on the assumption that honest accounts have identifiable psychological characteristics such as appropriate emotionality or irrelevant detail that are different from fabricated accounts. The most well-known approach to statement validation is that developed by Undeutsch (1989), known as statement validity analysis, which draws upon detailed consideration of the content of a statement, a procedure referred to as criteria-based content analysis (CBCA). Some studies have pointed to the effectiveness of this approach. For example, in their study of 43 interview statements from genuine and false rape cases, Parker and Brown (2000) showed that the CBCA factors did differentiate the two groups (as corroborated by forensic evidence, guilty pleas and withdrawal of allegation). However, in a Dutch study of 103 child sexual abuse allegations, Lamers-Winkelman (1999) reports only a weak relationship between the CBCA measure and case outcome, leading her to conclude that statement validity analysis should not be used to assess sexual abuse accounts from children.

It may be then that in many situations the most appropriate and the most effective means of identifying allegations that are fabricated come from empirical studies of the circumstances under which such false allegations are typically made. For example, the simple fact of a child's age can be a good indicator that an allegation is not false because studies show certain types of false allegations are not made by very young children. Clearly, general probabilities should not be used to make definitive judgements in any individual case but they do provide useful guidelines as to when more intensive examination of the allegation may be warranted. Whether or not this is a valid way of identifying false allegations is a topic awaiting further research.

Helping the police with their enquiries

From these broad areas of study psychologists are increasingly able to formulate answers to, or approaches to answering, a number of the specific questions faced during various stages of an investigation (Table 12.2).

Conclusions

There are three broad forms of contribution psychologists can make to investigations. These are: a) investigative inferences, b) the investigation process and c) the assessment and improvement of investigative information. Investigative psychology (IP) is the academic discipline that has emerged in response to the need for a more scientific basis to the 'offender profiling' advice given to investigators. The challenge at the heart of IP is to resolve the actions > characteristics (A > C) equations, which relate the set of an offender's actions in a crime to the set of his or her characteristics, such that these characteristics can be reliably inferred in the investigation context when the offender is unknown.

Psychological principles are being applied to the investigation process itself, to facilitate decision-making and to evaluate the information upon which those decisions are based. There is considerable psychological research that can be drawn upon to improve both the usefulness and detail and the accuracy and validity of investigative information. In particular, a number of specific psychological approaches to validity assessment have been developed

Key concepts and terms

Canter profiling equations

Investigative information

Investigative psychology

Offender profiling

Investigators' question	Informed by psychologists' understanding of:
What type of crime is this?	The differentiation of criminal action
What are the likely characteristics of the sort of individual who might commit a crime such as this?	Investigative inferences
Which of the possible suspects is most likely to have committed the crime?	Investigative inferences
Where is the offender most likely to live in relation to the crime?	Geographical offender profiling
Which other crimes are likely to have been committed by the same perpetrator(s)?	The consistency of criminal action
Are the decisions made during the investigation free from distortion and bias?	Decision-making under stress/cognitive load
Have the lines of enquiry pursued been determined systematically?	Decision-support tools
Can we get the witness to remember more?	How to interview a witness
Can we tell if a suspect is lying?	The detection of deception
Can we tell who wrote something?	Forensic psycholinguistics
Did this crime really happen?	False allegations
Did this person really do the crime they say they did?	False confessions

Table 12.2 Operational applications of investigative psychology

Sample essay titles

- Is offender profiling possible?

- What psychological processes are implied by the claim that there are links between an offender's actions and his/her characteristics?

- Why might investigators benefit from assistance from psychologists?

Further reading

Books

Canter, D.V. (1994). *Criminal Shadows*. London: HarperCollins (2006 edn, New York: Dorset Press.)

Canter, D.V. (2007). *Mapping Murder: The Secrets of Geographical Profiling*, (2nd Ed.). London: Virgin.

Canter, D., and Youngs, D. (2008a). *Investigative Psychology: Offender Profiling and the Analysis of Criminal Action*. Chichester: Wiley.

Keppel, R. (Ed.) (2004). *Offender Profiling: Readings in Crime Assessment and Profiling*. London: Thomson/Custom Publishing.

Journal articles

Canter, D., and Fritzon, K. (1998). Differentiating arsonists: A model of firesetting actions and characteristics. *Legal and Criminal Psychology*, 3, 73–96.

Salfati, G., and Canter, D. (1999) Differentiating stranger murders: Profiling offender characteristics from behavioural styles. *Behavioural Sciences and the Law*, 17, 391–406.

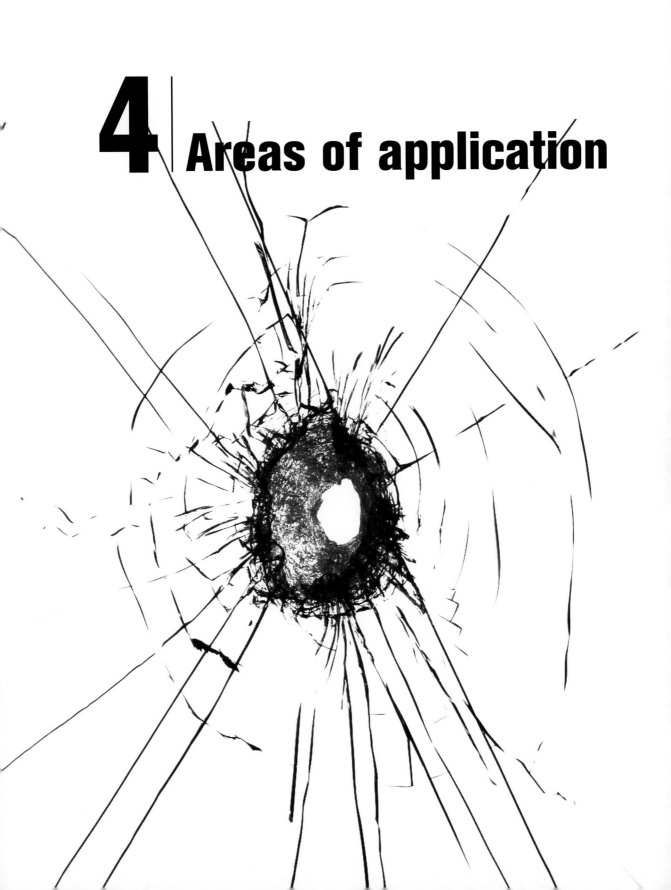

4 | Areas of application

13 Police psychology

Michelle Wright

This chapter examines the application of psychology to the recruitment, selection and training of police officers. The nature of the work carried out by police officers, work-related stress and the organizational culture in which police officers work is also outlined.

Learning outcomes

When you have completed this chapter you should be able to:

1. Understand the issues involved in the recruitment and selection of police officers.
2. Understand what advancements there are in UK police training.
3. Discuss the role of stress in policing.

The role of a police officer

Police officers will carry out many different tasks during their careers within the police service such as taking statements from victims and witnesses, interviewing suspects, managing traffic, carrying out administrative duties and maybe even engaging in covert operations. If they are involved in investigations they will deal with a diverse range of types of crimes such as delinquency and deviancy, property crime, domestic violence, rape, murder and even terrorism. All these involve officers utilizing different skills and abilities. The roles undertaken by a police officer will also differ as he or she moves up the ranks of the police organization. A uniformed constable walking 'the beat', protecting the community, a detective in overall charge of a murder enquiry and a Chief Constable who oversees the day-to-day functioning of a police force will all require different sets of skills. Due to the multifaceted nature of the work carried out by the police it has proved difficult to identify a set of core skills required by police officers. Nevertheless, the police service has a responsibility for ensuring the recruitment and selection of suitable individuals to serve as police officers.

Figure 13.1 The police carry out a much wider range of tasks than is often appreciated.
Source: MAX NASH/AFP/Getty Images.

Recruitment and selection

So how are police officers recruited? How are suitable candidates selected? And what are the qualities perceived to be desirable for those becoming a police officer? Working behind the scenes within police organizations across the world, occupational psychologists or police psychologists (as referred to in America) are employed to aid in the recruitment and selection of police officers. Such psychologists are also involved in the training and management of officers. The research literature on how psychology is drawn upon in the recruitment and selection process stems predominantly from America where the profession of police psychologist is more widely recognized. Bartol (1996) carried out a survey in America of 152 police psychologists to examine the work that they carry out. The results of this survey revealed that around one-third of police psychologists' work involved officer recruitment and selection. The application of psychology to policing in the UK is increasing with discussions provided in the literature by Ainsworth (2002), Hollin (1989), Ainsworth and Pease (1987) and Bull et al (1983).

Qualities of police officers

Does a particular type of individual apply to become a police officer? Do police officers differ in certain characteristics? And if so, can these characteristics provide an insight into the qualities required of police officers? In comparison to the rest of the population police officers have been found to be more conservative, extraverted and tough minded (Cook, 1977; Colman and Gorman, 1982). In a British study, Burbeck and Furnham (1984) examined the differences in personality traits of successful and unsuccessful applicants to the Metropolitan Police force using scores from the **Eysenck personality questionnaire (EPQ)** completed by 254 applicants. Successful candidates were found to be more extraverted and less neurotic than unsuccessful candidates.

Psychometric testing

In the American literature there has been much discussion about the use of **psychometric testing** to aid the police selection process. Psychometric tests are utilized to assess candidates' personality, attitudes, beliefs and values. Psychometric testing is used as a method of selecting in suitable candidates and selecting out those that are deemed unsuitable. The most commonly used psychometric tests for the selection into US law enforcement are the **MMPI** and the **IPI** (refer to Research methods box 13.1 for information on three sets of psychometric tests). The use of psychological testing brings an objective element to the selection process, whereas an interview panel may result in a subjective approach as interviewers bring their own prejudices and biases to choosing.

Research methods 13.1

Examples of psychometric tests

Minnesota multiphasic personality inventory (MMPI)

Developed by Drs Hathaway and McKinley (1940) at the University of Minnesota Hospital. The MMPI was designed to assess psychological disorders in the field of mental health. MMPI consists of ten clinical scales and three validity scales.

Inwald personality inventory (IPI)

Developed by Dr Inwald. The IPI consists of 310 'true-false' statements designed to identify a variety of personality and behavioural characteristics which are assessed over 25 clinical scales. The IPI is not a psychopathology test like the MMPI. The IPI was designed specifically for use in law enforcement selection.

Eysenck personality questionnaire (EPQ)

Developed by Hans and Sybil Eysenck (1975). The EPQ consists of 90 items scored across four scales: extraversion/introversion, neuroticism/stability, psychoticism/socialization and the lie scale. The EPQ was designed as a research rather than a diagnostic tool.

There have been numerous psychological studies which have examined the applicability and use of psychometric tests for police selection. A selected few of such studies are discussed here to illustrate their use in selecting police recruits.

Police selection studies

Cochrane, Tett and Vandecreek (2003) carried out a survey of 155 police agencies in America to explore the selection practices and procedures employed. Their findings revealed that psychological testing is now more readily used than it has been in the past. The most widely used psychometric test was the MMPI-2 followed by the CPI, 16PF and the IPI. The EPQ was found to be used less frequently for selecting suitable police candidates. Variations in the selection procedures used were found, with larger agencies relying more heavily on psychological testing than smaller agencies. There were also variations in the types of tests used for selecting candidates.

McCormick (1984) outlines criteria to be used for identifying good and bad cops derived from 120 police officers' MMPI profiles. The 'good cop/bad cop' (GCBC) criteria consist of 11 indicators of dysfunctional performance ranging from the number of resisting arrests filed by an officer to inefficient preparation for court.

Blau, Super and Brady (1993) aimed to extend McCormick's (1984) findings by examining the association between supervisors' performance evaluation and officers' MMPI scores. Blau et al (1993) found that 80 per cent of the officers' performance was correctly predicted using the GCBC criteria, thereby offering support for the use of the GCBC criteria for identifying individuals that are suitable or unsuitable for law enforcement at the pre-selection stage. However, a limitation of this study is the small sample size of 30 officers, which limits the generalization of the findings.

Shusman and Inwald (1991) used the MMPI and IPI to assess which of 246 male correctional officers were performing well and which were not. However, in using absenteeism, how often officers were late for duty and the number of times officers had had a disciplinary interview as measurements of bad performance, the study did not reveal anything about how well these officers actually performed at their job (Ainsworth, 2002).

In terms of on-the-job performance the IPI has been found to be a better predictor of job performance than the MMPI (Inwald and Shusman, 1984; Scogin et al, 1995). This may be related to the fact that the IPI was developed specifically for law enforcement selection (Inwald et al, 1982) whereas the MMPI was developed to assess psychiatric disorders in mental patients (Hathaway and McKinley, 1940). Nevertheless, the MMPI has been cited as the most used psychometric test for selecting out unsuitable police candidates (Cochrane et al, 2003).

Detrick and Chibnull (2002) examined whether police officer performance could be predicted using the IPI. They aimed to determine whether officers' performance on the job after working a year in the field as evaluated by their supervisors could be predicted from officers' pre-employment IPI scores. They examined the performance and IPI scores of 108 applicants. Supervisors rated officers' performance on a performance evaluation report form

(PERF) made up of five sections: conduct and discipline, job proficiency, neighbourhood policing, professionalism and job ability. Performance within each section was rated on a five-point scale. Multiple regression analysis was used to predict performance evaluation from officer demographics and IPI scores. Three of the IPI scales – family conflicts, guardedness and driving violations – were found to significantly predict supervisors' ratings of officers' performance on the job.

Schmidt and Hunter (1998) in a review of the literature on police selection found the best results were achieved when a general mental ability test was combined with a structured interview. In a study examining the use of psychometric testing and assessment centres, candidates' performance at an assessment centre more accurately predicted on-the-job performance than psychometric testing scores (Pynes and Bernardin, 1992).

Burbeck and Furnham (1984) in their study of the use of the EPQ to examine suitable and unsuitable candidates, outlined earlier, concluded that:

> ... the introduction of personality measures (particularly the EPQ) could prove useful both because they are simple, reliable and robust measures of individual differences and also because they provide standardized scores so making an objective comparison between individuals possible, provided proper caution is used in the interpretation of the results, and they are used to assist in selection and not as decision-makers in their own right. (Burbeck and Furnham, 1984: 262)

The use of psychometric testing is not without its faults. An issue of concern regarding the use of psychometric tests stems from the debate within personality theory as to whether personality is a fixed and stable trait (e.g. Eysenck, Cattell) or changes as a result of experience (e.g. Mischel, Bandura). Research on police personality testing has found support for both theoretical viewpoints. The notion that police culture and training impacts upon and can alter personality traits is referred to as the socialization model (Brown and Willis, 1985). The alternative view is that personality traits are stable over time. This is referred to in the literature as the pre-dispositional model (Colman and Gorman, 1982) which suggests that the values recruits join the police with will remain unaltered once they are trained and working in the field.

Another problem with the use of psychometric testing is that the criteria which should be included within police selection testing procedures are not yet apparent (Ainsworth, 2002). The research on the key attributes that are required of a suitable police candidate is inconclusive. Further psychological research, preferably in the form of longitudinal studies, is therefore needed because determining the key skills required by police officers will ensure the right individuals are recruited and selected for the job. Identifying suitable recruits is an extremely important issue because employing the wrong individual will cost a police force financially due to the high costs involved in training recruits and could also damage the reputation of a police force.

Police selection in England and Wales

So far the focus has been predominantly on studies from America and the selection procedures used. Across the 43 police forces in England and Wales there has been a recent standardization in the recruitment and selection of police officers (National Policing Plan, 2005–2008 – Home Office, 2005b). This has introduced more consistency in how police officers are recruited. There is now a national recruitment application form which is used by all forces. Each force has an operational assessment centre where recruits undergo a competency-based structured interview, a numeric and verbal logical reasoning test, two written exercises and four interactive exercises. Seven core competencies for undertaking the role of police constable are assessed (refer to Focus box 13.1 for details). These required competencies were put together by a Home Office working group.

Focus 13.1

Seven core competencies relevant to the role of police constable. (Source: Appendix A in *Police SEARCH: Structured Entrance Assessment for Recruiting Constables Holistically – Information for Candidates*. © Centrex [Central Police Training and Development Authority] 2003.)

1. *Respect diversity*. Considers and shows respect for the opinions, circumstances and feelings of colleagues and members of the public, no matter what their position, background, circumstances, status or appearance.
2. *Team working*. Develops strong working relationships inside and outside the team to achieve common goals. Breaks down barriers between groups and involves others in discussions and decisions.
3. *Community and customer focus*. Focuses on the customer and provides a high-quality service that is tailored to meet their individual needs. Understands the community that is served and shows an active commitment to policing a diverse society.
4. *Effective communication*. Communicates effectively, both verbally and in writing. Uses listening and questioning techniques to make sure that they and others understand what is going on and can effectively transfer ideas and information.
5. *Problem solving*. Gathers information from a range of sources. Analyses information to identify problems and issues, and makes effective decisions.
6. *Personal responsibility*. Takes personal responsibility for making things happen and achieving results. Displays motivation, commitment, perseverance and conscientiousness. Acts with a high degree of integrity.
7. *Resilience*. Shows resilience, even in difficult circumstances. Prepared to make difficult decisions and has the confidence to see them through.

The seven core competencies can be categorized into three types: job related, general skills and personality characteristics. The competencies which are considered to be related to the nature of the work of a police constable are community focus and respect and awareness of race and diversity issues. The key skills required are communication, problem-solving and ability to work in a team. The personality characteristics required are resilience and responsibility.

Police training

Once suitable candidates have been selected and recruited, the next stage is training. The role and type of training conducted is extremely important because it is this which prepares recruits to undertake their work as police officers effectively and efficiently. Police training tends to be 'in-house' – conducted within the organization, usually by police officers that have received some form of training qualification. Police training is an area where psychologists in Britain have not been utilized as extensively as in America (Hollin, 1989). However, the most notable input of British psychologists to police training occurred in the early 1980s in London. In 1982 the Metropolitan Police introduced a new training programme for police recruits, 'human awareness training' (HAT), which was later re-titled 'police skills training' (PST). The training programme focused on developing recruits in three main areas: interpersonal skills, self-awareness and community relations. An independent evaluation project was carried out over a five-year period by two psychologists – Ray Bull and Peter Horncastle (for full details see Bull and Horncastle, 1989, 1994; Horncastle and Bull, 1986).

Phase one was carried out at four time periods, at the start (week one) and end (week 20) of the training period and at six and 12 months during the recruits' probationary period. The impact of the training was measured using a set of questionnaires that measured social anxiety, self-esteem and interpersonal relations as well as recruits' views on the training programme. The second phase was conducted at 20, 40 and 66 weeks after initial training using the same questionnaires used in the first phase of the evaluation plus a self-monitoring questionnaire. An observational study of police officers interacting with members of the public was also carried out to supplement the questionnaire data.

The findings revealed a reduction in social anxiety of the recruits across the test periods, with levels of self-esteem showing little change on completion of the training programme. Officers who had received HAT training received fewer complaints against them during their first three years of service when compared with a matched control group. In terms of improvements in the skills that the HAT programme set out to enhance, the interpersonal skills component was considered to be the best aspect of the training, self-awareness reasonable and community relations poor. On completion of the evaluation, Bull and Horncastle recommended a number of modifications that they felt needed to be made to the training programme in light of their findings. These recommendations included enhancing officers' sympathy towards victims and improvement of the self-evaluation and awareness components of the training programme.

The evaluation conducted by Bull and Horncastle highlights the usefulness of the application of psychological knowledge to police training. It also illustrates the effective results that can be achieved when psychologists and the police work together to develop and implement a training course which incorporates psychological principles.

Advancements in UK police training

Ainsworth (2002) notes the reluctance of the police to accept psychological research and knowledge. However, there have been significant developments that have taken place with regards to this. This section outlines the advancements that have and are currently being made in the area of UK police training. There has been a call for the implementation of national training standards (Police Skills and Standards Organisation, 2002). An example of a recent standardization in police training is the Professionalizing Investigation Programme (PIP). PIP is an accreditation programme for investigators which is committed to a drive towards officers gaining academic qualifications and becoming familiar with academic literature that is of relevance and use to the field in which they work.

The National Centre for Policing Excellence (NCPE) was set up in 2003 as part of Centrex, the Central Police Training and Development Authority. The NCPE's role was to design and implement training programmes and establish professional standards and investigative doctrines to govern police work and procedures. The NCPE has set up a series of working groups with academics and practitioners to tap into their knowledge to aid in the writing of training documents and manuals. This consultation process demonstrates how psychological principles are beginning to be incorporated more readily into the world of policing. Further advances will hopefully be seen in the future as a result of the creation of the National Policing Improvements Agency (NPIA) which came into effect in April 2007.

Simulation exercises

There has also been a development in the way UK police are trained with the introduction and use of **simulation exercises** and immersive learning which are run on a computer system called Hydra. Hydra is a relatively new system utilized by the police for the training of officers in specialized roles and investigations. Different types of exercises have been designed for investigations such as serial rape, murder, hostage negotiation, child protection and firearms incidents. Hydra is an interactive computer simulation system that is used to create a detailed, real-time major investigation (Crego and Harris, 2000). The Hydra system is a useful and effective training tool for developing officer skills and experience. (For more information on Hydra refer to Applications box 13.1).

Applications 13.1

Immersive police training – Hydra

Hydra was designed by Jonathan Crego at the National Centre for Applied Learning Technologies (NCALT). Hydra is an immersive training exercise. Scenarios are developed that officers may be confronted with when working in the field. Hydra aims to immerse officers in the incident to produce a sense that they are investigating an incident for real.

The Hydra computer system is administered from a central control room by a team of facilitators. Information is sent simultaneously from the central control room to computers in separate syndicate rooms where the police officers taking part in the exercise are based. Officers are grouped into teams for the purpose of the exercise. The information officers have to work with comes in a range of formats (e.g. audio, visual or written). Officers have to assess the information received to set lines of enquiry for how they want the investigation to progress and make a series of critical decisions. All the decisions made are recorded in a decision log. The officers control how the situation they face unfolds by the decisions that they make during the course of the exercise.

For more information on Hydra see www.ncalt.com and www.incsid.org

The police simulation exercises have been used to study decisional activity under psychological stress (see Crego and Spinks, 1997). Hydra is also currently being utilized as a research tool by academics to examine what police work entails and the decision-making processes of officers (Crego and Alison, 2004). The use of Hydra to examine the decision-making processes of police officers relates to the field of naturalistic decision-making (NDM).

NDM researchers advocate that in order to understand how experts make decisions and the factors that influence the decision-making processes, decision makers should be observed undergoing tasks in the real world (Klein, 1993). Although Hydra is not the 'real world', the set-up of the simulated exercises and the immersive element means that it is as close as a researcher can get to observing police officers carrying out an investigation. Due to the scant literature on police decision-making, the examination of how decisions are made is an important area because research findings can be fed back to the police and be used to aid developments in police training.

Stress and police work

The concept of stress was developed by Selye (1956). Selye (1956) considered stress in terms of the physiological responses of the body to demands made upon it. No single definition of stress exists. Ainsworth and Pease (1987: 43) ask 'Is stress something that is imposed on you (a stimulus) or is it a way in which you react to the world (a response)?'. Many researchers approach stress from both angles, considering stress in terms of environmental stressors and how individuals respond to stress. Stress responses can be divided into three categories: physiological, psychological and behavioural (Schuler, 1980). Physiological symptoms consist of bodily changes such as increased heart rate and headaches. Psychological responses include apathy, forgetfulness and irritability. Behavioural changes include loss of appetite, disturbed sleeping patterns and increased smoking or alcohol habits.

Policing is considered to be one of the most stressful occupations (Brown and Campbell, 1994). Occupational stress is something which should be taken seriously because stress can impact upon the health and welfare of officers and affect job performance as a result of absenteeism or inability to focus on the job. There is an extensive literature on **stress in policing**, most of which stems from America (see Toch, 2002).

Police work stressors

One of the key psychological research studies on stress is the work carried out by Holmes and Rae (1967). They claimed that certain events we experience in our life can cause stress and increase our susceptibility to illness. Holmes and Rae's (1967) social readjustment rating scale (SRRS) lists 43 life events that are considered to be stressful. These events are ranked on a scale of stressfulness. The death of a spouse is rated as the highest stressful life event and the lowest is a minor violation of the law. However, there is likely to be variation in how individuals deal with stressful life events and the scale does not take this into account. The scale also neglects other factors that may play a role in stress and susceptibility to illness such as lifestyle and diet. Sewell (1983) has developed a critical life events scale specifically for law enforcement officers. The scale consists of 144 items. At the top of the scale is the death of a partner in the line of duty and at the lower end of the scale the completion of a routine report.

In a review of the literature on stress, Terry (1981) identified four categories of stressors which he termed external, internal, task and individual. External stressors included negative public opinion, bad media coverage and dissatisfaction with court sentences. Internal stressors included dissatisfaction with training and pay level. Task-related stressors focused on the nature of police work and included working in dangerous situations and the investigation of certain types of crime such as child abuse. Individual stressors included officers' concerns regarding their competence, success and safety. Terry's (1981) typology offers a useful framework for considering the stressors faced by police officers.

Cooper et al (1982) identified nine police work stressors. Work overload was considered the highest stressor with complaints against the police the lowest. Gudjonsson and Adlam (1983) have also examined stressors perceived to be stressful by the police. Ninety-three British police officers were asked to rate 45 situations that they could face in the line of duty. The highest rated, and therefore the situation considered to be the most stressful, was being taken hostage by terrorists. The lowest rated and least stressful situation was going into people's homes. Unpredictable and uncontrollable events were rated as most stressful, for example confronting a person with a gun and negotiating over hostages, which highlights the notion of control as a factor in police stress. This study differed from Cooper et al's (1982) in that officers were asked how stressful a situation would be if it took place rather than being asked about an actual situation they had experienced.

Research has revealed a difference in the stressors of officers of different ranks, which corresponds to officers' length of service and nature of duties performed. The main source of stress experienced by higher ranking officers is work overload, with lower ranking officers citing the dangers they face in routine policing such as having to deal with violent confrontations (Gudjonsson and Adlam, 1983). This highlights how the type of work carried out by different officers exposes them to different types of occupational stressors.

Stress management

Stress can be managed at an individual and organizational level. In the area of police stress the focus has tended to be on the management of stress at the organizational level (Bull et al, 1983). In two studies which asked officers about ways of managing job stress five organizational factors were identified: better training to cope with demanding situations, support from senior ranks, better familiarity with police procedures, improved police–community relations and fewer bureaucratic obstacles (Gudjonsson and Adlam, 1982; Gudjonsson, 1983, cited in Hollin, 1989: 144). Interestingly, no reference was made to the offer of counselling for officers who had experienced or witnessed a traumatic event. This may be because of the police's negative view and rejection of psychological services (Miller, 1995). This relates to the occupational culture of the police whereby counselling services are likely to be perceived as an inability to cope and frowned upon by colleagues. It is important for the police service to develop an understanding of what aspects of the job cause stress and also how individuals deal with stress to determine how best they can manage stress at an organizational level.

Critical incident stress debriefing is a procedure which has been developed recently and used in policing when officers have experienced a traumatic or critical incident (Bohl, 1995). Critical incident stress debriefing is usually carried out by a psychologist and involves asking officers to describe the incident in their own words and from their own viewpoint, followed by an examination of their thoughts and emotional reactions. An assessment of the individual's physical and psychological symptoms will be conducted and strategies for coping outlined.

Ross and Alison (1999) explored the effectiveness of critical incident stress debriefing (CISD) with Australian police officers who had been involved in a shooting incident. They compared two groups of 30 officers: one group had received CISD and one group had not. The two groups were examined for differences in maladaptive coping strategies and levels of anger. The findings revealed that the group which received CISD showed a significant reduction in anger levels and increased use of adaptive coping strategies. However, Ross and Alison (1999) emphasize the need for further research on CISD to also consider contextual life factors which may impact upon stress levels and coping strategies.

The police service has begun to recognize the detrimental effects stress can have on its officers and the ways in which stress can be identified and managed. In order to reduce stress levels in policing there needs to be a conscious move away from the perception that officers are tough and able to cope with anything the job throws at them. There also needs to be an acknowledgment and acceptance by officers that attending counselling and/or debriefing sessions aims to help them and does not reflect an inability to cope.

Police culture

Brown (2000: 259), in considering occupational culture as a factor in the stress experiences of police officers, comments how the 'particularities of the police occupational culture create a working climate and foster patterns of behaviour that are supportive of but can inhibit or exacerbate individuals adverse reactions to stressor exposure'. Police forces consist of predominantly male officers; it is therefore of no surprise that the police culture has a 'strong masculine ethos' (Brown, 2000). Females and ethnic minorities are still under-represented in the police force (Ainsworth, 2002). The police develop informal support systems with their colleagues but they do not discuss and share emotional issues (Stephens et al, 1997). This links back to the comments outlined above regarding the acceptance and acknowledgement of the need for counselling and critical incident debriefing to address the emotional pressures police officers may experience.

Conclusions

The role of a police officer is diverse and multifaceted which poses a challenge for selection. Attempts to obviate this have been made using psychometric testing in police recruitment and selection in the USA. However, research on the key attributes required for suitable police recruits is inconclusive. The use of assessment centres is now a standard procedure in the recruitment and selection process for police officers in the UK. Assessment involves a structured interview, role play exercises, numerical and verbal testing.

The training of police officers is generally conducted 'in-house', within the police organization. Training courses are rarely taught by psychologists. The most notable contribution of British psychologists to police training is an evaluation of the human awareness training programme for new recruits carried out by Bull and Horncastle (1989). However, there have been recent advancements in UK police training with the consultation and input from academics and practitioners in the development and implementation of training programmes and investigative doctrine by the National Centre for Policing Excellence (NCPE). This has included the utilization of simulation exercises; a form of immersive learning offers a unique and effective way of training officers in specialized roles and investigations.

Policing is one of the most stressful occupations. Work stressors vary according to the rank of officers and the policing tasks they are involved in. Stress needs to be managed at both an individual and organizational level. Psychological counselling and critical incident stress debriefing are two ways in which stress in policing can be addressed. Police culture impacts upon the stress experienced by officers. The tough, masculine ethos and informal support system means officers are likely to keep their emotional feelings bottled up and hold a negative view of psychological services.

Over recent years the police service in the UK has become much more open to input from psychologists, especially with regards to the training of officers and the development of training programmes, which marks a positive step forward. To further contribute psychological principles, theories and research into the recruitment, selection and training of police officers, the police service and psychologists must work together and foster closer links to further understanding of each other's line of work. The combination of practical knowledge and experience of police procedures and scientific endeavour will produce more effective developments within the field of psychology and policing.

Key concepts and terms

Critical incident stress
  debriefing (CISD)
Eysnck Personality
  Questionnaire (EPQ)
IPI

MMPI
Psychometric testing
Simulation exercises
Stress in policing

Sample essay titles

1. Discuss the advantages and disadvantages of the current methods used to recruit and select police officers.
2. How can psychology be used to advance the training of police officers?
3. Outline the key stressors related to police work and the ways in which stress can be managed.

Further reading

Books

Ainsworth, P.B. (2002). *Psychology and Policing*. Cullompton, Devon: Willan.

Brown, J.M., and Campbell, E.A. (1994). *Stress and Policing: Sources and Strategies*. Chichester: Wiley.

Bull, R., Bustin, R., Evans, P., and Gahagan, D. (1983). *Psychology for Police Officers*. Chichester: Wiley.

Toch, H. (2002). *Stress in Policing*. Washington, DC: American Psychological Association.

Journal articles

Bartol, C.R. (1996). Police psychology: Then, now and beyond. *Criminal Justice and Behaviour*, 23, 70–89.

Bull, R., and Horncastle, P. (1994). Evaluation of police recruit training involving psychology. *Psychology, Crime and Law*, 1, 143–149.

Ross, L., and Alison, L. (1999). Critical incident stress debriefing and its effects on coping strategies and anger in a sample of Australian police officers involved in shooting incidents. *Work and Stress*, 13, 2, 144–161.

14 Psychology in court

Michael R. Davis

This chapter provides an overview of **forensic psychology** in its most literal form – direct application to the courts. A brief historical review indicates that psychologists began delving into issues of direct relevance to the courts over a century ago. Since then four roles have been differentiated for the use of psychology in court: clinical, experimental, actuarial and advisory. Each of these is discussed with examples. The various strands of law in which psychologists play a role are described, including areas of criminal and civil law. The activities of psychologists in the pre-trial, trial and pre-sentencing phases of criminal cases are also discussed. Finally, the admissibility and application of various behavioural investigative techniques to the court setting is described.

Learning outcomes

When you have completed this chapter you should be able to:

1. Review the historical foundations of forensic psychology.
2. Understand the various areas of law in which psychologists practice.
3. Discuss the many roles that psychological evidence may take in court.
4. Consider the limited admissibility of behavioural investigative advice in court.

A brief history of psychology in the courts

As can be readily appreciated from the diverse chapters in this volume, modern forensic psychology is a field with considerable breadth of knowledge and application. However, in its most literal form, *forensic psychology* is concerned with 'the collection, examination, and presentation of evidence for judicial purposes' (Haward, 1981: 21). Indeed, the term forensic is derived from the Latin *forensis* – 'of the forum' – which referred to the Imperial Court of Rome (Haward, 1981; Gudjonsson and Haward, 1998). As such, it is perhaps not surprising that the beginnings of forensic psychology related directly to the court room. These can be traced to members of Wilhelm Wundt's first ever psychological laboratory at Leipzig in the late nineteenth century.

One of Wundt's students, Cattell (1895), began the academic study of legal psychology with experiments into the nature of testimony. However, the first forensic psychologist in its literal form was Schrenck-Notzing (1897) who gave evidence in a Munich court in 1896 during a murder trial. His testimony referred to experimental results on suggestibility and recall errors (Hale, 1980; Gudjonsson and Haward, 1998). In 1906 Sigmund Freud lectured to the Vienna judiciary about the benefits that psychology could bring to the legal system (Tapp, 1976; Brigham, 1999; Ogloff, 2000; Schuller and Ogloff, 2001). Two years later Munsterberg (1908), a former student of Wundt, published the first textbook of forensic psychology entitled *On the Witness Stand*. This volume urged the legal system to embrace psychological research, but Munsterberg was ultimately criticized by legal scholars for overstating his claims (Moore, 1907, Wigmore, 1909; see also Ogloff et al, 1996; Ogloff, 2000; Bartol and Bartol, 2006; Goldstein, 2007). Several further textbooks on legal psychology followed Munsterberg (e.g. Brown, 1926; McCarty, 1929; Burtt, 1931; Cairns, 1935).

Following the birth of clinical psychology, several legal cases from the United States addressed the admissibility of clinical psychologists' opinions regarding mental illness. For example, in *People v. Hawthorne* (1940), a clinical psychologist was barred from providing evidence in a criminal trial. However, the Michigan Supreme Court found that the trial court had erred. Furthermore, the civil case of *Hidden v. Mutual Life Insurance Co.* (1954) involved the testimony of a clinical psychologist which the trial judge subsequently instructed the jury to disregard. An appeals court ruled that this was also in error (Bartol and Bartol, 2006). Continued resistance by the psychiatric profession influenced trial courts until the case of *Jenkins v. United States* (1962), where a federal appeals court gave support to psychologists providing testimony regarding mental illness (Bartol and Bartol, 2006; Goldstein, 2007).

For a long time the admissibility of scientific evidence in the United States was dictated by the decision in *Frye v. United States* (1923). This stated that 'a scientific principle or discovery ... must be sufficiently established to have gained acceptance in the particular field in which it belongs' (p. 1014). However, in *Daubert v. Merrell Dow Pharmaceuticals* (1993) new rules for admissibility focused upon testability of theories and techniques, peer review and publication, and known potential error rates, in addition to the previous Frye standard of general acceptance (Zeedyk and Raitt, 1998; Rogers and Shuman, 2005). Nonetheless, these criteria were loosened somewhat in the case of *Kumho Tire Co. v. Carmichael* (1999), in which they were described as neither necessary nor sufficient for admissibility. This clearly gave greater latitude to the judiciary in considering expert testimony (Medoff, 2003; Morey et al, 2007).

In the United Kingdom, psychologists became quite active in providing evidence to the courts during the 1940s. However, this was provided in an indirect manner, as psychologists' opinions were generally incorporated into medical practitioners' reports. This changed in 1958 when a psychiatrist's inability to answer questions pertaining to psychological data in a report brought the matter into the open. It was ruled that the existing practice violated the rule of hearsay and that the psychologist in the case should be 'called as a "medical witness" in his own right' (Gudjonsson and Haward, 1998: 15).

Nonetheless, the range of psychological evidence that could be admitted was limited for some time by a decision in *R v. Turner* (1975). This suggested that evidence regarding psychological processes other than mental abnormality was not admissible because normal human behaviour is 'within the jury's common knowledge and experience' (Kapardis, 1997: 178). The Turner decision continued to constrain psychological evidence until the case of *R v. Sally Lorraine Emery (and another)* (1993), where evidence regarding domestic abuse was admitted and upheld on appeal. This has subsequently led to the admission of a wider range of psychological evidence (Colman and Mackay, 1995; Kapardis, 1997; Zeedyk and Raitt, 1998). Nonetheless, the judiciary in the UK and other Commonwealth nations appears to be more conservative than the USA when it comes to admitting evidence, ostensibly out of fear that the expert may usurp the function of the decision-maker (Zeedyk and Raitt, 1998). This makes decisions to admit newer forms of expertise considerably difficult (see Canter, 1997).

Roles of the psychologist in providing assistance to the courts

Haward (1981; see also Gudjonsson and Haward, 1998) identified four roles that the forensic psychologist may fulfil depending upon the nature of the legal case. These are the clinical, experimental, actuarial and advisory. In some instances the psychologist may fulfil more than one of these roles. In all but the advisory role, the psychologist is an expert witness. This means that, unlike other witnesses who are restricted to stating facts, psychologists are allowed to provide opinion evidence on issues that are considered outside the knowledge of the jury or judiciary (Cox, 1999; Kapardis, 1997; Ogloff and Polvi, 1998; Schuller and Ogloff, 2001; Hess, 2006). Expert witnesses, like all witnesses, are subjected to examination-in-chief by the party that called them, cross-examination and re-examination. However, it should be noted that psychologists may often submit reports and not have to give evidence in court. This may be because the report is not useful to the side that has called them, or particularly in the case of sentencing, if no particular questions arise. Accordingly, good report writing is crucial as in many cases it can obviate the need for court testimony.

The clinical role

The first role is the *clinical* or assessment role. This is the most common role for a psychologist involved in legal proceedings (Gudjonsson, 1985, 1996; Kapardis, 1997). The psychologist conducts an assessment interview in order to answer a particular referral question or series of questions. Depending upon the nature of the referral, the interview may include administration of a range of psychometric tests including personality, mental state and cognitive testing, as well as tests that focus solely upon forensic issues (e.g. competency, deception).

While this role is clearly similar to the traditional assessment activities of the treating clinical psychologist, there are important differences and the forensic assessor must adopt a different focus to their treating role. Of particular note is the absence of a traditional psychologist–client relationship. In a treating capacity the 'client' is generally the person being assessed or treated. In a forensic assessment situation the client is usually the referral source (e.g. solicitor, court or agency). Accordingly, informed consent of the examinee is required because any material discussed during the assessment interview may be included in the report that is provided to the referrer (Melton et al, 2007). Nonetheless, it is imperative that the forensic psychologist provide unbiased reports, regardless of whether their opinion pleases the referrer. In essence, the role adopted by a treating clinician is simply incompatible with the role of forensic assessor, which is one of truth-seeking. One particularly useful way of viewing this role was described by Dietz (1996: 156) who noted that it 'is the same as that of any other forensic scientist ... (the) touchstone for grappling with apparent moral conflicts ... (is to ask oneself) what the ideal forensic pathologist would do in a similar situation'.

Further differences involve the scope of the evaluation, which can be very narrow and is generally dictated by the referral question(s). Indeed, the examinee's well-being and needs are often of only secondary relevance. The forensic assessor must also take into consideration the likelihood of resistance or intentional distortion, which is something that is far less of a problem (if at all) when working in a therapeutic role (Melton et al, 2007). Accordingly, specialized psychometric tests may be employed and third party information is imperative.

The clinical role of the forensic psychologist has some obvious overlap with the work of the forensic psychiatrist. Indeed, forensic psychiatrists are often asked to opine on some of the same issues as the clinical–forensic psychologist. This is perhaps unsurprising. Grisso (1993) commented that both disciplines share theories and research findings that guide the logic of their decision-making. Nonetheless, Grisso (1993: 138) also suggested that the medical training of the psychiatrist, steeped as it is in the diagnosis, treatment and prevention of illness, favours their 'capacities to diagnose serious mental disorder'. Psychiatrists are also obviously better equipped to provide opinions on cases involving psychopharmacological or biological topics. In contrast, the training of the psychologist is grounded in an understanding of human behaviour more generally. This arguably better prepares psychologists to go beyond issues of mental disorder, to discuss personality, social and interpersonal functioning, cognitive abilities and the like. Psychologists also tend to use standardized tests, whereas psychiatrists tend to focus upon information gleaned from a clinical interview (Grisso, 1993; Gudjonsson and Haward, 1998). Of course, these are generalizations. There exist many psychiatrists with substantial knowledge of personality and social functioning, just as there are many psychologists with considerable expertise in the diagnosis of major mental illness. However, such crude division between the disciplines can be observed within the legal system, particularly in regard to the making of diagnoses. This will be discussed in more detail later in this chapter.

The experimental role

The second role described by Haward (1981) is the *experimental* role. As noted above, this was actually the first role that a psychologist played in a court of law (Schrenck-Notzing, 1897), long before the advent of clinical psychology. The experimental role includes two related activities (Kapardis, 1997). The more traditional meaning described by Haward (1981) involves the psychologist actually conducting an experiment that is directly relevant to the individual court case. An example of such an experiment is described by Kapardis (1997) in regard to a rape trial. In this case a crucial piece of evidence was the fact that the victim picked the defendant out of a 'voice parade'. To their credit, the police had apparently gone to great lengths to avoid bias in the procedure, by seeking advice from a linguist. However, despite the fact that all voices in the parade were apparently similar, only the defendant's voice was taken from a police interview. A psychologist subsequently conducted an experiment in which participants were asked to identify which voices were taken from a police interview. The defendant's voice was identified at a rate beyond chance. This evidence was deemed admissible at trial. The case resulted in a hung jury.

The second type of experimental role involves the psychologist testifying about the state of knowledge regarding a particular psychological topic or process that is relevant to the case (Pfeifer and Brigham, 1993; Kapardis, 1997; Schuller and Ogloff, 2001). For example, Loftus (1991) described testifying in numerous cases about the vagaries of eyewitness memory. In this way the psychologist takes a particularly instructive position while giving evidence.

Strong arguments can be made for the experimental role of the forensic psychologist. Meehl (1989: 521) described the commonsense, anecdotal beliefs of judges and laypeople as 'fireside inductions', and suggested that they often conflict with the empirical evidence of behavioural scientists. However, while sharing a distrust of these fireside inductions, Meehl posited that making generalized conclusions from some laboratory-based psychological research is 'equally dubious' when applied to the legal system. As such, Meehl suggested that quasi-experiments conducted in 'real-life' settings 'may often be the methodologically optimal data-source'. Similar opinions would seem to be held within the judiciary. For example, in the Australian case of *Attorney-General (NSW) v. John Fairfax Publications* (1999) empirical research regarding the likelihood of jurors recalling pre-trial publicity was adduced. The evidence was criticized because of differences between the experimental conditions and the circumstances of the trial. In their analysis of the case, Freckelton and McMahon (2002: 347) argued that 'a constructive legacy of the decision should be a greater sensitization ... to the kinds of factors that can distance experimental scenarios from curial contexts to a point where generalizations from the former become strained and spurious'.

The actuarial role

The third role is the *actuarial* role. This involves applying statistical probabilities to behaviours and events. This may be obtained from a literature search or by collecting new observational data (Gudjonsson, 1996; Gudjonsson and Haward, 1998). Haward (1981: 55) described several examples of the actuarial role, such as 'the probability of earning a living with a given IQ, the probability of finding two identical cars passing a road within a given period of time, (and) the probability of finding two persons with a given number of personal characteristics in the same town'. Unsurprisingly, this role is often adopted by statisticians or other professionals as well (see Focus box 14.1). It is perhaps the least common of the four roles (Gudjonsson and Haward, 1998).

Focus 14.1

The changing face of the expert witness in England

The role of 'expert evidence' in a court of law can be pivotal to the outcome of a trial. Expert witnesses are the only type of witness able to provide admissible evidence based on opinions, and must have a depth of knowledge in a subject which is more than that of a layman. In criminal courts, this expertise can vary greatly from paediatricians to handwriting experts. However, in light of high-profile cases, such as the conviction of Sally Clark for the murder of her two children in 1999 based on the expert testimony of Sir Roy Meadow, the Court of Appeal is introducing new measures to protect both the expert witness and those convicted of an offence. Sir Roy Meadow adopted the 'actuarial' role of expert evidence and testified that the likelihood of two children dying from sudden infant death syndrome (SIDS) in the same family was around 75,000,000:1. However, the Royal Statistical Society contested this evidence. They argued that if environmental and genetic factors were taken into account, this likelihood was reduced to around 100:1. Approximately 300 cases in which Sir Roy Meadow had testified were subsequently reviewed by the Court of Appeal and the role of expert witnesses were scrutinized in a government report led by Sir Liam Donaldson.

The new expert witness

Following the General Medical Council's ruling of 'serious professional misconduct' that was successfully contested by Sir Roy Meadow the Court of Appeal has introduced new measures to protect expert witnesses in the courts. This includes immunity to being sued in civil courts – a right currently only held by non-expert witnesses. This right has not been extended to the ability for expert witnesses to become exempt from professional body rulings on their conduct in criminal trials.

A new central body has also been proposed which is likely to be called the National Knowledge Service, and is specifically aimed at National Health Service professionals who give expert evidence in courts. The central service would provide a central source of expert witnesses who would receive mentoring, supervision and peer review. This would be a very positive step forward for expert witnesses who provide a valuable service to court cases but have as yet had minimal regulation.

The advisory role

The final role is the *advisory* role. This involves advising lawyers about the psychological evidence of other experts, pointing out weaknesses and thus assisting in the preparation of cross-examination strategies (Haward, 1981). By its very nature this role is a destructive one, but can be seen as a form of peer review. Nonetheless, it is important that the advisor draws attention to clearly unsound material without becoming an advocate (Gudjonsson and Haward, 1998).

Figure 14.1 A modern courtroom in use.
Source: © Corbis Premium RF/Alamy.

The law and psychology

The two main strands of law are **criminal law** and civil law. These two areas differ in several ways. Criminal law involves cases that are considered to be in the public interest. For example, someone may be assaulted by another person, however the case is usually brought against the offender by the Crown Prosecution Service in England (in Scotland it is the Procurator Fiscal; Gudjonsson and Haward, 1998). Thus, the victim technically does not play a role in the proceedings (other than possible witness[1]) and compensation of the victim plays no role in proceedings. The desired outcome is punishment of the offender. In contrast, civil law involves actions that are taken by one party against another with the desired outcome being compensation. Furthermore, the legal standard of proof differs. In criminal law the prosecution must prove guilt *beyond a reasonable doubt*. In civil cases a somewhat lesser standard of proof *on the balance of probabilities* is required (Rose, 2001). The next section will provide an overview of areas in which psychologists may provide evidence within these two types of law, with a focus upon law from the UK. This is a far from exhaustive review but does provide a general summary of the relevant areas of law.

---

[1]This is the usual method of prosecution. Nonetheless, 'any citizen possessing prima-facie evidence of a crime may prosecute' (Gudjonsson and Haward, 1998: 121).

Criminal law

The bulk of forensic psychological literature pertains to the criminal law (Wayte et al, 2002). Within criminal proceedings there are essentially three phases in which psychologists may become involved: pre-trial, trial and pre-sentence.

In the pre-trial phase, the main issue requiring the assistance of a mental health professional is that of fitness to plead (known in the USA as 'competency to stand trial'). According to Briscoe and colleagues (1993), there are five criteria for determining fitness to plead and stand trial in England and Wales: the ability to plead with understanding to the indictment; the ability to comprehend the details of evidence; the ability to follow court proceedings; the knowledge that a juror can be challenged; and the ability to instruct one's legal team.

As can be appreciated, mental illness is important in relation to fitness. Accordingly, in the UK these cases have been traditionally referred to psychiatrists. Nonetheless, Gudjonsson and Haward (1998) noted that psychologists are becoming increasingly involved. Intellectual and neuropsychological assessments may be of relevance in this regard. Standardized tests of malingering and deception may also be of considerable use (Melton et al, 2007). Furthermore, several specialist competency assessment tools have been developed in North America which address the varying domains of functioning that are required by relevant law (see Grisso, 2003; Melton et al, 2007). Nonetheless, as they were developed in the USA or Canada, the applicability of each tool to jurisdictions such as the UK would need to be reviewed prior to use.

Within the trial phase, two main elements need to be proven beyond a reasonable doubt: *actus reus* (the guilty act) and *mens rea* (intent to commit the act). *Actus reus* requires a voluntary physical act. For example, if person X pushed person Y's arm into person Z, person Y would not be criminally responsible because the act was not voluntary. The rare defence of automatism is one example, in which the defendant commits the act while unconscious due to "head injury, hypnotic suggestion, shock created by bullet wounds, or metabolic disorders (such as anoxia, hypoglyc(a)emia, or the involuntary ingestion of alcohol or drugs)" (Melton et al, 2007: 219).

Perhaps the most well known defence regarding *mens rea* is the insanity defence. While this is primarily the domain of psychiatrists within the UK, it is useful to look at this defence in some detail because psychologists are sometimes involved in order to complement a psychiatric evaluation (Gudjonsson and Haward, 1998). The modern insanity defence, indeed the foundation for the insanity defence in the UK, the USA, Canada, Australia, New Zealand, and numerous other nations, can be traced to the case of Daniel McNaughton in 1843. McNaughton was charged with the murder of the private secretary to the Prime Minister. He claimed that 'The Tories in my native city have compelled me to do this. They follow and persecute me wherever I go, and have entirely destroyed my peace of mind. They followed me to France, into Scotland, and all over England; in fact, they follow me wherever I go' (as cited in Memon, 2006: 234). McNaughton was found not guilty on the ground of insanity and controversy ensued. As a result of debate in the House of Lords, their Lordships were asked to determine the wording of the insanity defence. Their response became known as the *McNaughton rules* which are: 'at the time of the committing of the act, the party accused was labouring under such a defect of reason, from disease of the mind, as not to know the nature and quality of the act he was doing, or, if he did know it, that he did not know he was doing what was wrong' (Tindal L.C.J., as cited in Memon, 2006: 237). Clearly assessment in these cases requires that attention be paid to the presence of mental illness, the possibility of malingering, and a focus upon third party sources of information (Gutheil, 2002).

In regard to other issues pertaining to *mens rea*, British psychologists have chiefly been involved in issues of duress and coercion, absentmindedness and diminished responsibility (Gudjonsson and Haward, 1998). The latter applies in cases of homicide and is a partial defence that reduces the charge of murder to manslaughter. It requires an 'abnormality of mind' that 'substantially impaired' the defendant's 'mental responsibility for his acts' (Homicide Act, 1957, as cited in Gudjonsson and Haward, 1998).

In regard to the pre-sentence phase, psychologists are often asked to provide reports that are relevant to mitigation, treatment options and the risk of recidivism (Melton et al, 2007). Over the past three decades the latter has become a prominent focus in the forensic mental health literature. Monahan (1981) reviewed the extant literature and found that mental health professionals were accurate in only one out of three violence predictions. This can be contrasted with current risk assessment approaches which perform well above chance (Douglas et al, 1999; Davis and Ogloff, 2008).

The modern literature suggests that risk opinions made on the basis of unstructured, intuitive clinical judgement are inadequate. Greater accuracy can be attained by using either an actuarial prediction tool or a structured professional judgement (SPJ) scheme. The formar involves a mechanical process whereby risk factors are coded and tallied to form a score that relates to a probability estimate. This indicates how many people in the development sample, at that score or category, went on to re-offend during a defined follow-up period. This can then be compared to the base rate of offending within the development sample. In contrast, SPJ schemes also require careful coding of a series of risk factors, after which the clinician makes a structured judgement of low, moderate or high risk. Both approaches have demonstrated comparable predictive validity, although the SPJ approach enables some advantages in regard to risk management planning (see Davis and Ogloff, 2008). Risk assessment is also of considerable relevance in cases of post-sentence detention, such as the UK's Dangerous and Severe Personality Disorder Programme (Barrett and Byford, 2007).

Activity 14.1

Actuarial risk assessment

Consider two child sex offenders. The first is a 35-year-old married man who has been found guilty of molesting his daughter for the past 11 years while she was aged 4–14. The second is a single 23-year-old man who had 'consensual' sexual intercourse with a 14-year-old boy four hours after meeting him in a local park. Neither man has any prior criminal history for sexual or non-sexual offences. Neither has a history of substance abuse. Neither man has ever received treatment for a mental illness. Clinical psychologists indicate that neither man suffers from a psychotic illness. With this information, you have been asked to provide an opinion about the risk that each man may pose for committing further sexual offences. From the limited information described here, who would you consider to pose the greatest risk and what information would you focus on to make this judgement? One solution is provided at the end of this chapter.

Civil law

Psychologists are also involved as experts in civil disputes within the UK. For example, in regard to the law of torts (i.e. 'wrongs'), compensation is the goal. Psychologists have been involved in cases in which a particular trauma, emotional distress or cognitive impairment is claimed to have been sustained. Conditions such as post-traumatic stress disorder and acute stress disorder are common afflictions to be assessed. Once again, the possibility of deception and malingering must be considered (Melton et al, 2007). Psychologists are also involved in areas of children's and family law. This includes areas such as child abuse and neglect, and child custody in cases of divorce.

Behavioural investigative advice in court

As the name suggests, the field of **behavioural investigative advice** (i.e. investigative psychology or criminal investigative analysis) was developed to provide assistance to police investigations (as discussed in Chapter 12). Nonetheless, there have been some attempts to have such analyses admitted in court proceedings. Overall, these attempts have not been particularly successful. In regard to offender profiling, perhaps the most sensationalized of all behavioural investigative techniques, one ill-fated attempt was made in the British homicide case of *R v. Stagg* (1994) The trial judge rejected the evidence and was quite pessimistic about profiling ever being admitted, although he did acknowledge its likely investigative utility (Ormerod, 1999). It is perhaps difficult to see how profiling evidence could be admitted in criminal trials, as it would appear to impinge directly upon the 'ultimate issue' (i.e. the issue to be decided by the jury).

The psychological autopsy, similar to a process known as equivocal death analysis, is a technique in which the lifestyle of a deceased person, as well as the circumstances of their death, are analyzed in order to provide an opinion as to the likely mode of death (i.e. natural causes, accident, suicide or homicide; Canter, 1999; Davis, 2005). Attempts have also been made to have such analyses admitted at trial. In the UK these have not been successful. For example, in the case of *R v. Gilfoyle*, a man was convicted of murdering his pregnant wife who died from hanging. A psychological autopsy conducted by a professor of psychology suggested that suicide was a likely mode of death, but this was deemed inadmissible (see Canter, 2005a).

However, evidence of a similar nature was admitted in the Northern Ireland case of Torney (1996, as cited in Gudjonsson and Haward, 1998). In this case a police officer was charged with the murders of his wife, son and daughter. He claimed that his son had gone 'berserk' and killed his mother and sister before committing suicide. A psychologist reviewed the case material and testified that the scene was not consistent with this scenario. Rather, he suggested that a carefully planned execution was more likely. This evidence was admitted and the defendant was convicted of all three murders.

Behavioural investigative advice would appear to have been more successful in being admitted to courts within the USA. In regard to the psychological autopsy, Ogloff and Otto (2003) noted that the technique has been chiefly admitted within civil courts, but added that there has been reluctance to permit testimony regarding mode of death. Rather, testimony limited to the decedent's state of mind prior to death is more likely to be allowed. Ogloff and Otto also noted that psychological autopsies have been allowed in cases of insurance and workers' compensation, but not in regard to testamentary capacity or intestate succession, which suggests that the courts are uncomfortable with psychological autopsies that opine on the ultimate issue. They also note that criminal courts have been less willing to admit such evidence.

As the name suggests, linkage analysis is a technique in which separate crimes are linked by reference to their behaviour (Hazelwood and Warren, 2003). This technique has been admitted during several criminal trials in the USA. The first of these was in *Delaware v. Pennell* (1989), where an FBI behavioural scientist gave evidence suggesting that three murders had behavioural similarities. In the case of *Louisiana v. Code* (1993), such evidence was used to link four further murders to a defendant already charged with four murders. In both of these cases the decision to admit the linkage analysis was upheld on appeal (Alison et al, 2002). Nonetheless, in the more recent case of *New Jersey v. Fortin* (2000) such evidence was limited. The expert was allowed to testify about aspects of his analysis, but was not allowed to state an opinion as to whether two cases were indeed linked (Risinger and Loop, 2002).

Conclusions

In its most literal form, forensic psychology is concerned with 'the collection, examination, and presentation of evidence for judicial purposes' (Haward, 1981: 21). The field has grown considerably since the first experimental psychologist gave expert evidence in court in 1897. Present-day forensic psychology comprises four broad roles: clinical, experimental, actuarial and advisory. Forensic psychologists provide opinions on a range of topics within both criminal and civil law and have managed to be admitted in areas that were previously the domain of the psychiatrist. Even the field of investigative psychology, developed to assist police investigations, has seen some limited application in the courts, although this has largely been seen to encroach upon the ultimate issue. Nonetheless, advances made within the field of forensic psychology over the past century have clearly been enormous.

Activity 14.2

Actuarial risk assessment solution

One tool that you might consider using is the Static-99 (Hanson and Thornton, 1999). This is a 10-item actuarial tool that is comprised exclusively of 'static' (i.e. relatively unchanging) risk factors. The first offender has no risk factors on this instrument. He is above the age of 25, has been married, has not been charged with non-sexual violence in his index offence, has no previous charges or convictions, and has not committed a sexual offence against someone outside of his family, a stranger or a male. A score of zero places this offender in the 'low' category of risk. In the studies on which this measure was developed, 13 per cent of offenders who had a score of zero went on to sexually re-offend over 15 years. This is half the base rate in the development sample (which was 26 per cent).

In contrast, the second offender has five risk factors. He is under the age of 25, has never been in a cohabiting relationship, and has committed a sexual offence against a victim who is outside of his family, a stranger and a male. A score of five places this man in the 'moderate–high' category of risk. In the development studies, 40 per cent of offenders who had a score of five went on to sexually re-offend over 15 years. This is considerably higher than the base rate of 26. Thus, based on static risk factors, the second offender would appear to pose a higher risk of sexual recidivism than the first offender.

Those conducting risk assessments generally do not rely exclusively on the results of the Static-99. Indeed, the manual for the instrument indicates that it 'does not address all relevant risk factors for sexual offenders' (Harris et al, 2003: 3. Nonetheless, it does provide a useful anchor point for conducting a risk assessment.

Acknowledgements

The author would like to thank Professors David Canter and James Ogloff for their helpful suggestions and Laura Hammond for contributing material for the 'focus box'.

Key concepts and terms

Behavioural investigative advice

Criminal law

Expert evidence

Forensic psychology

Sample essay titles

- Given the McNaughton rules, discuss why schizophrenia may, in some conditions, be relevant to a claim of insanity while antisocial or dissocial personality disorder is not?

- Discuss reasons why testimony that addresses the ultimate issue should not be admitted in court.

- What are the main roles for psychologists in court?

- In what sorts of civil court cases might psychology be relevant?

Further reading

Books

Goldstein, A.M. (Ed.) (2007). *Forensic Psychology: Emerging Topics and Expanding Roles*. Hoboken, NJ: Wiley.

Gudjonsson, G.H., and Haward, L.R.C. (Eds) (1998). *Forensic Psychology: A Guide to Practice*. London: Routledge.

Melton, G.B., Petrila, J., Poythress, N.G., and Slobogin, C. (2007). *Psychological Evaluations for the Courts: A Handbook for Mental Health Professionals and Lawyers*, (3rd Ed.). New York: Guilford.

Ogloff, J.R.P. (Ed.) (2002). *Taking Psychology and Law into the Twenty-First Century*. New York: Kluwer Academic/Plenum.

Weiner, I.B., and Hess, A.K. (Eds) (2006). *The Handbook of Forensic Psychology*, (3rd Ed.). Hoboken, NJ: Wiley.

Journal articles

Brigham, J. (1999). What is forensic psychology anyway? *Law and Human Behavior*, 23, 273–298.

Cattell, J.M. (1895). Measurements of the accuracy of recollection. *Science*, 2, 761–766.

Douglas, K.S., Cox, D.N., and Webster, C.D. (1999). Violence risk assessment: Science and practice. *Legal and Criminological Psychology*, 4, 149–184.

Risinger, D.M., and Loop, J.L. (2002). Three card monte, monty hall, modus operandi and 'offender profiling': Some lessons of modern cognitive science for the law of evidence. *Cardozo Law Review*, 24, 193–285.

15 Psychology in prison

Kevin Rogers

This chapter begins with a short history of punishment before giving an overview of prison life and the types of offences for which people are imprisoned. It then examines the psychological effect on people who, having committed an offence, have been sentenced to a term of imprisonment. The approaches to reducing re-offending through accredited offending behaviour programmes are considered with an explanation of the psychological issues involved. Finally, the chapter briefly examines the work of a **forensic** psychologist based in a prison environment.

Learning outcomes

When you have completed this chapter you should be able to:

1. Know what it is like to be in prison.
2. Understand the types of offences for which people are imprisoned.
3. Discuss the psychological impact of imprisonment.
4. Consider the methods undertaken to reduce re-offending, including offending behaviour programmes offered to prisoners.
5. Understand the work of a prison-based forensic psychologist.

The prison 'experience'

Throughout history, imprisonment has been based upon the notion that those who wronged society should be punished through the suffering of the body. During the Middle Ages, punishments for offending ranged from hanging nd mutilation to whipping and fining. By 1275 prisoners were forced to lie on bare earth and given bread and water every other day. Some prisoners were even loaded with weights and chains until they were crushed to death.

In the late 1600s and early 1700s, juries were sometimes hesitant to send criminals to the gallows and thus a guilty verdict was not always passed. Alternatives at the time were to offer criminals a pardon if they joined the army or navy, or transportation to the Americas or Australia.

In 1777, the punishment emphasis enforced by jailers was on penal work, which included the physical labour of the tread wheel and crank. If the number of revolutions from either was not achieved, flogging or missed meals were the usual punishments.

By the turn of the nineteenth century, a system known as 'silent and separate' was used either to maintain a regime of silence or to keep prisoners in solitary confinement, the idea being that prisoners could not 'infect' each other with criminal ways.

The Prisons Act of 1878 brought all prisons under the control of a national system run by the Prison Commission and later the Prison Department. As a result, prison commissioners were appointed to inspect all prisons and submit annual reports on the prisons to Parliament. The Act led to the closure of the worst prisons in the country and set the tone for the future by adopting the principle of prisons being for reformation rather than punishment. It was believed that reformation and deterrence should now be the main objectives of prisons. Thankfully, the trend towards rehabilitation has continued to the present day where prisoners are more likely to be encouraged to address their offending behaviour through education, behavioural programmes and one-to-one interventions.

But what is it like for someone coming into prison for the first time? Experiences of prison can vary from person to person and from prison to prison. However, for those in jail for the first time, expectations can sometimes be far harsher than the reality. That does not mean that prison is easy, far from it. First impressions often leave people feeling frightened, depressed, anxious, and with a whole multitude of other negative emotions. Most of the trouble prisoners encounter while in prison is due to people's dependency on drugs and tobacco and the resultant bullying which takes place when personal supplies run low. It is little wonder, then, that those imprisoned for the first time are most at risk of suicide.

When a prisoner first arrives at prison, there are a few measures which need to take place. These are undertaken to ensure the prisoner has everything they need and to call attention to any problems they may have, such as a medical complaint. The first thing that happens is that the prisoner's property is listed by an officer and put into safe-keeping. Some of the items can be kept in the prisoner's cell, the rest will be returned to them at the end of their sentence. Once the prisoner has had a shower and been allocated their prison number, they are seen by a member of the health care team. It is important that every prisoner is medically assessed so that they can be given the proper care that they need while they are in prison. All the information gathered is treated as confidential – just like going to a normal GP.

Shortly after arriving at prison, the prisoner will have an interview with a member of the probation staff, or a 'personal officer'. A personal officer is a prison officer who has been allocated to individual prisoners. The reception interview is another chance for the prisoner to discuss any problems they may have. Prison staff are there to help if there is anything the prisoner does not understand or if they need any advice or support.

To help prisoners settle into prison life, an induction session has been developed to explain how the prison works and what each prisoner's responsibilities are. It also helps prisoners to think about making the best use of their time in custody. Of course, from time to time, prisoners may have worries or problems that they might need to speak to someone about. Their personal officer or the officer in charge of their wing or unit is there to talk problems through with prisoners. In addition, prisoners can talk to a prison 'listener' who is trained by the Samaritans or the prison's chaplain.

Adapting to prison regime can be difficult because so many things are different. There are new rules and regulations to become accustomed to, new behaviour norms and respective routines to understand, new social hierarchies and a different 'prison' language to get used to. There will be some overcrowding, annoying and frustrating levels of noise and distraction with little personal space or privacy. It can be difficult to sleep properly with radios played at intolerable volumes, the noise of keys turning loudly in locks, gates banging shut and loud arguments. The food is basic, starchy and dull. Prisoners have to learn to wait for everything: a phone call, a shower, any mail, even the answer to a question. Time can become distorted: days slip by, but each hour could seem like an eternity to those with nothing to occupy their minds.

Upon conviction and entry into the prison system, all prisoners are allocated a classification mark in accordance with their level of security risk (Price, 2000). This is based upon recommendations made by Lord Mountbatten in his 1966 report *Prison Escapes and Security* (Home office, 1996). It followed the escape from HMP Wormwood Scrubs in London of the spy George Blake. Employed by MI6 after the war and sent first to Korea and then to Berlin, Blake had volunteered his services to the KGB. He was eventually caught and, some five years earlier in 1961, had been sentenced to 42 years imprisonment which was, at that time, the longest determinate sentence ever passed in a British court.

As well as recommending the building of a single maximum-security prison on the Isle of Wight, Lord Mountbatten suggested four distinct categories of prisoner, which he suggested were necessary to improve prison security. These categories are as follows:

- *Category A*. 'Prisoners who must in no circumstances be allowed to get out, either because of security considerations affecting spies, or because their violent behaviour is such that members of the public or the police would be in danger of their lives if they were to get out.'

- *Category B*. Prisoners for whom 'the very high expenditure on the most modern escape barriers may not be justified, but who ought to be kept in secure conditions'.

- *Category C*. Prisoners who 'lack the resource and will to make escape attempts, but have not the stability to be kept in conditions where there is no barrier to escape'.

- *Category D*. Prisoners 'who can reasonably be entrusted to serve their sentences in open conditions'.

Table 15.1 shows a 'typical' day in the life of a prisoner. Their time is dictated by the prison regime and one day is pretty much the same as the day before and the day before that. Notable exceptions to this would be for example, 25 December, when prisoners would go to chapel for a Christmas Day service, enjoy extra time out of cell, have a traditional Christmas lunch and involve themselves in inter-wing quizzes or competitions such as volleyball, pool and weightlifting.

7.30	Breakfast
8.30	Work or education
11.30	Lunch and lock up in cell
1.30	Return to work/education
4.30	Finish work and return to cell area
5.30	Tea and lock up
6.30–8.30	Association/ education/group work
8.30	Lock up for the night

Table 15.1 Prison – a day in the life...

Figure 15.1 A typical UK prison cell.

Prisoners cannot refuse to work if there is work available unless they have been judged 'medically unfit'. Work includes activities such as assembly, packing, data inputting, recycling, charity workshops, etc. The money is paid into a prison account in the prisoner's name. Prisons have a shop or 'canteen' in which prisoners may purchase phone calls, stamps, tobacco, extra food, etc.

People in prison

The population of prisons in England and Wales has risen in recent years, increasing to 85 per cent since 1993. With approximately 81,000 people currently incarcerated in prison, research shows that England and Wales lock up more prisoners per head of the population than any other country in Western Europe, and far in excess of countries such as Germany, France, Italy, Denmark and Ireland. This represents a 15 per cent increase since 1999 (International Centre for Prison Studies 2007).

A review of recent statistics, unfortunately, does not make encouraging reading. On 4 September, 2007, the prison population in England and Wales stood at 80,762, a rise of 1549 on the year before (Prison Statistics, Sept. 2007). England and Wales has the highest imprisonment rate in Western Europe at 148 per 100,000 of the population. France has an imprisonment rate of 85 per 100,000 and Germany has a rate of 95 per 100,000. The number of prisoners in England and Wales has increased by 29,800 in the last 15 years. In 1995, the average prison population was 50,962; today, that figure stands at 80,762. Previously, it had taken nearly four decades (1958–1995) for the prison population to rise by 25,000 (Home Office, 2003).

As discussed earlier, different people's experience of prison can vary. Obviously there is a vast difference between serving a short sentence and long-term imprisonment. This results not so much from one's experience while in prison, but the fact that it can be harder to remain unaffected psychologically. It will take longer to re-adjust to the outside world on release as it will have changed dramatically and thus old skills will have to be improved or new ones learnt.

Being in prison on remand can be mentally and emotionally taxing because of the uncertainty regarding length of sentence, and the stress of an approaching court case. Women in prison experience additional problems as not only are they likely to be imprisoned further away from family and friends due to the scarcity of female prisons in comparison to male, but one in three women in prison are driven to self-harm, often as a way of coping with the psychological stress they encounter (Home Office, 1997).

The observed agreement on the most depressing effects of confinement is that the majority of prisoners who have served time in prison return to the outside world with little or no permanent, clinically diagnosable psychological disorder as a result (Haney, 1997).

Imprisonment does not, ordinarily, make people crazy although some researchers who are openly cynical about whether the difficulties of incarceration convert into psychological harm admit that, for at least some, incarceration can generate damaging, long-term change (Andrews et al, 1990). Most agree that the more psychologically demanding the type of imprisonment, the greater the number of people who will suffer and the deeper the damage that they will experience (Andrews et al, 1990).

As well as the more clinically diagnosable effects of imprisonment, such as worthlessness, anger, depression and low self-esteem, psychologists have to deal with the broader and more understated psychological changes that transpire in the everyday course of adapting to prison life. Haney (2001) described these as:

Dependence on institutional structure and contingencies

The prison system demands that prisoners give up their freedom of choice and the independence to decide things for themselves, which can be a painful and difficult adjustment for most people. Over time, prisoners may become progressively more dependent on the institution to make decisions for them to the extent that they become increasingly anxious when their previous freedom and autonomy is returned.

Hyper-vigilance, interpersonal distrust and suspicion

Prisons are clearly dangerous places from which there is no exit or escape. It is necessary to become hyper-vigilant and ever-alert for signs of threat or personal risk. Because there are people in their close surroundings ready to take advantage of any sign of weakness, interpersonal doubt and suspicion often result. Some male prisoners learn to project a 'hard man' image, believing that unless they can credibly project an aura that conveys the ability for violence they are likely to be dominated and exploited throughout their sentence. This has a direct link to:

Emotional over-control, alienation and psychological distancing

Developing this image requires the prisoner's emotional responses to be carefully measured and, as a result, they struggle to control and suppress their own internal emotional reactions to events around them. Prisoners who struggle at both an emotional and behavioural level to develop a 'prison mask' that is unrevealing and impenetrable risk alienation from themselves and others. They may acquire an emotional void which becomes habitual and incapacitating in social situations and relationships, and find that they have formed an enduring and unbridgeable distance between themselves and other people.

Social withdrawal and isolation

Some prisoners display a tendency to protect themselves by hiding behind a cloak of social invisibility and becoming as low-key and as discreetly detached from others as possible. This self-imposed social retreat and isolation may mean that they completely withdraw themselves from everything; they do not allow themselves to trust anyone, and cope with the stresses of prison life by living a secluded life of quiet distraction. In some, more extreme cases, especially when combined with prisoner indifference and loss of the ability to instigate behaviour on their own, the pattern is remarkably similar in nature to that of clinical depression. It is common for prisoners serving long-term sentences to be particularly susceptible to this type of psychological adjustment.

Incorporation of exploitative norms of prison culture

As well as having to follow the recognized and established rules of the institution, prisoners are forced to accept the unofficial rules and norms that are part of the unwritten but critical prisoner code which, at some level, must be adhered to or the risk of repercussion faced. For some, this means protecting themselves from the dangerousness and deprivations of the immediate environment by accepting all of its informal norms, including some of the most exploitative and extremist values of prison life. It is unfortunate that prisoners typically are given no alternative culture to which to ascribe or in which to participate.

As noted earlier, prison culture looks down on any sign of weakness and susceptibility, and discourages the expression of sincere emotions or familiarity. Some prisoners embrace this in a way which encourages a keen investment in one's reputation for toughness, and promotes an attitude towards others in which even apparently irrelevant verbal abuse, disrespect or physical infringements must be responded to speedily and intuitively, often with decisive force. In some cases, the failure to take advantage of weakness is often seen as a symbol of weakness itself and viewed as provocation for manipulation. In male prisons, it may encourage a type of hypermasculinity in which power and control are overestimated as critical parts of one's identity.

Obviously, if one adopts these principles completely, it generates huge obstacles to significant interpersonal communication with the outside world; it prevents searching for suitable assistance with problems, and leaves an overwhelming reluctance to trust other people through fear of manipulation. It can also lead to what appears to be spontaneous over-reaction, hitting out at people in response to token provocation. This happens particularly with people who have not been socialized into the norms of prisoner culture, in which the preservation of interpersonal respect and personal space are so sacrosanct. Yet these things are often as much a part of the process of prison life as adapting to the formal rules that are obligatory in the institution, and they are equally difficult to relinquish upon release.

Diminished sense of self-worth and personal value

As previously stated, once incarcerated, prisoners are denied their basic right to privacy and relinquish control over everyday features of their very being that most people on the outside take for granted. They live in a small, sometimes extremely confined and deteriorating space, have little or no say in choosing the person with whom they must share the cell space, have no option over when they must get up or go to bed, when or what they eat, when they shower or even when they exercise. All are aware that the degraded circumstances under which they exist help to continually remind them of their compromised social status and stigmatized social role as prisoners. As a result, a diminished sense of self-worth and personal value may exist. In some cases of institutionalization, prisoners may come to internalize the belief that they deserve the degradation and stigma to which they have been subjected while imprisoned.

Post-traumatic stress reactions to the pains of imprisonment

The fact that a high percentage of people currently in prison have experienced some form of childhood distress means, among other things, that the austere, castigatory and callous nature of prison existence may characterize a type of 're-traumatization' experience for many of them. That is, some prisoners find the inflexible and unyielding strictness of prison life, the unsolicited immediacy of violent encounters and the likelihood of being mistreated through physical and/or sexual assaults, the need to traverse the controlling objectives of others, the dearth of legitimate esteem and regard for their well-being in the surrounding environment, is an all too familiar experience. Time spent in prison may renew not only the recollections but the disabling psychological reactions and consequences of these earlier damaging experiences.

These difficulties are often treated by psychologists on an individual basis, usually in a one-to-one format using **cognitive behaviour** methods over an agreed time span and number of sessions. Any change in mood or behaviour is monitored by wing staff and reported to psychologists on a regular timescale with interventions amended accordingly.

Although everyone who comes into prison is subjected to many of the above-stated pressures of institutionalization, and will tend to respond in various ways with varying degrees of psychological change associated with their adaptations, it is important to note that there are some prisoners who are much more vulnerable to these pressures and the overall pains of imprisonment than others. These will include mentally ill and developmentally disabled prisoners and those held in solitary confinement.

Addressing the problem of offending behaviour

As well as addressing individual issues such as those listed in preceding paragraphs, forensic psychologists have to focus on addressing the problem of offending behaviour so that issues around reducing recidivism can be attended to. In recent times, a quantity of contemporary ways of interacting with prisoners have been devised which have been developed from the cognitive behaviour approach. As a method of working with offenders, this approach has a number of substantial qualities and benefits. McGuire (2000) suggests these are that:

- It is theoretically driven.

- It is firmly grounded in a considerable amount of empirical research.

- Large-scale research into the outcomes of work with repeat offenders can be reduced by the application of methods based on the cognitive behaviour approach.

McGuire (2000) does not suggest that this approach or methods based upon it have all the answers but instead argues that: 'There are still many large questions to be answered, some yet to be asked; numerous problems to be solved, further ideas to be tested and room for many innovations and developments'.

Cognitive behaviour therapy (CBT) is based on the theory that most unwanted thinking patterns and emotional and behavioural reactions are learned over a long period of time. The aim is to identify the thinking that is causing those unwanted feelings and behaviours and learn to replace them with more positive thoughts. The cognitive behaviour approach is evident in a number of accredited offending behaviour programmes offered to prisoners by the Prison Service. CBT helps prisoners to make sense of overwhelming problems they may experience by breaking them down into smaller parts. This makes it easier to see how they are connected and how they themselves can be affected by it. These parts are:

- A situation (a problem, event or difficult situation).

From this can follow:

- Thoughts.

- Emotions.

- Physical feelings.

And this will determine:

- Actions.

Each one of these areas can affect the others. How you think about a problem can affect how you feel physically and emotionally. It can also alter what you do about it.

Interventions with offenders in H.M. Prison Service (England and Wales) were first introduced in 1992; these were Reasoning and Rehabilitation (RandR) in 1992 and Thinking Skills in 1993. The Reasoning and Rehabilitation programme was developed by Ross and Fabiano in Canada in the 1970s (Ross and Fabiano, 1985; Porporino and Fabiano, 2000). The Thinking Skills programme, which later became known as Enhanced Thinking Skills (ETS; Clark, 2000), was developed by the Prison Service using the RandR structure as a model (Ross and Fabiano, 1985).

Before the 1980s, there was a great deal of deliberation on the efficacy of offending behaviour groupwork interventions. A number of meta-analytic reviews of effectiveness research, published from the mid 1980s onwards, provided evidence that such interventions with offenders could produce a small but significant decrease in recidivism (Garrett, 1985; Lösel and Köferl, 1989; Andrews et al, 1990; Izzo and Ross, 1990; Lipsey, 1992; Lipton et al, 1998). In addition, this research, known jointly as 'What Works', served to emphasize the components necessary for a structured intervention to be most efficient in reducing recidivism. The general consensus was that using cognitive behaviour approaches produced the maximum decline (Cooke and Philip, 2001). With this method as the starting point, well-designed interventions matched to the needs and abilities of the offender and delivered systematically are likely to produce the greatest effect (McGuire and Priestley, 1995). Collective meta-analytical evidence suggests that interventions which incorporate all these factors can reduce the base rate of offender reconviction by around 10 per cent (Hollin, 1999).

Focus 15.1

An example of CBT with a prisoner

Situation: You're expecting a visit from your partner. She has promised to arrive by 2pm. At 2:15, you're escorted to the visits room and she's not there.

	Helpful	**Unhelpful**
Thoughts	Perhaps she's stuck in traffic or missed the bus. She'll be here soon	She's found someone else. She's dumped me and can't face me to tell me
Emotional feelings	Happy, positive, in high spirits	Angry, upset, jealous, low, sad, rejected
Physical	None – feel comfortable	Stomach cramps, low energy, feel sick
Action	Wait quietly, get a coffee and chat with prison staff	Go back to the wing, telephone her tonight, accuse her of being unfaithful and tell her exactly what I think of her

The same situation has led to two very different results, depending on how you thought about the situation. How you think this has affected how you felt and what you did. In the example in the right-hand column, you've jumped to a conclusion without very much evidence for it – and this matters, because it's led to:

- A number of uncomfortable feelings.

- An unhelpful behaviour.

If you go back to the wing feeling depressed, you'll probably brood on what has happened and feel worse. If you get in touch with the other person, there's a good chance you'll feel better about yourself. If you don't, you won't have the chance to correct any misunderstandings about what they think of you – and you will probably feel worse.

This is a simplified way of looking at what happens. The whole sequence, and parts of it, can also feedback like this:

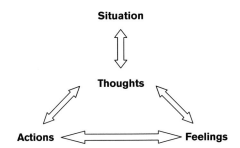

Figure 15.2

This 'vicious circle' can make you feel worse. It can even create new situations that make you feel worse. You can start to believe quite unrealistic (and unpleasant) things about yourself. This happens because, when we are distressed, we are more likely to jump to conclusions and to interpret things in extreme and unhelpful ways.

In order to improve the efficacy of programmes, the Prison Service introduced a system of accreditation in 1996 (Lipton et al, 2000). This is to make certain that the Prison Service offers effective interventions, and is necessarily a thorough and challenging process. The accreditation criteria are based on evidence of what works to reduce re-offending, drawn from independent reviews of studies of a large number of varied interventions and programmes for offenders. In broad terms, effective interventions are those which:

■ Use methods that are relevant to offenders' learning styles (see Table 15.2).

■ Are well designed to address specific factors associated with offending.

■ Are delivered as designed.

Each accredited programme of intervention used in the Prison Service is designed around the following criteria:

■ *A clear model of change*: There must be an explicit model to explain how the programme is intended to bring about relevant change in offenders. The programme's theory manual must explain who the programme is for and which areas of risk it will reduce. It must specify how it will do this and what is achieved at each stage of the programme. It must describe why this combination of targets and methods is likely to work with the offenders selected. Evidence from existing research must be given to support the

Activists learn best from activities where:	Reflectors learn best from activities where:
There are new experiences to learn from They can engross themselves in 'here and now' activities There are a range of diverse activities There is high visibility They can generate ideas without constraints They are thrown in at the deep end They are involved with other people They can 'have a go'	They can observe/think over activities They can stand back from events They are allowed time to think and prepare They can research/review They are asked to produce reports They can exchange views in a protected environment They can operate to their own deadlines
Theorists learn best from activities where:	**Pragmatists learn best from activities where:**
They are offered interesting theories There is time to explore ideas There is opportunity to question They are intellectually stretched There are structured situations with a clear purpose They can read about logical ideas/concepts They can analyse success or failure They can participate in complex situations	There are links between the topic and their job They can try things out and receive feedback They can emulate the model provided They are shown techniques which are applicable to their job They can implement what has been learned The learning activity has validity They can concentrate on practical issues

Table 15.2 Offenders' learning styles. Research by Honey and Mumford (1986) suggested that the way in which people learn new skills can be divided up into four distinct areas: activists, reflectors, theorists and pragmatists.

approach. The methods and exercises in the programme manual have to fit with the theory manual.

- *Selection of offenders*: There must be clear specification of the types of offender for whom the programme is intended, and the methods used to select them. The programme has to identify the characteristics of the offenders selected. These should include the nature of the offences which the programme is tackling, risk, motivation, learning style, gender and race. The measures used to assess these must be described. Standard measures developed and validated by the Prison and Probation Services are preferred. The programme must have ways for dealing with offenders who have started and are then found to be unsuitable.

- *Targeting a range of dynamic risk factors*: A range of dynamic risk factors known to be associated with re-offending must be addressed in an integrated manner within the programme. We know that people who offend very often share certain characteristics or experiences. These are risk factors. Some are fixed (i.e. static or non-changeable) factors, such as previous convictions and family background. Some are changeable (i.e. dynamic) factors such as attitudes and behaviours. Programmes target changeable areas. The areas chosen must be explained. An effective programme targets areas of dynamic risk which are well established. Alternatively, the programme must provide evidence to justify targeting other factors.

- *Effective methods*: There must be evidence to show that the treatment methods used are likely to have an impact on the targeted dynamic risk factors. The methods on the panel's approved list are those that have been proved to be effective with offenders. Cognitive behaviour methods work well with most types of offenders, including sex offenders. These focus directly on changing thinking and behavioural patterns and the way thoughts, feelings and behaviours interact. Structured therapeutic communities attempt to change the lifestyle of people with drug or alcohol addictions or other patterns of antisocial behaviour. If other methods are selected, existing research or a testable theory is put forward.

- *Skills orientated*: The programme must facilitate the learning of skills that will assist participants in avoiding criminal activities and facilitate their involvement in legitimate pursuits. It must teach skills which help participants live and work without re-offending. These can include literacy, numeracy, how to find work, make and keep relationships, general problem-solving and other skills relevant to the participants' lives. How skills are selected and taught and how participants' learning is evaluated must be described.

- *Sequencing, intensity and duration*: The amount of treatment provided must be linked to the needs of programme participants, with the introduction of different treatment components timed so that they complement each other. Length matches risk. Offenders who have high fixed risk, e.g. a history of antisocial behaviour, need programmes long enough to change established attitudes and habits. For lower risk offenders, a shorter programme is sufficient. Those with many, but potentially changeable, risk areas need enough time to work on these.

- *Engagement and motivation*: The programme must be structured to maximize the engagement of participants and to sustain their motivation throughout. Staff should be positively committed to the programme. The content and the methods of teaching should match the way participants learn best and motivate them to want to change.

- *Continuity of programmes and services*: There must be clear links between the programme and the overall management of the offender, both during a prison sentence and in the context of community supervision. Relevant information is shared. Key agencies concerned with protection of the public are kept informed to aid work with victims, and monitor offenders.

- *Maintaining integrity*: There must be provision to monitor how well the programme functions, and a system to modify aspects of it that do not perform as expected.

- *Ongoing evaluation*: There must be provision built into the programme to evaluate the efficacy of it. Checks are done to ensure that staff are properly selected, trained and supervised and that the programme is run as intended. Failure in any of these areas can undermine effectiveness and make it impossible to evaluate what does actually work. Further checks are made on whether there are improvements in the risk areas targeted and reconviction is reduced. Research into making programmes more effective is continued.

Accredited offending behaviour programmes

Past research tells us that we will not help offenders to lead law-abiding lives by simply locking them away for 23 hours a day with one hour of exercise. Therefore, every prison establishment offers prisoners access to a structured regime of work, education and offending behaviour programmes.

Offending behaviour programmes are treatment programmes designed to ascertain the reasons why prisoners offend and reduce and monitor these factors. As well as reducing risk, programmes support risk assessment and the risk management of offenders. The Prison Service, through the Offending Behaviour Programmes Unit (OBPU), currently provides a number of different offending behaviour programmes (excluding drug treatment programmes, which are provided through the National Drug Programme Delivery Unit [NDPDU]) which have been fully or provisionally accredited by the Correctional Services Accreditation Panel (CSAP). The objective for 2005/06 was 7000 offenders completing these programmes. International evidence from systematic reviews of effective practice on reducing re-offending tends to maintain the use of cognitive behaviour offending behaviour programmes and interventions with offenders. Current evidence in the UK is principally based on quasi-experimental or non-experimental evaluation studies, which make it difficult to accredit the outcomes to the effects of the treatment or intervention. More often than not, the results can be attributed to selection or other effects if not poor implementation. Outcome studies therefore need to be based on more effective research design. At the same time, adequate focus should be placed on implementation to ensure that programmes are delivered as intended so that theory failure and implementation failure do not confound evaluation of effectiveness.

The Offending Behaviour Programmes Unit offers the following description of these programmes.

Enhanced Thinking Skills (ETS)

ETS is a 20-session, 40-hour course based on the premise that much antisocial behaviour stems from offenders' inability to reach their goals in pro-social ways, because they lack various cognitive skills. These deficiencies are not related to intelligence or educational attainment, but are related to styles of thinking and attitudes which lead to anti-social behaviour. The cognitive skills lacking include impulse control, flexible thinking, social perspective taking, values/moral reasoning, reasoning, and interpersonal problem solving. Such deficits have been reported by many researchers working with offenders, including Bowman and Auerbach (1982), Young (1984), Arbothnot and Gordon (1986) and Ross,

Fabiano and Ewles (1988). ETS is the programme most frequently delivered, with over 40,000 offenders having completed this course within HMPS over the past 12 years.

Session	Content
Pre-course session	An opportunity for group members to get to session know each other and to be introduced to topics in the course. Tutors also increase awareness of group in the value of monitoring their own thoughts
1	Relationships between thoughts and behaviour are explored and the first step of the problem-solving strategy is explained
2	Involves a number of exercises aimed at demonstrating the importance of stopping and thinking (second step of the problem-solving strategy) before making a decision. Having considered how errors in information processing occur, techniques to avoid behaving impulsively are covered
3	Covers steps 3 and 4 of the problem-solving strategy. Group is encouraged to explore how 'good' information can help in decision-making and what type of information is most useful
4	Continues the development of the problem-solving strategy, through the introduction of the second part of the decision-making process – consideration of consequences
5	This session introduces the final two steps of the problem-solving strategy – planning and action. The strategy is then reviewed and practised
6	Having completed the problem-solving strategy, group members explore the influence of past experiences, group membership and levels of personal involvement on our beliefs
7	This session introduces the group to the idea that there are different ways of behaving which can affect interactions with others. Also examines the differences between aggressive, assertive and passive behaviours
8	Session 8 covers perspective taking and highlights how seeing a situation from a number of perspectives can be important in understanding the facts
9	Two related social skills are covered in this session, listening and asking for help
10	This session provides another opportunity to take part in a perspective taking exercise. The second half of the session involves the first in a series of moral dilemmas which encourage the group to think about the reasoning they use to reach value-laden decisions

Continued ...

. . . Continued

Session	Content
11	Session 11 begins with another moral dilemma which raises the issue of loyalty and trust. This is followed by the social skill convincing others. Tutors highlight the differences between this skill and manipulation or bullying
12	At this stage, the group should have an understanding of the link between thinking and behaviour, will have developed a problem-solving strategy and have begun developing perspective taking and social skills strategies. The first part of session 12 focuses on identifying and managing irrational thinking. The second part introduces the skill responding to failure and offers a way of dealing with irrational thoughts when you have been told you have failed at something
13	This session offers the opportunity to review how emotions affect us and how we can identify emotions in ourselves and others. The second part of the session is a moral dilemma on an issue with a high emotional content
14	Session 14 looks at working with others on problem-solving tasks. This requires keeping an open mind, planning, cooperation and guarding against selfishness. The moral debate raises the issue of what is fair and just for society and individual responsibility
15	The first part of the session looks at the issues of rules and how they are essential to enable people to live and work together. The moral debate examines issues of trust and deception and informal versus legal and formal rules
16	This session examines negotiation, involving a combination of problem-solving with social skills. It is also pointed out that not everything is negotiable
17	Session 17 further develops the group's repertoire of skills by presenting how to respond to others. It gives them a strategy for dealing with occasions when others try to convince them of something or when someone attempts to manipulate or cajole them. The moral debate focuses on an emotive issue where several of the characters are under pressure from others to make an irreversible decision
18	This session brings together all the main aspects of the course and demonstrates how the various points fit together. Group members work through the whole problem-solving strategy and present a chosen solution for a problem they have thought of
19	This session focuses on the implementation of solutions generated by the group to real-life problems
20	The final session reviews the course by means of a quiz. Group members then produce individual action plans for areas they feel they need further work in

Table 15.3 A general overview of ETS

Session 15 assignment
Think of an example of both a formal and informal rule and consider the purpose of each rule.
Formal rule
Purpose
Informal rule
Purpose

Table 15.4 Example of an ETS out-of-session assignment

Cognitive Skills Booster Programme

This programme is run by both the Prison and Probation Service and is designed to reinforce learning from general offending programmes (such as ETS) through skills rehearsal and relapse prevention.

Controlling Anger and Learning to Manage It (CALM)

The CALM programme is not designed to target offenders who have a poor institutional history of anger/aggression alone. It is aimed at those for whom anger/aggression features as a factor in either current or previous offending. Within this context, institutional behaviour provides additional information on the level of need. All referrals must meet the criteria of a previous or current offence which involved the expression of anger or another intense emotion. This criterion excludes the use of instrumental aggression that is used to achieve a purpose (e.g. street robbery).

The CALM programme has been developed specifically to meet the needs of offenders in managing emotions associated with the occurrence of aggression and antisocial behaviour. It uses a cognitive behaviour approach to teach offenders skills in managing anger and other emotions.

There are a number of programmes on offer which specifically target violent and sexual offenders, these are:

Cognitive Self Change Programme (CSCP)

This programme targets high-risk violent offenders and includes group and individual sessions. It equips prisoners with skills to help them control their violence and avoid re-conviction. It is aimed at offenders with a history of violent behaviour and is suitable for those whose violence is reactive and/or instrumental.

Sex Offender Treatment Programmes (SOTP)

In order for a sex offender to stop offending, he or she needs to be motivated to do so and needs to possess the insight, skills and strategies to avoid risk and control temptation. The Prison Service SOTP is based on established cognitive behaviour principles of the type known to be most effective in reducing risk of re-offending. The cognitive behaviour approach to treatment teaches clients to understand and control thinking, feelings and behaviour to achieve this goal.

A range of programmes are available for sexual offenders, providing a menu which is offered according to the level of risk and need of the offender. These are:

Core programme

The treatment goals of this programme include helping offenders develop understanding of how and why sexual offences were committed to increase awareness of victim harm issues and to develop meaningful life goals as part of a relapse prevention plan. The programme is targeted at male medium- and high-risk sex offenders. It challenges thinking patterns and develops victim empathy and relapse prevention skills.

Extended programme

This supplementary programme for high-risk offenders covers five treatment needs areas: dysfunctional thinking styles; emotion management; offence-related sexual fantasy; intimacy skills; and inadequate relapse prevention plans. It is targeted at male high- and very-high-risk sex offenders.

Adapted programme

Treatment goals are similar to the core programme, but treatment methods are adapted to suit learning-disabled sex offenders across all risk levels. The programme is designed to increase sexual knowledge, modify offence-justifying thinking, develop ability to recognize feelings in themselves and others, to gain an understanding of victim harm, and develop relapse prevention skills.

Rolling programme

This programme covers the same topics as the core programme but with less emphasis on obtaining an adequate offence account, and more emphasis on relationship skills and attachment deficits. It is targeted at male low- and medium-risk sex offenders, but sex offenders who have completed primary treatment programmes and who are serving long sentences can attend as a 'top up' programme.

Booster programme

This programme is designed to provide an opportunity for offenders to refresh their learning in treatment and to prepare for additional relapse prevention and release work.

Healthy Relationships Programme (HRP)

This intervention is designed for male offenders who demonstrate a risk of being violent to an intimate female partner. High-risk offenders receive a high-intensity programme while lower risk offenders receive a moderate-intensity programme. Both programmes target attitudes supporting or condoning domestic violence, poor emotional control, skills deficits and motivational issues.

Chromis

Chromis is a complex and intensive programme that aims to reduce violence in high-risk offenders whose level or combination of psychopathic traits disrupts their ability to accept treatment and change. Chromis has been specifically designed to meet the needs of highly psychopathic individuals and provides participants with the skills to reduce and manage their risk.

Prison Addressing Substance Related Offending (PASRO)

PASRO is a cognitive behaviour groupwork programme designed to address drug dependence and related offending. The programme targets offenders who are dependent on one or more drugs, or a combination of drugs and alcohol. Participants should be at risk of re-offending with a historical link between their substance dependence and offending or a likelihood that future untreated substance dependence would lead to re-offending.

The work of a forensic psychologist based in prison

Let me attempt to explain further what forensic psychologists based in prisons are and what we do. We are not typically 'profilers' as seen in movies such as *Silence of the Lambs*; that is generally the province of those in law enforcement, they are a rarity in this field. The word 'forensic' is derived from the Latin *forum*, the place where trials were conducted in Roman times. The current use of 'forensic' denotes a relationship between one professional field such as medicine, pathology, chemistry, anthropology and psychology, with the adversarial legal system (Goldstein, 2003).

Forensic psychologists work mainly in the Prison and Probation Services to develop intervention techniques and treatment programmes for use with both offenders and people under supervision. They develop one-to-one or group treatment interventions for offenders, people on community orders and others under supervision to address their offending behaviour and/or their psychological needs, for example, to manage depression, anger or anxiety. Using expertise based on psychological theory and research, forensic psychologists work closely with other professionals and agencies both in the assessment and treatment of individuals, and in the development of institutional policy and working practices.

Forensic psychology is concerned with the behaviour of individuals and with organizations within the judicial and penal systems, such as:

- offenders;

- victims;

- witnesses;

- judges and juries;

- prisoners and prison staff.

Much of the work of a forensic psychologist focuses on therapy in correctional settings where tasks typically involve:

- Carrying out one-to-one assessments, often to assess the risk of re-offending (e.g. for lifers being released into the community or sex offenders after a treatment programme) or of suicide, self-injury or other high-risk behaviour.

- Presenting findings from assessments to a wider staff audience.

- Developing and evaluating the contribution of assessment techniques such as psychometrics.

- Undertaking research projects to evaluate the contribution of specific service elements, policy initiatives or group programme developments, e.g. exploring programme 'drop-out' rates or evaluating a group programme.

- Participating in delivery or management of nationally recognized cognitive behaviour group programmes, e.g. Enhanced Thinking Skills, or severe personality disorder and sex offender treatment programmes.

- Checking and monitoring treatment groups to ensure standards and quality.

- Overseeing the training of Prison/Probation Service staff.

- Preparing risk assessment reports.

- Overseeing the provision of support during serious incidents.

- Advising prison governors on incidents such as riots, demonstrations and hostage taking.

- Liaising with and providing consultancy to hospital staff, prison officers, the police, social workers, probation officers, representatives of the judicial and legal systems and university staff.

- Attending team and area meetings.

Other tasks include:

- Management and administration.

- Analysing local, area and national policy to develop strategies for continuous improvement.

■ Casework notes and court work, sometimes including attendance and providing expert witness testimony.

Key concepts and terms

Accreditation   Forensic
Cognitive behaviour

Sample essay titles

■ Taking into consideration the 'What Works' literature, critically evaluate its usefulness in the punishment or rehabilitation debate.

■ Consider ways in which you might intervene with a prisoner displaying anger management problems towards other prisoners.

■ Why is skills-based training used in accredited offending behaviour programmes?

Further reading

Books

Hollin, C.R. (1989). *Psychology and Crime: An Introduction to Criminological Psychology*. London: Routledge.

Hollin, C.R. (Ed.) (2001). *Handbook of Offender Assessment and Treatment*. Chichester: Wiley.

Howitt, D. (2002). *Forensic and Criminological Psychology*. London: Prentice Hall.

McGuire, J. (Ed.) (1995). *What Works: Reducing Reoffending – Guidelines from Research and Practice*. Chichester: Wiley.

Needs, A., and Towl, G.J. (2003). *Applying Psychology to Forensic Practice*. Oxford: Blackwell.

Towl, G.J., and Crighton, D.A. (1996). *The Handbook of Psychology for Forensic Practitioners*. London: Routledge.

Journal articles

Andrews, D.A., Zinger, I., Hoge, R.D., Bonta, J., Gendreau, P., and Cullen, F.T. (1990). Does correctional treatment work? A clinically relevant and psychologically informed meta analysis. *Criminology*, 28, 369–404.

Izzo, R.L., and Ross, R.R. (1990). Meta-analysis of rehabilitation programmes for juvenile delinquents. *Criminal Justice and Behaviour*, 17, 134–142.

Ogloff, J.R.P., and Davis, M.R. (2004). Advances in offender assessment and rehabilitation: contributions of the risk-need-responsivity approach. *Psychology, Crime and Law*, 10, 229–242.

16 Concerning victims

Jonathan S. Ogan

The chief component of any crime, namely the victim, has been largely ignored in many areas of criminology and crime psychology. However, there is a growing concern with the people who suffer crime, an area of study that has come to be known as '**victimology**'. This chapter will focus on the victim, their characteristics and how victimization occurs.

Learning outcomes

When you have completed this chapter you should be able to:

1. Understand the concept of *victimology* and how the topic has moved away from the individual (micro level) to the wider scope of societal attitudes to victimization (macro level).
2. Consider how some characteristics make some people more open to victimization.
3. Know about the contexts of interpersonal crimes in terms of how the victim and offender meet in time and space.
4. Discuss how some victim characteristics may provide a 'pen picture' of the type of offender responsible for the crime.

Origins and development of victimology

Early research into victimology focused principally on the victim and offender within a crime, examining how these two agents came together and the types of crime that resulted. One piece of work in this vein can be found in Von Hentig's seminal work *The Criminal and his Victim*. Although written in the 1940s, it remains a classic on the subject of victimology. Ostensibly Von Hentig's book aimed to be an overview of criminology. However, it is through his final chapter focusing upon the victim and offender that the book has become most influential. Indeed, his chapter was the first in-depth analysis of the victim and the offender and has been acknowledged as the coining of the term the 'victim and offender relationship'. This term relates to the strength of relationship that exists between victim and offender. It is best viewed as a form of sliding scale or continuum, ranging from the intense and dynamic relationships found within the family, e.g. between husband/wife, parent and child, etc., to that where there is no discernible relationship present, such as crimes involving total strangers.

Other studies, notably Mendelsohn (1940), took the subject of victimology to a different level of interpretation and examined how far the victim's actions may have contributed to their victimization. In studying this form of victimology, Mendelsohn and subsequent researchers studied accident causation models to examine the chaining of events and what roles the victim and offender 'performed' during the crime. This led to the phrase 'victim facilitation', or the extent to which the victim contributed to the crime. Indeed, in a subsequent paper Mendelsohn (1956) questioned the role of women as 'victims' within sexual assault. He suggested that as women's sexual organs were internal they should have, in some way, been able to thwart their sexual assault. This viewpoint marked a shift from the relationship between victim and offender and moved towards the theoretical interpretation to societal reaction as to how a person becomes labelled as a victim.

This diversity of the subject is reflected in the definition provided by Foster (2001):

Victimology is a field of research that covers a wide range of offender/victim relations and attendant issues such as societal attitudes to rape. (Foster, 2001: 125)

Clearly, the topic has a wide-ranging set of issues that recognizes the dynamics found within the victim and offender relationship. This is often referred to as the micro level of victimology. In addition, victimology also covers the wider context of social attitudes to crime, victims and victimization, which is termed macro level victimology. The focus of this chapter will be upon the former, namely the micro level of the victim and offender relationship, and later what that tells us about the type of person most likely to have committed a serious interpersonal crime. However, the first step will be to identify the characteristics of the victim.

Figure 16.1 Who becomes a victim?
Source: © Janine Wiedel/Photofusion.

What makes a victim?

As noted earlier, Von Hentig's (1948) last chapter principally focused upon the interpersonal contexts in which victimization occurs and identified 13 types of victim. These attributes were:

- Young.

- Female.

- Old.

- Mentally defective (sic).

- Immigrants (sic).

- Minorities.

- Dull normals (sic).

- Depressed.

- Acquisitive.

- Wanton.

- Lonesome/heartbroken.

- Tormentor.

- Fighting victim.

While some of his terminology appears to be endowed with the negative stereotyping of some victim types, it has to be recognized that Von Hentig was writing in a different era using what was then considered appropriate terminology. Moreover, he was making the perceptive observation that people from different backgrounds and people with learning disabilities or mental illness were more prone to exploitation from others. This is a good point to start from as it shows that not all people are open to the same level of risk or forms of victimization. Indeed, Von Hentig's list can be compressed into two broad areas: victim demographics (age, gender, etc.), and victim lifestyle/habits.

Karmen (2001) identifies further factors that can impact on victimization whereby the target/victim has a number of risk factors that can be viewed as a form of continuum. If you examine the factors below, some objects may be more desirable than others, and aspects of security may also vary between target objects/people and so on.

Karmen cites four factors:

1. Attractiveness. This refers to whether the target object is in high demand so that the offender can sell it on to others, e.g. a top marque car or mobile phone. This list is ever changing as 'sat nav' devices are now particularly sought after. Previously it was laptops.
2. Proximity. This dimension relates to whether the offender can access the target either geographically or by person-to-person interaction. Some victims are selected simply because they are close at hand and so the offender does not have to travel great distances.
3. Deviant place. These are locations where crime can flourish. This tends to be where high numbers of people meet in time and place. Also, the police may seldom patrol them. Under these conditions they can become 'crime hot spots'. Logically, those people who frequent these areas will be at a higher risk of victimization than those who do not visit these 'hot spots'.
4. Vulnerability. This dimension refers to the target's ability to resist an attack. Ostensibly, the notion is of a person's vulnerability, e.g. elderly, very young or infirm; however, this may also relate to a building where the security is poor.

The above section helps to explain both the individual and thematic factors that may lead to someone becoming a victim, but neglects the roles of both offender and the setting in which the crime occurs.

Wrong place, wrong time: How the offender and victim meet

According to Hindelang, Gottfredson and Garofalo (1978), four conditions have to be met before any form of predatory crime can occur. These conditions are:

-   First, there are the two actors of victim and offender. Moreover, similarly to Cohen and Felson (1979), the two components must somehow meet in time and location.

-   Second, there must be some form of targeting by the offender of a suitable victim present in the area. (Here, there is an implicit acknowledgement of a victim 'type'.)

-   Third, there must be a propensity of one person (the offender) to victimize the other (the victim).

-   Fourth, the offender believes that force, or the threat of violence, will secure the target of their crime.

The transaction between victim and offender is best explained by understanding the circumstances that bring the potential victim and offender together. This is governed by their social and occupational activities and is termed **routine activity theory** (RAT). In essence, RAT refers to lifestyle and the places that one finds oneself in on a regular, hence the term 'routine', basis. Taking this a step further, Cohen and Felson (1979) argue that both the offender's legal and illegal activities will be interdependent upon each other. Thus, an offender will commit their crimes as a routine extension of their non-criminal day-to-day recreational and occupational activities.

It is the merging together of theories by Cohen and Felson (1979) and Hindelang et al (1978) that truly encapsulates the processes of victimization as these two sets of theorists address the following aspects:

1. The offender is motivated to offend against someone.
2. There is an identifiable victim.
3. The circumstances in which victim and offender meet in time and space.

Hindelang et al (1978) also suggest that the likelihood of victimization is raised when the victim enters areas of higher criminal activity (crime 'hot spots' as these high crime rate zones are called) at greater frequency than, for example, someone who only makes what can be characterized as a fleeting visit to the same area. In addition, people of similar lifestyles will tend to congregate together in greater frequency than non-similar groups. Therefore, people who interact together in much higher degrees of contact are more likely to become victimized by the same type of people. A very simple example is what the media have labelled as 'gangland hits' – murders committed by rival gang members. Here, the old saying 'birds of a feather flock together' aptly sums up this particular type of interpersonal context.

Focus 16.1

Added dangers for the commercial sex worker

The murders in 2006 in Suffolk of five commercial sex workers (prostitutes) have highlighted the added dangers that these women face and how the factor of lifestyle impacts on their proneness to victimization. In relation to their activities, consider how sex workers will be more open to assault and homicide. For example, as commercial sex work is illegal, they have to carry out their activities away from the relative safety of public settings. Thus, they tend to make 'ideal' victims in terms of the offender targeting their victim. Indeed, Church et al (2001) note the dangers that sex workers face in terms of sexual and physical assault, especially those working outdoors.

In a similar vein, if a serious crime is committed against a sex worker, it is difficult for the police to gain information from this group of people because the police are often regarded as the 'enemy' by sex workers as they arrest them for soliciting (offering sex for money). Second, their clients are also committing an illegal act and so are highly unlikely to come forward to volunteer information to help police with their enquiries. Moreover, problems exist in the wider social context because the general public are less likely to be concerned over such crimes as the victims are considered criminal themselves.

A further point to note in terms of added vulnerability is that Church et al (2001) recognize that a significant number of sex workers have an

Continued ...

... Continued

alcohol or drug dependency and so are a) in a desperate need to obtain money to maintain their addiction, and b) likely to be under the influence of drugs/alcohol, making them less able to defend themselves and make decisions as to whether their potential client looks 'safe'. This may be termed 'compound vulnerability': their initial characteristic, i.e. a commercial sex worker, makes them vulnerable to victimization. This is further compounded by added vulnerabilities such as being intoxicated, making them less able to decide on who is a 'safe' client or be clear-headed enough to extricate themselves from difficult situations with their 'clients', a lifestyle that is a very far cry from the sugary romance of Julia Roberts' character in *Pretty Woman*.

Victim selection

So far, there has been an implicit recognition of what makes the 'right sort of victim' from the offender's perspective, but we have not touched upon how this targeting of a 'soft' victim occurs. In explaining victim targeting, Lord et al (2002) likened the offender's victim selection strategies to those of a predator. They reasoned that the offender would identify suitable victims that conform to three criteria:

1. Desirability. This refers to the appeal of the resource need or 'target'. Thus, any form of 'target', whether a victim or an object such as cash or goods, could easily fit into this model.
2. Accessibility. This aspect relates to ease of approach and escape routes that the offender could use.
3. Vulnerability. This refers to how susceptible the target looks to attack. In relation to inanimate objects, this could mean a lack of security. In terms of a victim, this might be someone out alone on an empty street.

The utility of this model can be explored by the following hypothetical example of child sex-related abduction:

A young child outside of their home would be noted by the paedophile as a sexual target (desirability). They are out on their own with no-one about (vulnerability), the offender has a vehicle and is ready to abduct the child and speed away from the scene (accessibility). The presence of these conditions would lay this child open to a greater risk of victimization. However, if the same child is outside the home but this time out with their brothers and sisters, walking on the same street at a busy time when other folk are about, then this child would be less likely to be abducted.

As noted before, this model has utility in explaining property as well as interpersonal crimes and supplies a basic guide on crime prevention of property crimes. For example, if someone visibly uses a 'top of the range' mobile phone (desirability) outdoors and all alone (vulnerability), where there are a number of side streets to escape down (accessibility), then they have greater risk of their phone, i-pod or whatever being stolen. However, if they can reduce any of these factors, they will reduce their level of victimization. A good example here is health promotion: some campaigns inform us that if we want to reduce our chances of having coronary heart disease (CHD) we should eat less fatty food, reduce salt and take more exercise. Unfortunately, this does not mean that if we adopt this lifestyle we will never suffer from CHD, but the lifestyle change will reduce the likelihood of suffering some form of CHD. Similarly, in terms of victimization we may never be totally *safe*, but by taking certain precautions we can make ourselves *safer*.

By pulling together the strands of research in victim types, and how the victim and offender come together, we can present a much more comprehensive model to explain the processes involved in victimization (see below). It can be seen that crime does not occur in a vacuum; instead a number of factors come into play that will increase or, by avoiding certain situations, reduce the chance of victimization.

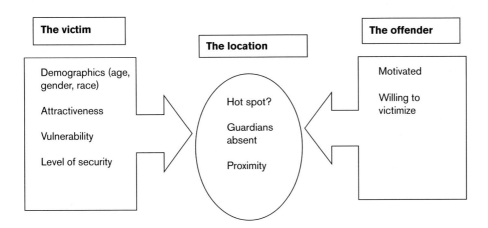

Figure 16.2 An integrated model of victimization.

Messner and Tardiff (1985) take this further and contend that crime is not a random set of variables comprising victim, location and offender that haphazardly come together; instead they contend that predictions can be made as to the interpersonal and social contexts in which certain crimes will occur. They also apply the principles of RAT to hypothesize that victimization will reflect typical social roles. For example, they argue that women are traditionally linked to domestic activities and thus are more susceptible to victimization in their own home than anywhere else. Conversely, men's activities take them outside the home setting on a regular basis and so make them liable to victimization by other young males engaging in a similar recreational activity, such as 'pub brawls' and football hooliganism. However, at a practical level this type of male-on-male violence is a very broad typology and so does not provide any fruitful strategies to reduce the pool of suspects under investigation. However, when we examine a much younger age group – child victims – there appears to be a more useful investigative aspect assumed by the victim in a criminal investigation.

Child sex abuse

In terms of violent offences against children, the routine activity (or lifestyle) of the victim becomes a critical factor in which type of person is likely to have committed the offence. Lord et al (2002) argue that a set of elements come into play that determine the relationship between the child's age and the strength of the relationship between the victim and the offender. The differing levels of relationship are based upon aspects of the child's age, their increasing independence from their families and how this is manifested in the frequency of solitary community activities that they engage in. Therefore, it can be seen that the vulnerability of very young children makes them more dependent on parental care and so their homicide is home-based, involving a parental figure, whereas scholars of high-school age are more susceptible to homicidal victimization by strangers.

On another dimension, Kuznetsov, Pierson and Harry (1992) believe that the victim's age is an important factor in defining sex abuse and creating offender typologies. Analyzing a large dataset of sexual offences (n = 827) they categorized the victims into three groups, broadly mirroring the ages of adulthood, adolescence and childhood. The three subsets revealed some interesting findings that set the offenders into three distinct groups.

Those offending against children were described as chronic sex offenders. Typically they were related to the victim, or knew their victim well, and so, due to the length of relationship in which they could effectively 'groom' the victim towards sexual compliance, and so used less force than the other groups.

Those offending against adolescents were more likely to be married and have children and would offend against both their own children and children who were strangers to them. In terms of personality or character the offenders appeared to be successful members of the community with very little setting them apart from the non-abusing member of society. Indeed, Kuznetsov et al (1992) described this as a veneer of normalcy.

However, those offending against adults tended to have more chaotic lifestyles and were described as antisocial, unmarried and younger in age than the other two groups of abusers. They also had criminal convictions for a variety of non-sexual offences and were most likely to carry a weapon to commit the sexual offence. The varied criminal career is a useful investigative point to note as it indicates that such offenders are not fixated in terms of their criminal careers and so are not *solely* sex offenders; instead they would be expected to have a police record involving a number of varied offences.

Child sexual homicide

While Kuznetsov et al (1992) have produced some interesting rules of thumb linking victim age to perpetrator characteristics, a more detailed appraisal of offender characteristics can be found in later research by Boudreaux, Lord and Durtra (1999) who studied the abduction and homicide of children. In a similar fashion to Kuznetsov et al (1992), Boudreaux et al (1999) break down the offences in terms of victim age groups and by overt motivation. As a brief summary, Boudreaux et al (1999) found that the sexual abductee homicide types listed below were likely to be committed by the following types of offenders.

High school children abductions (15–17 years of age)

These crimes involved a male offender with an average age of 26 years: 88 per cent were Caucasian. Fifty-seven per cent were strangers, 36 per cent were acquaintances and only 7 per cent were from the victim's immediate family. In 3 per cent of the cases the offender lived at the crime scene, increasing to 24 per cent living within one mile, 33 per cent living between one and five miles, and 21 per cent living over five miles from the victim's home. The method of death typically involved strangulation (in 43 per cent of the cases) or stabbing (31 per cent).

Elementary school children abductions (6–11 years of age)

These offences typically involved a male offender with an average age of 29.30 years: 86 per cent were Caucasian. Fifty-one per cent were strangers, 40 per cent were acquaintances and 15 per cent were family members. Eighteen per cent of the offenders lived at the crime scene, 34 per cent lived within one mile, and 16 per cent lived between one and five miles from the offence. Method of death followed a similar pattern to high school victims involving strangulation (44 per cent), knife wounds (17 per cent), blunt force injury (15 per cent) or suffocation (10 per cent).

Pre-school children abductions (3–5 years of age)

These offences involved a male offender with an average age of 26.40 years: 73 per cent of the offenders were Caucasian. Seventy per cent were acquaintances, while 30 per cent were strangers. The offence site (abduction site) demonstrated the highly localized nature of these crimes, involving a neighbour abducting a neighbour's child. Twenty-seven percent of children were abducted in the street, and 18 per cent were abducted from their yard. The offenders' living location mirrored the local nature of the crimes – 60 per cent lived within a mile of the crime scene. Use of weaponry is rare due to the young age of the victims, the cause of death typically being manual violence involving strangulation (38 per cent) with the same percentage of victims being suffocated.

As we discovered earlier in this chapter, these typologies form the basis of what can be called **age-specific interactions** that are in turn based upon the victim's routine activities. For instance, as the younger victim would seldom be unaccompanied out of the family setting, these children are abducted close to their home, whereas adolescents would be more adventurous and engage in more community activities with wider circles of acquaintances who in turn may victimize them. This is an important point to note. Finkelhor (1997) refers to these differing contexts of abuse as **developmental victimology**. In essence, this describes how the age of the child will affect the contexts in which the abuse occurs, together with the type of victim and offender relationship, such as whether the offender is a family member, family 'friend' or stranger.

Another important point to note is that Boudreaux et al's (1999) work is a statistical account of child abduction homicide covering a number of crime elements such as the weapon used and distance travelled by the offender. This marks their findings as being probabilistic in nature, featuring basic descriptive statistics (e.g. percentages and averages). As such, this offers the investigator a tangible guide as to the type of person responsible. Also, by virtue of a percentage being supplied, their research also presents a potential error rate. For example, if you read the full paper you will see that in the abduction homicide of all high school children 83 per cent are white; therefore by default 17 per cent will not be.

In conclusion, it can be seen that the victim's age as shown by Lord et al (2002) and Finkelhor (1997) can be indicative of the form of victim and offender relationship, i.e. the young child is more likely to be victimized by an offender who is a close family member, whereas the older child has an increased likelihood of stranger abuse. Moreover, an examination of Boudreaux et al's (1999) paper shows that the victim's age group can provide a much richer picture of the person responsible and the circumstances in which the crime occurs.

Conclusions

This chapter has covered the emergence of victimology in terms of its early emphasis on the victim and offender relationship to the wider perspective of the sociological interpretation of labelling a victim. This cultural shift towards the societal interpretation of crime and victimization neglects the victim and what their characteristics will tell us about the crime and the offender. The chapter has also demonstrated how the victimization process occurs, showing how both the victim and offender's attributes and recreational activities can all play their part in predicting who is likely to be victimized. In terms of the investigative aspects of victimology, this chapter has shown that there are limits to the victimological aspects of male-on-male adult violence in so much as the victim will tend to mirror the offender's demographics and lifestyle. However, the research findings reviewed in this chapter suggest that a form of 'investigative victimology' can be applied to provide fruitful lines of enquiry while investigating violent crimes against children.

Key concepts and terms

Age-specific interactions
Developmental victimology

Routine activity theory
Victimology

Sample essay titles

- To what extent can victim characteristics aid identification of who has victimized them?

- Individuals are responsible for their own victimization. Discuss.

Further reading

Books

Karmen, A. (2001). *Crime Victims: An Introduction to Victimology*, (4th Ed.). London: Wadsworth.

Walklate, S. (2001). *Gender, Crime and Criminal Justice*. Cullompton, Devon: Willan.

Useful websites

www.homeoffice.gov.uk (A good source of victim and recorded crime statistics in the UK, along with details of Government initiatives.)

www.victimology.nl/ (A useful international website that holds a number of news items on the developments of victimology, with links to other relevant sources of information.)

www.ncvc.org (An American website of the National Criminal Victim Center, useful for crime and victim statistics.)

www.rainn.org/ (A website of the Rape Abuse and Incest National Network [RAINN] that provides the reader with information on serious sexual crimes in America.)

www.fbi.org (The FBI's website, a useful resource for their national crime figures and research findings on a variety of topics.)

17 The future of psychology and crime

David Canter

The many processes that give rise to changes in the nature of criminality are discussed. They include the obvious issues of the internet and related technologies as well as the associated globalization, including easier travel between countries. Related changes in society also need to be considered. The changing family structure and role of women as well as the emerging ideological battles between different religious and ethical frameworks all create fertile ground in which new forms of criminality will grow. Psychologists seem destined to chase these trends rather than be ahead of them, but a revised evolutionary perspective that recognizes that crimes will emerge to fill the environmental niches that are available could change this. Such a perspective will require closer integration between psychological, sociological and technical approaches to crime.

Learning outcomes

When you have completed this chapter you should be able to:

1. Discuss the changes in the world that are relevant for considering the developing nature of crime and criminality.
2. Appreciate how offenders and their actions evolve in relation to their social and personal context.
3. Consider the possible significance of psychology for helping to prevent crime.
4. Appreciate the challenges to psychological research that are inherent in the evolving nature of crime and criminality.
5. Understand that there are many questions about the psychology of crime that still remain to be answered.

Changes in how we live

Criminal actions operate on the opportunities available, whether this is other people or property that those people own. Therefore as the opportunities change, so do the crimes. If psychologists are to play any role in understanding, predicting or managing crimes then the unfolding opportunities and their implications for human behaviour need to be understood. The variety and range of emerging opportunities for crime are mind-boggling. They include those listed in Table 17.1.

Developments	Opportunities for criminals
Increased wealth throughout the world, while there are still big differences between the rich and the poor	More wealth to be stolen or fought over, with plenty of people feeling injustices
A greater number of consumer goods, often smaller and more portable	More desirable objects that are easier to steal
Information and communication being stored and transmitted electronically around the world	Access to crucial information such as identities and bank accounts can be obtained in cyberspace
Developments in technology	Technology becomes a target as well as a tool for criminality
Open borders between many countries	Criminals can move without hindrance
Increased ease of movement around the world	Criminals can move much greater distances
Improved crime prevention	More violent crime to overcome protective devices

Table 17.1 Developments and emerging opportunities for crime

Activity 17.1

Consider any of the items in the list provided of changes in society over the last 10 years and discuss the implication it has for how particular crimes may be committed and who may commit them. Does this challenge any psychological explanations of crime?

These economic and technological changes are also being joined by big social changes which drive and are driven by some similar processes as well as having their own momentum. As indicated in Table 17.2, they carry implications for the nature of criminals and their criminality as much as for the sorts of offences they commit. Many of these changes have direct implications for how individuals see the world and their fundamental ethical stands.

Social changes	Implications for criminals
Breakdown of traditional religious and moral frameworks combined with re-emergence of fundamentalist belief systems	The origins of offenders may be in wider areas of society and from unusual backgrounds
Reduction in the power of the nuclear family and family discipline	Criminogenic backgrounds more widely dispersed through social groups
Wider education and increased technological skills and availability	The increasing ease of use of many emerging technologies means more offenders have the skills needed to abuse them
The increased cultural mix of many cities	Offenders drawn from a wider ethnic and cultural background

Table 17.2 Social changes of relevance to the nature of offenders

There are two important points about the nature of criminals that derive from these changes. On the one hand, those who may have become a certain type of criminal in the past may in the future turn to different sorts of crime. So bank robbers may turn to penetration of internet accounts and stalkers may harass their victims over e-mail, or through Facebook and YouTube. On the other hand, new forms of criminal are emerging, driven by the re-emerging fundamentalist beliefs or the excitement they see in cybercrime. In the past centuries anarchists and urban guerrillas also attacked because of their beliefs in an unjust world, and young men broke into houses because of the thrills that provided. But it is an open question as to whether the terrorists and hackers of today are drawn from the same psychological mix as their analogous counterparts from a hundred years ago.

Psychologists are thus faced with the question of whether those who would offend are likely to be the same sorts of people as they would have been in the past, but now acting in different ways, or whether new sorts of people are becoming criminal. This raises the fundamental question of whether the sorts of explanations and categorizations of crime and criminals that have been such a dominant part of the present volume will still be relevant in the future or whether some rather different approaches to the psychology of crime will be necessary.

A really evolutionary theory of crime

One way of conceptualizing the future of crimes is to recognize that crime has always emerged in relation to the context and opportunities for breaking the norms of society. This is a much more solidly evolutionary approach to crime than the rather bizarre search for atavistic origins of offending within humanity's distant animal heritage. It sees behaviour as emerging in response to the niches that are made available by the way people relate to each other. Such behaviour may well be passed down from one generation to the next in many different ways, but it will continually evolve in relation to changing circumstances.

This evolution is partly a product of changes within the direct experiences of individuals, either within the family or in the culture and ideology to which that person is exposed. It is also partly a product of changes in the opportunities for crime and the way those opportunities are assessed by those who, for whatever reason, have the potential for criminality. Thus when ships had no ready contact with the shore and spent many months at sea with valuable cargo, piracy was a constant threat. It still is a problem in those parts of the world where a rapid response from law enforcement is unlikely. Highwaymen could similarly rob stagecoaches because of their isolation on some journeys. Today there are some forms of crime that only occur on very long train journeys, such as thieves who politely offer fellow travellers biscuits that are laced with sedatives so that they can steal from them when they are knocked out by the drug. Or the 'door-pushers' that Canter (2005b) describes in Las Vegas who take advantage of the vast number of hotel doors in that city to look for the very small number that are not locked properly so they can steal from what the hotel guest has left in the room.

The many forms of opportunity for crime that the internet provides have predictably spawned a new generation of criminals for whom this is their hunting ground. However, the increase in security also requires those who would steal or rob to find new ways of getting away with their crimes. They may decide to be more violent, attacking people to steal their cars, when in the past they would just have stolen the car and jump started it. It is noticeable how many fewer aeroplane hijackings there have been since airport security has been strengthened, but the number of kidnappings has increased.

The question for psychologists in all this is whether these changes are bringing new sorts of people into criminality or whether criminals have always been the same but find their outlets in different ways. The answer is probably a bit of both. It is certainly the case that the sort of people who would have sold snake oil as a panacea in Victorian times will now have websites selling equally useless products. It is even the case that people who stalked an estranged loved one in the past by sitting outside her house or sending her endless letters will these days fill her answer-phone with messages and bombard her with e-mails. Therefore many of the psychological processes discussed in this volume will still be relevant for many of the crimes of the future. It may even be suggested that the young drop-out that Charles Dickens portrays in *Oliver Twist* as stealing from gentlemen on the street, under the management of Fagin, a criminal mastermind, may now be set to work at computer terminals by a latter-day Fagin to send fraudulent offers of business contracts by e-mail.

Activity 17.2

The crimes they are a changing

Which of the following are truly new areas of criminality which require rather new forms of psychological explanation and which are really well-established forms of crime that are now carried out in a new way or a different context from earlier? What offences are missing from this list?

If you want to find out what they are, just use a www search engine such as Google.

Figure 17.1 New technology opens up new opportunities for crime.
Source: Olivier Pirard/Rex Features.

- Advanced fee (419) fraud e-mails
- Car-jacking
- Cyber-stalking
- 'Happy-slapping'
- Computer hacking
- Hoax e-mails
- Identity fraud
- Phishing
- Suicide bombing
- Urban terrorism

Figure 17.2 The aftermath of terrorist bombing in London.
Source: Rex Features.

Activity 17.3

Consider any of the crimes listed that are chosen because they are not mentioned in the rest of the book and discuss how psychology may elucidate their causes and help various agencies who may have to deal with them. Does any of this imply the development of new research methodologies?

The changing culture and opportunities are probably also drawing some people into criminality who in earlier generations would not have been the sorts of people who would have committed crimes. The fundamentalist young men and women who become suicide bombers may have some counterparts in earlier generations, but as Canter (2006) suggests, the psychological processes that are now at play may have some rather different emphases. Others may regard the possibility of defrauding large anonymous organizations, such as insurance companies, as not really a crime at all, when in times past those same people would have had such direct contact with the same companies that they would never have thought of cheating them.

It is therefore an open question as to the extent that there will emerge new forms of crime or new forms of criminal.

Crime prevention

One issue that has not really been touched on directly in the present book is the contribution that psychology can make to the reduction and prevention of crime. Of course, one of the most powerful ways in which psychologists help is by reducing the number of people who become criminal and, of those that do, reducing the number who return to crime after being caught. There is still an open question about how much psychologists really can offer to either of these. Yet as discussed in earlier chapters some progress is being made in the managing of offenders in prisons and mental hospitals. Perhaps even more important is the contribution that educational and child psychologists can make to children who have difficulties in their early years.

Many offenders try to avoid capture and do find the risk of apprehension a serious constraint on their criminality. So the contribution that investigative psychology is making to the development of decision-support systems for the police such as geographical profiling (Canter, 2005b) and help to crime analysts, as discussed by Clarke and Eck (2003), are important ways in which crime reduction is being assisted by behavioural science.

The understanding of how criminals make decisions and the situations they choose to commit crimes also is elucidated by the sorts of considerations in earlier chapters. These perspectives are finding their way into more general criminological considerations about **crime prevention**. Indeed, this is one area in which the borders between criminal psychology and traditional criminology are very vague. The cognitive processes of an offender may lead to a distortion in his or her understanding of what targets are safe to attack or worthwhile attacking. This may be reflected in criminological processes such as 'repeat victimization' as discussed by Farrell (2005) for example. Yet there have been no detailed attempts to link these two perspectives together.

In general, psychological and social psychological perspectives on offenders have been remarkably absent from the consideration of crime prevention. This is in part due to the difference, noted in the opening chapter, between the focus of criminologists and of psychologists. Those who see themselves as studying crime tend to deal with volume crime and often characterize their work as being as much about delinquency and deviance as about criminality. They thus tend to be considering young offenders involved in relatively minor crimes. Crime prevention thus focuses on deterrence and target hardening. But as we have seen in our chapters on rape and homicide, these more serious crimes tend to be perpetrated by older offenders and there is more of a possibility of their having some obvious mental disorder (although, as we saw in Chapter 4, that relationship is not as clear cut as might be expected). It is these older more serious offenders with whom criminal psychologists often work. Bridging these two realms is an important future development for a more thorough approach to crime prevention.

Changing roles

Throughout this book a great variety of roles for crime psychologists have been described as well as a range of contexts in which they operate. These exist in many different sorts of institutions and working with many different agencies. There seems to be no reduction in the contributions of psychology to the understanding and management of crime. It therefore seems very likely that the contributions of psychologists will continue to expand relating to new areas of crime control and new ways of dealing with offenders, often in unpredictable ways.

Some of these developments will doubtless relate to the new forms of crime that are emerging as well as the recognition of emerging forms of criminality. One significant example, explored in Chapter 6, is the identification of harassment, or in popular parlance 'stalking', as a crime. By creating laws that deal with this behaviour specifically the way is open for the search for treatment programmes or other ways of managing this behaviour, which in the past would just have been regarded as a nuisance.

The realms of psychological expertise are also broadening and whenever the expertise becomes established enough for wider recognition there are pressures to draw it into court cases. One unusual example described by Canter (2008) is the use of environmental psychology principles to support the case for human rights abuse in prison solitary confinement. Other examples of new, emerging expert evidence are reviewed by Kennedy and Sakis (2008), dealing for example with the liability that organizations may have for creating environments that facilitate criminality. The specification of new syndromes, such as 'battered wife syndrome', also creates opportunities for psychological evidence in court, although not without its difficulties as Kennedy (2008) makes clear.

In all of this the professional psychologist offers an ethical framework and opinion rooted wherever possible in empirical research. As in so many other areas of human progress the scientific tradition eventually survives over other more subjective, biased approaches.

The challenge to research

It is research and a scientific basis that distinguishes psychology from personal opinion and ideology. However, as has emerged many times throughout this volume, there are many challenges to carrying out crime psychology research. Modern psychology grew out of laboratory and clinical studies, mainly with institutional subject groups. But crime has to be studied on the streets. Examining how people may cheat in laboratory experiments or if they will generate aggressive behaviour having watched a film of violence are so far removed from the rough and tumble of the day-to-day world outside of the controlled circumstances of a laboratory that such pure studies can only hint at genuine processes. People in institutions are also subject to so many significant pressures that their reactions have to be carefully evaluated before any generalizations can be made.

Once psychologists get out of their institutions and laboratories they discover that they do not have all the answers to all the world's problems. Crime, like many other areas of human activity, requires a fundamentally multidisciplinary approach. A burglary or violent assault in a public house, a fraud carried out over the internet, or a terrorist attack can never be fully understood only from the examination of the individual involved. Their social, economic, political and cultural context all play a part and thus need to be integrated into our understanding. The changing nature of crime and criminality, as well as the broadening **roles of psychologists**, therefore provides very severe challenges to how psychological studies of criminals are carried out.

Conclusions

The consideration of a wide range of human activity in the present volume has stretched the boundaries of what is often regarded as 'psychological'. The methodologies for the studies described are also often a long way from the ethereal purity to which many academic psychologists aspire. There has been virtually no mention of 'control groups', or 'dependent' variables; hardly a single analysis of variance has been mentioned. Some may see this as indicating the weakness of the field because it lacks what they regard as scientific rigour. But the rapid development of criminal psychology indicates otherwise. It suggests that by developing research tools and approaches that are relevant to the questions to be answered, rather than shaping the questions to fit the tools available, a fruitful discipline is emerging, which very many people find to be extremely valuable. It is really still too early to determine how this discipline will unfold, but the considerable interest in it from the current generation of students does show that it certainly has a vibrant future.

Crime psychology is still very much part of the broader science and profession of psychology. It therefore is very likely to continue to influence its parent discipline. It can be seen to be leading to a rather different sort of psychology from that which is often considered mainstream. The study of crime requires psychologists to consider very carefully not only the more obvious ethical and professional implications of what they do, but also the consequences of their growing involvement with the many and various agencies that deal with crime and criminals. There may be a general message here for the way in which the practice of psychology changes when it engages with real world issues.

Key concepts and terms

Crime prevention
Evolutionary theory of crime

Role of psychologists
Social developments

Sample essay titles

You will certainly need to consider this book as a whole in answering these essays, not just the details in the present chapter.

- Which do you think is most likely to change in the future: the types of crimes that are committed or the sorts of people who commit crimes?

- How might psychologists contribute to crime prevention?

- What roles do you see for crime psychologists?

- Is there any difference between criminal psychology and criminology?

- Can crime be studied in a laboratory?

- Does the study of criminal psychology have relevance to understanding non-criminal behaviour?

Further reading

Books

Canter, D., and Zukauskiene, R. (Eds) (2008). *Psychology and Law: Bridging the Gap*. Aldershot: Ashgate.

Tilley, N. (Ed.) (2005). *Handbook of Crime Prevention and Community Safety*. Cullompton, Devon: Willan.

Journal articles

Association of British Insurers (2000). Future crime trends in the UK. London: Association of British Insurers http://projects.bre.co.uk/frsdiv/crimetrends/Crime_Trends_Report.pdf

Witte, A.D. (1993). Some thoughts on the future of research in crime and delinquency. *Journal of Research in Crime and Delinquency*, 30, 513–524.

References

Agnew, R. (1984). Appearance and delinquency. *Criminology*, 22, 421–440.

Agnew, R. (1990). The origins of delinquent events: An examination of offender accounts. *Journal of Research in Crime and Delinquency*, 27, 267–294.

Aichhorn, A. (1925). *Wayward Youth*. New York: Meridian Books.

Ainsworth, P. (2001). *Offender Profiling and Crime Analysis*. Cullompton, Devon: Willan.

Ainsworth, P.B. (2002). *Psychology and Policing*. Cullompton, Devon: Willan.

Ainsworth, P.B., and Pease, K. (1987). *Police Work*. London: The British Psychological Society and Methuen.

Akers, R. (1977). *Deviant Behaviour: A Social Learning Approach*, (2nd Ed.). Belmont: Wadsworth.

Akers, R., Krohn, M., Lanza-Kaduce, L., and Radosevich, M. (1979). Social Learning and Deviant Behaviour: A Specific Test of a General Theory. *American Sociological Review*, 44, 636–655.

Aldridge, M.L., and Browne, K.D. (2003). Perpetrators of spousal homicide: A review. *Trauma, Violence and Abuse*, 4, 265–276.

Alison, L., Bennell, C., Mokros, A., and Ormerod, D. (2002). The personality paradox in offender profiling: A theoretical review of the processes involved in deriving background characteristics from crime scene actions. *Psychology, Public Policy, and Law*, 8, 115–135.

American Psychiatric Association (2000). *Diagnostic and Statistical Manual of Mental Disorders, Text Revision*. (4th Ed.). Washington, DC: American Psychiatric Association.

Amir, M. (1971). *Patterns in Forcible Rape*. University of Chicago Press, Chicago.

Andrews, D.A., Zinger, I., Hoge, R.D., Bonta, J., Gendreau, P., and Cullen, F.T. (1990) Does correctional treatment work? A clinically relevant and psychologically informed meta analysis. *Criminology*, 28, 369–404.

Arbuthnot, J., and Gordon, D.A. (1986). Behavioural and cognitive effects of a moral reasoning development intervention for high risk behavior-disordered adolescents. *Journal of Consulting and Clinical Psychology*, 54, 208–216.

Arrigo, B.A., and Purcell, C.E. (2001). Explaining paraphilia and lust murder: Toward an integrated model. *International Journal of Offender Therapy and Comparative Criminology*, 45, 6–31.

Arseneault, L., Tremblay, R.E., Boulerice, B., Seguin, J.R. and Saucier, J-F. (2000a). Minor physical anomalies and family adversity as risk factors for violent delinquency in adolescence. *American Journal of Psychiatry*, 157, 917–923.

Arseneault, L., Moffitt, T.E., Capsi, A., Taylor, P.J., and Silva, P.A. (2000b). Mental disorders and violence in a total birth cohort: Results from the Dunedin Study. *Archives of General Psychiatry*, 57, 979–986.

Association of British Insurers (2000). Future Crime Trends in the UK. London: Association of British Insurers. http://projects.bre.co.uk/frsdiv/crimetrends/Crime_Trends_Report.pdf

Attorney-General (NSW) v. John Fairfax Publications (1999). NSWSC 318.

Baldwin, J. (1993). Police Interview Techniques: Establishing Truth or Proof? *British Journal of Criminology*, 33, 325–352.

Ball, J., Rosen, L., Flueck, J.A., and Nurco, E.N. (1981). 'The criminality of heroine addicts; when addicted and when off opiates.' In: J.A. Inciardi (Ed.), *The Drugs Crime Connection*. Beverly Hills, CA: Sage, 39–66.

Bandura, A. (1976). 'Social learning analysis of aggression.' In: E. Ribes-Inesta and A. Bandura (Eds), *Analysis of Delinquency and Aggression*. Hillsdale, NJ: Lawrence Erlbaum.

Bank, L., Forgatch, M.S., Patterson, G.R., Fetrow, R.A. (1993). Parenting practices of single mothers: Mediators of negative contextual factors. *Journal of Marriage and the Family*, 55, 371–384.

Barker, M. (2000). 'The criminal range of small-town burglars.' In: D. Canter and L. Alison (Eds), *Profiling Property Crimes*. Aldershot: Dartmouth Publishing, 57–106.

Barrett, B., and Byford, S. (2007). Collecting service use data for economic evaluation in DSPD populations: Development of the secure facilities service use schedule. *British Journal of Psychiatry*, 190 (suppl. 49), s75–s78.

Bartlett, F.C. (1932). *Remembering: A Study in Experimental and Social Psychology.* Cambridge: Cambridge University Press.

Bartol, C.R. (1991). *Criminal Behaviour: A Psychosocial Approach*, (3rd Ed.). Englewood Cliffs, NJ: Prentice Hall.

Bartol, C.R. (1996). *Police psychology: Then, now and beyond. Criminal Justice and Behaviour*, 23, 70–89.

Bartol, C.R. (1999). *Criminal behaviour: A psychosocial approach*, (5th Ed.). Upper Saddle River, NJ: Prentice-Hall.

Bartol, C.R., and Bartol, A. M. (2006). 'History of forensic psychology.' In: I.B. Weiner and A.K. Hess (Eds), *The Handbook of Forensic Psychology*, (3rd Ed.). Hoboken, NJ: John Wiley, 3–27.

Beaton, A., Cook, M., Kavanagh, M., and Herrington, C. (2000). The psychological impact of burglary. *Psychology, Crime and Law*, 6, 33–43.

Becker, H. (1963). *Outsiders: Studies in the Sociology of Deviance.* New York: Free Press.

Beeghley, L. (2003). *Homicide: A Sociological Explanation.* Latham, MD: Rowan and Littlefield.

Bennett, T. (1998). *Drugs and Crime: The Results of Research in Drug Testing and Interviewing Arrestees.* Home Office Research Study 183. London: Home Office.

Bennett, T., and Wright, R. (1984). *Burglars on Burglary.* Aldershot: Gower.

Bernasco, W., and Luykx, F. (2003). Effects of attractiveness, opportunity and accessibility to burglars on residential burglary rates of urban neighbourhoods. *Criminology*, 41, 981–1001.

Bernasco, W., and Nieuwbeerta, P. (2004). How do residential burglars select target areas? A new approach to the analysis of criminal location choice. *British Journal of Criminology*, 45, 296–315.

Bevis, C., and Nutter, J.B. (1977). 'Changing street layouts to reduce residential burglary.' In: G. Rengert and J. Wasilchick (1986), *Suburban Burglary. A Time and a Place for Everything.* Springfield, IL: Charles C. Thomas, 85.

Bijleveld, C., and Smit, P. (2006). Homicide in the Netherlands: On the structuring of homicide typologies. *Homicide Studies*, 10, 195–219.

Black (1963). In: M. Maguire and T. Bennett (1982), *Burglary in a Dwelling.* London: Heinemann, 65.

Blackburn, R. (1994). *The Psychology of Criminal Conduct: Theory, Research and Practice.* Chichester: Wiley.

Blau, T.H., Super, J.T., and Brady, L. (1993). The MMPI good cop/bad cop profile in identifying dysfunctional law enforcement personnel. *Journal of Police and Criminal Psychology*, 9, 1–4.

Blumstein, A., Cohen, J., and Farrington, D. (1988). Criminal career research: Its value for criminology. *Criminology*, 26, 1–36.

Bohl, N. (1995). 'Professionally administered critical incident debriefing for police officers.' In: J.T. Reese, J.M. Horn, and C. Dunning (Eds), *Critical Incidents in Policing.* Washington, DC: US Government Printing Office.

Bond, C.F. Jr., and DePaulo, B.M. (2006). Accuracy of deception judgments. *Personality and Social Psychology Review*, 10, 214–234.

Bonta, J., Law, M., and Hanson, K. (1998). The prediction of criminal and violent recidivism among mentally disordered offenders: A meta-analysis. *Psychiatric Bulletin*, 123, 123–142.

Borgatti, S., Everett, M., and Freeman, L. (2002). Ucinet 6.109 for Windows: Software for Social Network Analysis. Harvard, MA: Analytic Technologies.

Boudreaux, M., Lord, W., and Durtra, R. (1999) Child abduction: Age-based analyses of offender, victim, and offense characteristics in 550 cases of alleged child disappearance. *Journal of Forensic Sciences*, 44, 539–553.

Bowlby, J. (1944). Forty four juvenile thieves. *International Journal of Psychoanalysis*, 25, 1–57.

Bowlby, J. (1952). *Maternal Care and Mental Health*. Geneva: World Health Organization.

Bowman, P.C., and Auerbach, S.M. (1982). Impulsive youthful offenders; multimodal cognitive behavioural treatment programme. *Criminal Justice and Behaviour*, 9, 432–454.

Brandt, D. (2006). *Delinquency, Development, and Social Policy*. New Haven: University Press.

Brewer, K. (2000). *Psychology and Crime*. London: Heinemann.

Brewer, N., and Williams, K.D. (Eds) (2005). *Psychology and Law: An Empirical Perspective*. London: Guilford.

Brigham, J. (1999). What is forensic psychology anyway? *Law and Human Behaviour*, 23, 273–298.

Briscoe, O., Carson, D., d'Orban, P., et al. (1993). 'The law, adult mental disorder, and the psychiatrist in England and Wales.' In: J. Gunn and P.J. Taylor (Eds), *Forensic Psychiatry: Clinical, Legal and Ethical Issues*. London: Butterworth-Heinemann, 21–117.

Brookman, F. (2005). *Understanding Homicide*. Portland, OR: Sage.

Brown, B.B., and Altman, I. (1981). 'Territoriality and residential crime: A conceptual framework.' In: P.J. Brantingham and P.L. Brantingham (Eds), *Environmental Criminology*, Prospect Heights, IL: Waveland, 55–76.

Brown, J. (2000). 'Occupational culture as a factor in the stress experiences of police officers.' In: F. Leishman, B. Loveday and S. Savage (Eds), *Core Issues in Policing*, (2nd Ed.). Harlow: Pearson Education.

Brown, J.M., and Campbell, E.A. (1994). *Stress and Policing: Sources and Strategies*. Chichester: Wiley.

Brown, L., and Willis, A. (1985). Authoritarianism in British police: Importation, socialisation or myth? *Journal of Occupational Psychology*, 58, 97–108.

Brown, M.R. (1926). *Legal Psychology: Psychology Applied to the Trial of Cases, to Crime and its Treatment, and to Mental States and Processes*. Indianapolis, IN: Bobbs-Merrill.

Brown, S.L., and Forth, A.E. (1997). Psychopathy and sexual assault: Static risk factors, emotional precursors, and rapists subtypes. *Journal of Consulting and Clinical Psychology*, 65, 848–857.

Browne, K., and Herbert, M. (1997). *Preventing Family Violence*. Chichester: Wiley.

Brownmiller, S. (1975). *Against our Will: Men, Women and Rape*. New York: Simon and Schuster.

Brugman, D., and Aleva, E. (2004). Developmental delay or regression in moral reasoning by juvenile delinquents? *Journal of Moral Education*, 33, 321–338.

Budd, T. (1999) *Burglary of Domestic Dwellings: Findings from the British Crime Survey*. Home Office Statistical Bulletin, issue 4/99. London: Home Office.

Budd, T., Sharp, C., and Mayhew, P. (2005). *Offending in England and Wales: First Results from the 2003 Crime and Justice Survey*. Home Office Research Study No. 275, London: Home Office.

Bull, R., and Horncastle, P. (1989). 'An evaluation of human awareness training.' In: R. Morgan and D.J. Smith (Eds), *Coming to Terms with Policing*. London: Routledge.

Bull, R., and Horncastle, P. (1994). Evaluation of police recruit training involving psychology. *Psychology, Crime and Law*, 1, 143–149.

Bull, R., Bustin, R., Evans, P., and Gahagan, D. (1983). *Psychology for Police Officers*. Chichester: Wiley.

Burbeck, E., and Furnham, A. (1984). Personality and police selection: Trait differences in the successful and non-successful applicants to the Metropolitan Police. *Personality and Individual Differences*, 5, 257–263.

Burt, M.R. (1980). Cultural myths and supports for rape. *Journal of Personality and Social Psychology*, 38, 217–230.

Burtt, H.E. (1931). *Legal Psychology*. New York: Prentice-Hall.

Cairns, H. (1935). *Law and the Social Sciences*. New York: Harcourt Brace.

Campbell, J.C. (1986). Nursing assessment of risk of homicide for battered women. *Advances in Nursing Science*, 8, 36–51.

Campbell, J.C. (1995). 'Prediction of homicide of and by battered women.' In: J.C. Campbell (Ed.), *Assessing the Risk of Dangerousness: Potential for Further Violence of Sexual Offenders, Batterers, and Child Abusers*. Newbury Park, CA: Sage, 96–113.

Cannon-Bowers, J., Salas, E., and Converse, S. (1993). 'Shared mental models in expert team decision making.' In: N. Castellan (Ed.), *Individual and Group Decision Making: Current Issues*. Hillsdale, NJ: Erlbaum, 221–246.

Canter, D. (1989). Offender profiling. *The Psychologist*, January, 12–16.

Canter, D. (1994). *Criminal Shadows*. London: Harper Collins.

Canter, D. (1995). 'Psychology of offender profiling.' In: R. Bull and D. Carson (Eds), *Handbook of Psychology in Legal Contexts*. Chichester: Wiley, Chapter 4.5, 343–335.

Canter, D.V. (1997). The status of the expert in legal proceedings. *Forensic Update*, 51, 29–35.

Canter, D.V. (1999). 'Equivocal death.' In: D.V. Canter and L.J. Alison (Eds), *Offender Profiling Series: Vol. 2. Profiling in Policy and Practice*. Aldershot: Ashgate, 123–156.

Canter, D. (2000). 'Destructive organisational psychology.' In: D. Canter and L. Alison (Eds), *The Social Psychology Of Crime: Groups, Teams and Networks*. Aldershot: Ashgate.

Canter, D.V. (2005a). 'Suicide or murder? Implicit narratives in the Eddie Gilfoyle case.' In: L. Alison (Ed.), *The Forensic Psychologist's Casebook: Psychological Profiling and Criminal Investigation*. Cullompton, Devon: Willan, 315–333.

Canter, D.V. (2005b). *Mapping Murder: The Secrets of Geographical Profiling*. London: Virgin.

Canter, D. (2006). The Samson syndrome: is there a kamikaze psychology? *21st Century Society*, 1, 107–127.

Canter, D.V. (2007). *Mapping Murder: The Secrets of Geographical Profiling*, (2nd Ed.). London: Virgin.

Canter, D. (2008). 'In the kingdom of the blind.' In: D. Canter and R. Zukauskiene (Eds), *Psychology and Law: Bridging the Gap*. Aldershot: Ashgate, 1–22.

Canter, D., and Alison, L. (Eds) (1999). *Interviewing and Deception*. Aldershot: Ashgate/Dartmouth.

Canter, D.V., and Alison, L. (2000a). *Profiling Propery Crimes*. Aldershot: Ashgate/Dartmouth.

Canter, D., and Alison, L. (Eds) (2000b). *The Social Psychology of Crime: Groups, Teams and Networks*. Aldershot: Ashgate.

Canter, D., and Alison, L.J. (2003). Converting evidence into data: The use of law enforcement archives as unobtrusive measurement. *The Qualitative Report*, 8, 151–176.

Canter, D., and Fritzon, K. (1998) Differentiating arsonists: A model of firesetting actions and characteristics. *Legal and Criminal Psychology*, 3, 73–96.

Canter, D., and Heritage, R. (1990). A multivariate model of sexual offence behaviour: developments in 'offender profiling'. *Journal of Forensic Psychiatry*, 1, 185–212.

Canter, D., and Larkin, P. (1993). The environmental range of serial rapists. *Journal of Environmental Psychology*, 13, 63–69.

Canter, D.V., and Wentink, N. (2004). An empirical test of the Holmes and Holmes serial murder typology. *Criminal Justice and Behavior*, 31, 489–515.

Canter, D., and Youngs, D. (2003). 'Beyond "offender profiling": The need for an investigative psychology.' In: D. Carson and R. Bull (Eds), *Handbook of Psychology in Legal Contexts*, (2nd Ed.). Chichester: Wiley, 171–205.

Canter, D., and Youngs, D. (2008a). *Investigative Psychology: Offender Profiling and the Analysis of Criminal Action*. Chichester: Wiley.

Canter, D., and Youngs, D. (2008b). 'Geographical offender profiling: Applications and opportunities.' In: D. Canter and D. Youngs (Eds), *Principles of Geographical Offender Profiling*. Aldershot: Ashgate, 3–24.

Canter, D., and Zukauskiene, R. (Eds) (2008). *Psychology and Law: Bridging the Gap*. Aldershot: Ashgate.

Canter, D., Missen, C., and Hodge, S. (1996). Are serial killers special? *Policing Today*, 22–28.

Canter, D., Hughes, D., and Kirby, S. (1998). Paedophilia: Pathology, criminality, or both? The development of a multivariate model of offence behaviour in child sexual abuse. *Journal of Forensic Psychiatry*, 9, 532–555.

Canter, D.V., Bennell, C., Alison, L.J., and Reddy, S. (2003a). Differentiating sex offences: A behaviourally based thematic classification of stranger rapes. *Behavioral Sciences and the Law*, 21, 157–174.

Canter, D., Kaouri, C., and Ioannou, M. (2003b). 'The facet structure of criminal narratives.' In: S. Levy and D. Elizur (Eds), *Facet Theory: Towards Cumulative Social Science*. Ljubljana: University of Ljubljana, 27–38.

Canter, D.V., Alison, L.J., Alison, E., and Wentink, N. (2004). The organized/disorganized typology of serial murder: myth or model? *Psychology, Public Policy, and Law*, 10, 293–320.

Carter, R.L. and Hill, K.Q. (1975). *The Criminal's Image of the City*. New York: Pergamon.

Cassel, E., and Bernstein, D. (2007). *Criminal Behaviour*. Hillsdale, NJ: Lawrence Erlbaum.

Cattaneo, L.B., and Goodman, L.A. (2003). Victim-reported risk factors for continued abusive behaviour: Assessing the dangerousness of arrested batterers. *Journal of Community Psychology*, 31, 349–369.

Cattell, J.M. (1895). Measurements of the accuracy of recollection. *Science*, 2, 761–766.

Cavanaugh, M., and Gelles, R.J. (2005). The utility of male domestic violence offender typologies: new directions for research, policy and practice. *Journal of Interpersonal Violence*, 20, 155–66.

Celio, M., Karnik, N.S., and Steiner, H. (2006). Early maturation as a risk factor for aggression and delinquency in adolescent girls: a review. *International Journal of Clinical Practice*, 60, 1254–1262.

Centrex (2005). Structured Entrance Assessment for recruiting constables holistically. Information for candidates. Centrex.

Chappell, P. (1965). 'The development and administration of the English criminal law relating to offences of breaking and entering.' In: M. Maguire and T. Bennett (1982), *Burglary in a Dwelling*. London: Heinemann, 25.

Charles (1998), cited in Mawby, R.I. (2001), *Burglary*. Cullompton, Devon: Willan, 66.

Chiffriller, S.H., Hennessy, J.J., and Zappone, M. (2006). Understanding a new typology of batterers: Implications for treatment. *Victims and Offenders*, 1, 79–97.

Chung, H., and Steinberg, L. (2006). Relations between neighbourhood factors, parenting behaviours, peer deviance and delinquency among serious juvenile offenders. *Developmental Psychology*, 42, 319–331.

Church, S., Henderson, M., Barnard, M., and Hart, G. (2001) Violence by clients towards female prostitutes in different work settings: Questionnaire survey. *British Medical Journal*, 323, 524–525.

Clark, D. (2000). *Theory Manual for Enhanced Thinking Skills*. Prepared for the Joint Prison Probation Service Accreditation Panel.

Clarke, R., and Eck, J. (2003). *Becoming a Problem-solving Crime Analyst in 55 Steps*. London: Jill Dando Institute of Crime Science. (Available from www.jdi.ucl.ac.uk)

Cochrane, R.E., Tett, R.P., and Vandecreek, L. (2003). Psychological testing and the selection of police officers. A national survey. *Criminal Justice and Behaviour*, 30, 511–537.

Cohen, A.K. (1955). Delinquent Boys. Glencoe: Free Press.

Cohen, L.E., and Felson, M. (1979). Social change and crime rate trends: A routine activity approach. *American Sociological Review*, 44, 588–608.

Cohen, M.L., Seghorn, T.K., and Calmas, W. (1969). Sociometric study of the sex offender. *Journal of Abnormal Psychology*, 74, 249–255.

Coid, J.W. (1992). DSM-III Diagnosis in criminal psychopaths: A way forward. *Criminal Behaviour and Mental Health*, 2, 78–94.

Coleman, C., and Norris, C. (2000). *Introducing Criminology*. Cullompton, Devon: Willan.

Colman, A.M., and Gorman, P.L. (1982). Conservatism, dogmatism and authoritarianism in police officers. *Sociology*, 16, 1–11.

Colman, A.M., and Mackay, R.D. (1995). Psychological evidence in court: Legal developments in England and the United States. *Psychology, Crime and Law*, 1, 261–268.

Colwell, A., Hiscock, C., and Memon, A. (2002). Interviewing techniques and the assessment of statement credibility. *Applied Social Psychology*, 16, 287–300.

Cook, P.M. (1977). Empirical survey of police attitudes. *Police Review*, 85, 1042–1045.

Cooke, D.J. (1998). 'Cross-cultural aspects of psychopathy.' In: T. Millon, E. Simonsen, M. Birket-Smith, and R.D. Davis (Eds), *Psychopathy: Antisocial, Criminal and Violent Behavior*. New York: Guilford, 260–276.

Cooke, D.J. (2000). 'Current risk assessment instruments.' In: *Report of the Committee on Serious Violent and Sexual Offenders*. Edinburgh: Scottish Executive, 151–58. SE/2000/68. Available online from: www.scotland.gov.uk/maclean.

Cooke, D.J. (2008). 'Psychopathy and an important construct: Past, present and future.' In: D. Canter and R. Zukauskiene (Eds), *Psychology and Law: Bridging the Gap*. Aldershot: Ashgate, 167–190.

Cooke, D.J., and Michie, C. (2001). Refining the construct of psychopathy: Towards a hierarchical model. *Psychological Assessment*, 13, 171–188.

Cooke, D.J., and Philip, L. (2001). 'To treat or not to treat? An empirical perspective.' In: C.R. Hollin (Ed.), *Handbook of Offender Assessment and Treatment*. Chichester: Wiley.

Cooke, D.J., Michie, C., Hart, S.D., and Clark, D.A. (2004). Reconstructing psychopathy: Clarifying the significance of antisocial and socially deviant behavior in the diagnosis of psychopathic personality disorder. *Journal of Personality Disorders*, 18, 337–357.

Cooper, C.L., Davidson, M.J., and Robinson, P. (1982). Stress in the police service. *Journal of Occupational Medicine*, 24, 30–36.

Cornish, D.B., and Clarke, R.V.G. (1986) (Eds). *The Reasoning Criminal: Rational Choice Perspectives on Offending*. New York: Springer-Verlag.

Councell, R. (2003). *Prison Statistics: England and Wales 2002*. London: National Statistics Cm5996. Available online from: www.archive2.official-documents.co.uk.

Cox, K. (1999). 'Psychologists as expert witnesses.' In: D.V. Canter and L.J. Alison (Eds), *Offender Profiling Series: Vol. 2. Profiling in Policy and Practice*. Aldershot: Ashgate, 189–206.

Craissati, J., and Hodes, P. (1992). Mentally ill sex offenders, the experience of a regional secure unit. *British Journal of Psychiatry*, 161, 846–849.

Crego, J., and Alison, L. (2004). Control and legacy as functions of perceived criticality in major incidents. *Journal of Investigative Psychology and Offender Profiling*, 1, 207–225.

Crego, J., and Harris, C. (2000). Do NDM and CDM theories mark the end of a continuum? Or does a hybrid approach better describe team based decision-making problem solving processes with the management of critical incidents? Retrieved November 2001 from www.minerva-hydra.org.uk/draft2000.htm

Crego, J., and Spinks, T. (1997). 'Critical incident management.' In: R. Flin, E. Salas, M. Strub and L. Martin (Eds), *Decision Making Under Stress. Emerging Themes and Applications.* Aldershot: Ashgate.

Cromwell, P.F., Olson, J.N., and Avary, D.A.W. (1991), *Breaking and Entering.* Newbury Park, CA: Sage.

Crowe, R.R. (1974). An adoption study of antisocial personality. *Archives of General Psychiatry*, 31, 785–791.

Cullen, F.T., Gendreau, P., Jarjoura, G.R., and Wright, J.P. (1997). Crime and the bell curve: Lessons from intelligent criminology. *Crime and Delinquency*, 3, 387–411.

Cusson, M. (2001). 'Control: Social.' In: N.J. Smelser and P.B. Baltes (Eds), *International Encyclopedia of the Social and Behavioral Sciences.* Oxford: Elsevier Science, 2730–2735.

Daubert v. Merrell Dow Pharmaceuticals Inc. 509 U.S. 579 (1993).

Davis, M.R. (2005). The psychological autopsy: Structured guidelines for conducting equivocal death analyses. Paper presented at the 25th annual congress of the Australian and New Zealand Association of Psychiatry, Psychology, and Law (ANZAPPL), November 2005, Wellington, New Zealand.

Davis, M.R. (2006). Linking behaviour to characteristics: Evidence-based practice and offender profiling. Paper presented at the 8th International Investigative Psychology Conference, December 2006, London, England.

Davis, M.R., and Ogloff, J.R.P. (2008). 'Key considerations and problems in assessing risk for violence.' In: D.V. Canter and R. Zukauskiene (Eds.), *Psychology, Crime and Law: New Horizons – International Perspectives.* Aldershot, UK: Ashgate.

De Becker, G., and Associates (2000). Domestic violence method (DV MOSAIC). Available at www.mosaicsystem.com/dv.htm

Deibert, G., and Miethe, T. (2003). Character contests and dispute related offences. *Deviant Behavior: An Interdisciplinary Journal*, 24, 245–267.

Delaware v. Pennell (1989). 584 A. 2d 513 (Del. Super. Ct. 1989).

Delisi, M., and Sherer, A.M. (2006). Multiple homicide offenders: Offence characteristics, social correlates, and criminal careers. *Criminal Justice and Behaviour*, 33, 367–391.

Department of Health (2000). *Reforming the Mental Health Act.* London: HMSO.

Department of Health (2001). *Changing the Outlook: A Strategy for Developing and Modernising Mental Health Services in Prisons.* London: Department of Health. Available at www.phrn.nhs.uk/workstreams/mentalhealth/ChangingTheOutlook.pdf

DePaulo, B.M., Lindsay, J.J., Malone, B.E., Muhlenbruck, L., Charlton, K., and Cooper, H. (2003). Cues to deception. *Psychological Bulletin*, 129, 74–118.

Detrick, P., and Chibnull, J.T. (2002). Prediction of police officer performance with the Inwald Personality Inventory. *Journal of Police and Criminal Psychology*, 17, 9–17.

Dietz, P.E. (1996). The quest for excellence in forensic psychiatry. *Bulletin of the American Academy of Psychiatry and the Law*, 24, 153–163.

Dietz, P.E., Hazelwood, R., and Warren, J. (1990). The sexually sadistic criminal and his offences. *Bulletin of the American Academy of Psychiatry and the Law*, 18, 163–178.

Directorate Research Study No. 171. London: Home Office.

Dobash, E.R., Dobash, R.P., Cavanagh, K., and Lewis, R. (2000). *Changing Violent Men.* Thousand Oaks, CA: Sage.

Dobash, R.E., and Dobash, R.P. (1992). The myth of sexual symmetry in marital violence. *Social Problems*, 39, 71–87.

Dodge, K.A. (1986). 'A social information processing model of social competence in children.' In: M. Perlmutter (Ed.), *Minnesota Symposium on Child Psychology.* Hillsdale, NJ: Erlbaum.

Douglas, J., Ressler, R., Burgess, A., and Hartman, C. (1986). Criminal profiling from crime analysis. *Behavioral Science and the Law*, 4, 401–421.

Douglas, J.E., Burgess, A.W., Burgess, A.G., and Ressler, R.K. (1992). *Crime Classification Manual: A Standard System for Investigating and Classifying Violent Crime*. New York: Simon and Schuster.

Douglas, K.S., and Dutton, D.G. (2001). Assessing the link between stalking and domestic violence. *Aggression and Violent Behavior*, 6, 519–546.

Douglas, K.S., Cox, D.N., and Webster, C.D. (1999). Violence risk assessment: Science and practice. *Legal and Criminological Psychology*, 4, 149–184.

Downes, D., and Rock, P. (1982). *Understanding Deviance: A Guide to the Sociology of Crime and Rule Breaking*. Oxford: Clarendon.

Dutton, D.G., Saunders, K., Starzomski, A., and Bartholomew, K. (1994). Intimacy, anger and insecure attachment as precursors of abuse in intimate relationships. *Journal of Applied Social Psychology*, 24, 1367–1386.

Egger, S.A. (1984). A working definition of serial murder and the reduction of linkage blindness. *Journal of Police Science and Administration*, 12, 348–357.

Egger, S.A. (1990). *Serial Murder: An Elusive Phenomenon*. New York: Praeger.

Egger, S.A. (1998). *The killers among us: An examination of serial murder and its investigation*. New Jersey: Prentice Hall.

Einstadter, W. (1969). The social organisation of armed robbery. *Social Problems*, 17, 64–83.

Ekman, P. (2001). *Telling Lies: Clues to Deceit in the Marketplace, Politics and Marriage*. New York: W.W. Norton.

Ekman, P., O'Sullivan, M., and Frank, M.G. (1999). A few can catch a liar. *Psychological Science*, 10, 263–266.

Elbow, M. (1977). Theoretical considerations of violent marriages. *Social Casework*, 58, 515–526.

Emerson, R.M., Ferris, K.O., and Gardner, C.B. (1998). On being stalked. *Social Problems*, 45, 289–314.

Erikson, E. (1968). *Identity: Youth and Crisis*. New York: W.W. Norton.

Eysenck, H.J. (1977). *Crime and personality* (3rd Ed.). London: Paladin.

Eysenck, H.J., and Eysenck, S.B.G. (1975). *The Eysenck Personality Questionnaire Manual*. London: Hodder and Stoughton.

Eysenck, H.J., and Gudjonsson, G.H. (1989). *The Causes and Cures of Criminality*. New York: Plenum.

Farrell, G. (2005). 'Progress and prospects in the prevention of repeat victimization.' In: N. Tilley (Ed.), *Handbook of Crime Prevention and Community Safety*. Cullompton, Devon: Willan, 143–170.

Farrington, D.P. (1987). 'Epidemiology.' In: Quay, H.C. (Ed.), *Handbook of Juvenile Delinquency*. Chichester: Wiley, 33–61.

Farrington, D.P. (1991). 'Childhood aggression and adult violence: Early precursors and later outcomes.' In: D.J. Pepler and K.H. Rubin (Eds), *The Development and Treatment of Childhood Aggression*. Hillsdale, NJ: Erlbaum.

Farrington, D.P. (1992). Criminal career research in the United Kingdom. *British Journal of Criminology*, 32, 521–536.

Farrington, D.P., and Lambert, S. (1994). Differences between burglars and violent offenders, *Psychology, Crime and Law*, 1, 107–116.

Farrington, D.P., and West, D.J. (1990). 'The Cambridge study in delinquent development: A long term follow up of 411 London males.' In: G. Kaiser and H.J. Kerner (Eds), *Criminal: Personality, Behaviour, Life History*. Heidelberg: Springer-Verlag.

Farrington, D.P., Snyder, H.N., and Finnegan, T.A. (1988). Specialization in juvenile court careers. *Criminology*, 26, 461–488.

Farrington, D.P., Coid, J.W., Harnett, L.M., Jolliffe, D., Soteriou, N., Turner, R.E., and West, D.J. (2006). *Criminal careers up to age 50 and life success up to age 48: New findings from the Cambridge Study in Delinquent Development*. Home Office Research Study No. 299. London: Home Office.

Fazel, S., and Danesh, J. (2002). Serious mental disorder in 23,000 prisoners: A systematic review of 62 surveys. *The Lancet*, 359, 545–550.

Fazel, S., and Grann, M. (2006). The population impact of severe mental illness on violent crime. *American Journal of Psychiatry*, 163, 1397–1403.

Feeley, T.H., and deTurck, M.A. (1998). The behavioral correlates of sanctioned and unsanctioned deceptive communication. *Journal of Nonverbal Behavior*, 22, 189–204.

Feist, A., Ashe, J., Lawrence, J., McPhee, D., and Wilson, R. (2007). *Investigating and Detecting Recorded Offences Of Rape*. Home Office Online Research Report, 18/07. London: Home Office.

Feldman, P. (1993). *The Psychology of Crime*. Cambridge: Cambridge University Press.

Fesbach, S. (1964). The function of aggression and the regulation of aggressive drive. *Psychological Review*, 71, 257–272.

Finkelhor, D. (1997). 'The homicide of children and youths: A developmental perspective.' In: G. Kaufman Kantor and J. Jasinski (Eds), *Out of the Darkness: Contemporary Perspectives on Family Violence*. Thousand Oaks, CA: Sage.

Finney, A. (2006). *Domestic Violence, Sexual Assault and Stalking: Findings from the 2004/05 British Crime Survey*. Home Office Online Research Report, 12/06. London: Home Office.

Fisher, R., and Geiselman, R. (1992). *Memory-Enhancing Techniques for Investigative Interviewing: The Cognitive Interview*. Springfield , IL: Charles C. Thomas.

Ford, C.V. (1996). *Lies! Lies!! Lies!!: The Psychology of Deceit*. London: American Psychiatric Press.

Ford, R. (2006). Yobs Want an ASBO as a Badge of Honour. *The Times*, Thursday 2 November, 1–2.

Forrester, D., Chatterton, M., and Pease, K. (1988). *The Kirkholt Burglary Prevention Project, Rochdale*. London: HMSO (Crime Prevention Unit Paper no. 13).

Foster, D. (2001). *Author Unknown*. London: Macmillan.

Fox, J.A., and Levin, J. (1998). Multiple homicide: Patterns of serial and mass murder. *Crime and Justice*, 23, 407–455.

Fox, J.A., and Levin, J. (2003). Mass murder: An analysis of extreme violence. *Journal of Applied Psychoanalytic Studies*, 5, 47–64.

Frank, M.G. (2005). 'Research methods in detecting deception research.' In: J. Harrigan, R. Rosenthal and K. Scherer (Ed.), *The New Handbook of Methods in Nonverbal Behavior Research*. Oxford: Oxford University Press, 341–365.

Freckelton, I., and McMahon, M. (2002). Social science research and experimentation in Australian Criminal Proceedings: Prejudicial pre-trial publicity and psychological research. *Journal of Law and Medicine*, 9, 347–367.

Freedman, B.J., Rosenthal, L., Donahoe, C.P., Schlundt, D.G., and McFall, R.M. (1978). A social behavioural analysis of skills deficits in delinquent and non-delinquent adolescent boys. *Journal of Consulting and Clinical Psychology*, 46, 448–462.

Frye v. United States, 293 F.1013 (D.C. Cir. 1923).

Fuller, J.L., and Thompson, W.R. (1978). *Foundations of Behavior Genetics*. Mosby: St. Louis.

Garrett, C.J. (1985). Effects of residential treatment in adjudicated delinquents. *Journal of Research in Crime and Delinquency*, 22, 287–308.

Geiselman, R.E., Fisher, R.P., MacKinnon, D.P., and Holland, H.L. (1985) Eyewitness memory enhancement in the police interview: Cognitive retrieval mnemonics versus hypnosis. *Journal of Applied Psychology*, 70, 401–412.

Gelles, R.J. (1994). Research and advocacy: can one wear two hats? *Family Process*, 33, 93–96.

Gelles, R.J., and Cornell, R. (1985). *Intimate Violence in Families*. Newbury Park, CA: Sage.

Gerberth, V.J., and Turco, R.N. (1997). Antisocial personality disorder, sexual sadism, malignant narcissism, and serial murder. *Journal of Forensic Science*, 42, 49–60.

Gibson, E. (1975). *Homicide in England and Wales 1967–1971*. Home Office Research Study No. 31. London: HMSO.

Glaeser, E., Sacerdote, B., and Scheinkman, J. (1996). Crime and social interactions. *The Quarterly Journal of Economics*, 111, 507–548.

Glueck, S., and Glueck, E. (1956). *Physique and Delinquency*. New York: Harper.

Goldstein, A.M. (2003). *Handbook of Psychology, Volume 11*. Chichester, Wiley.

Goldstein, A.M. (2007). 'Forensic psychology: Toward a standard of care.' In: A.M. Goldstein (Ed.), *Forensic Psychology: Emerging Topics and Expanding Roles*. Hoboken, NJ: Wiley, 3–41.

Gondolf, E.W. (1988). Who are those guys? Toward a behavioural typology of batterers. *Violence and Victims*, 3, 187–203.

Goodkind, S., Ng, I., and Sarri, R.C. (2006). The impact of sexual abuse in the lives of young women involved or at risk of involvement with the juvenile justice system. *Violence Against Women*, 12, 456–477.

Goring, C. (1913). *The English Convict: A Statistical Study*. London: Darling and Sons.

Granhag, P.A., and Stromwall, L.A. (2004) (Eds). *Deception Detection in Forensic Contexts*. Cambridge: Cambridge University Press, 229–250.

Granhag, P.A., and Vrij, A. (2005). 'Detecting deception.' In: N. Brewer, and K. Williams (Eds), *Psychology and Law: An Empirical Perspective*. New York: Guilford, 43–92.

Greenall, P.V., and West, A.G. (2007). A study of stranger rapists from the English high security hospitals. *Journal of Sexual Aggression*, 13, 151–167.

Gresswell, D.M. (1991). *Multiple Murder in England and Wales: An Analysis*. Unpublished Doctoral Dissertation, Birmingham University.

Gresswell, D.M., and Hollin, C.R. (1994). Multiple murder: A review. *British Journal of Criminology*, 34, 1–14.

Grisso, T. (2003). *Evaluating Competencies: Forensic Assessments and Instruments*, (2nd Ed.). New York: Kluwer Academic/Plenum.

Grisso, T. (1993). The differences between forensic psychiatry and forensic psychology. *Bulletin of the American Academy of Psychiatry & the Law*. 21, 133–145.

Groth, A.N. (1979). *Men Who Rape: The Psychology of the Offender*. New York: Plenum.

Groth, A.N., Burgess, A.W., and Holmstrom, L.L. (1977), Rape: power, anger, and sexuality. *American Journal of Psychiatry*, 134, 1239–1243.

Grove, W.M., Eckert, E.D., Heston, L., Bouchard, T.J., Segal, N., Lykken, D.T. (1990). Heritability of substance abuse and antisocial behaviour: a study of monozygotic twins reared apart. *Biological Psychiatry*, 27, 1293–1304.

Gudjonsson, G. (1992). *The Psychology of Interrogations, Confessions and Testimony*. Chichester: Wiley.

Gudjonsson, G.H. (1985). Psychological evidence in court: Results from the BPS survey. *Bulletin of the British Psychological Society*, 38, 327–330.

Gudjonsson, G.H. (1996). Forensic psychology in England: One practitioner's experience and viewpoint. *Legal and Criminological Psychology*, 1, 131–142.

Gudjonsson, G.H., and Adlam, K.R.C. (1983) Personality patterns of British police officers. *Personality and Individual Differences*, 4, 507–512.

Gudjonsson, G.H., and Haward, L.R.C. (Eds) (1998). *Forensic Psychology: A Guide to Practice*. London: Routledge.

Gutheil, T.G. (2002). 'Assessment of mental state at the time of the criminal offense: The forensic examination.' In: R.I. Simon and D.W. Shuman (Eds), *Retrospective Assessment of Mental States in Litigation: Predicting the Past*. Washington, DC: American Psychiatric Publishing, 73–99.

Hale, M. (1980). *Human Science and Social Order: Hugo Munsterberg and Origins of Applied Psychology*. Philadelphia: Temple University Press.

Hamberger, L.K., Lohr, J.M., Bonge, D., and Tolin, D.F. (1996). A large sample empirical typology of male spouse abusers and its relationship to dimensions of abuse. *Violence and Victims*, 11, 277–292.

Hammond, L., Wagstaff, G.F., and Cole, J. (2006). Facilitating eyewitness memory in adults and children with context reinstatement and focused meditation. *Journal of Investigative Psychology and Offender Profiling*, 3, 117–130.

Haney, C. (1993). Psychology and legal change: The impact of a decade. *Law and Human Behaviour*, 17, 371–398.

Haney, C.W. (1997). The psychological impact of incarceration: Implications for Post-Prison Adjustment. Craig Haney, University of California, Santa Cruz.

Haney, C. (2001). The Psychological Impact of Incarceration: Implications for Post-Prison Adjustment. Retrieved 18 September 2007 from http://aspe.hhs.gov/hsp/prison2home02/haney.pdf

Haney, C. (2008). 'The consequences of prison life: Notes on the new psychology of prison effects.' In: D. Canter and R. Zukauskiene (Eds), *Psychology and Law: Bridging the Gap*. Aldershot: Ashgate, 143–166.

Hanneman, R., and Riddle, M. (2005). *Introduction to Social Network Methods*. Riverside, CA: University of California, Riverside. Published online; available at http://faculty.ucr.edu/~hanneman/nettext/

Hanson, R.K., and Thornton, D. (1999). *Static-99: Improving Actuarial Risk Assessments for Sex Offenders*. Ottawa: Department of the Solicitor General of Canada.

Hare, R.D. (1991). *Hare Psychopathy Checklist – Revised*. Toronto: Multi-Health Systems.

Hare, R.D. (1993). *Without Conscience: The Disturbing World of the Psychopaths Among Us*. New York: Guilford.

Hare, R.D. (1999). Psychopathy as a risk factor for violence. *Psychiatric Quarterly*, 70, 181–197.

Hare, R.D. (2003). *Hare Psychopathy Checklist – Revised*, (2nd Ed.). Toronto: Multi-Health Systems.

Hargreaves, D.H. (1980). Classrooms, schools and juvenile delinquency. *Educational Analysis*, 2, 75–87.

Harlan, H. (1950). Five hundred homicides. *Journal of Criminal Law and Criminology*, 40, 736–752.

Harris, A., Phenix, A., Hanson, R.K. and Thornton, D. (2003). *Static – 99 coding rules revised – 2003*. Ottawa. Department of the Solicitor General of Canada.

Harrower, J. (1998). *Applying Psychology to Crime*. London: Hodder and Stoughton.

Hart, S.D. (1998). The role of psychopathy in assessing risk for violence: Conceptual and methodological issues. *Legal and Criminological Psychology*, 3, 121–137.

Hart, S.D., Kropp, P.R., Laws, D.R., Klaver, J., Logan, C., and Watt, K.A. (2003). *The Risk for Sexual Violence Protocol (RSVP): Structured Professional Guidelines for Assessing Risk of Sexual Violence*. Burnaby: Mental Health, Law, and Policy Institute, Simon Fraser University.

Hartwig, M., Granhag, P.A., Strömwall, L.A., and Andersson, L.O. (2004). Suspicious minds: Criminals' ability to detect deception. *Psychology, Crime and Law*, 10, 83–95.

Harty, M.A., Shaw, J., Thomas, S., et al. (2004). The security, clinical and social needs of patients in high security psychiatric hospitals in England. *Journal of Forensic Psychiatry and Psychology*, 15, 208–221.

Hathaway, S.R., and McKinley, J.C. (1940). A multiphasic personality schedule (Minnesota): I. Construction of the schedule. *Journal of Psychology*, 10, 249–254.

Haward, L.R.C. (1981). *Forensic Psychology*. London: Batsford Academic and Educational.

Hawkins, J., and Weis, J. (1985). The social development model: An integrated approach to delinquency prevention. *Journal of Primary Prevention*, 6, 73–97.

Hazelwood, R.R., and Burgess, A.W. (1987). *Practical Aspects of Rape Investigation: A Multidisciplinary Approach*. New York: Elsevier.

Hazelwood, R.R., and Warren, J.I. (2003). Linkage analysis: Modus operandi, ritual, and signature in serial sexual crime. *Aggression and Violent Behavior*, 8, 587–598.

Healy, W., and Bronner, A.F. (1936). *New Light on Delinquency and its Treatment*. New Haven, CT: Yale University Press.

Henry, D., Tolan, P., and Gorman-Smith, D. (2001). Longitudinal family and peer group effects on violence and nonviolent delinquency. *Journal of Clinical Child Psychology*, 30, 172–186.

Hess, A.K. (2006). 'Serving as an expert witness.' In: I.B. Weiner and A.K. Hess (Eds), *The Handbook of Forensic Psychology*, (3rd Ed.). Hoboken, NJ: Wiley, 652–697.

Hickey, E. (2002). *Serial Murderers and their Victims*, (3rd Ed.). Belmont, CA: Wadsworth.

Hidden v. Mutual Life Insurance Co. (1954). 217 F.2d 818 (4th Cir. 1954).

Higgins, J.P., and Thies, A.P. (1981). Social effectiveness and problem-solving thinking of reformatory inmates. *Journal of Offender Counselling Services and Rehabilitation*, 5, 93–98.

Hindelang, M., Gottfredson, M.R., and Garofalo, J. (1978). *Victims of Personal Crime: An Empirical Foundation for a Theory of Victimization*. Cambridge, MA: Ballinger Books.

Hirschi, T. (1969). *Causes of Delinquency*. Berkeley, CA: University of California Press.

HM Prison Service (2007). *Prison Statistics 2007*. Retrieved 18 September 2007 from www.hmprisonservice.gov.uk

Hodelet, N. (2001). Psychosis and offending in British Columbia: Characteristics of a secure hospital population. *Criminal Behaviour and Mental Health*, 11, 163–172.

Hodge, S., and Canter, D. (1998). Victims and perpetrators of male sexual assault. *Journal of Interpersonal Violence*, 13, 222–239.

Hodgins, S., Mednick, S.A., Brennan, P.A., Schulsinger, F., and Engberg, M. (1996). Mental disorder and crime: Evidence from a Danish birth cohort. *Archives of General Psychiatry*, 53, 489–496.

Hodgskiss, B. (2003). Lessons from serial murder in South Africa. *Journal of Investigative Psychology and Offender Profiling*, 1, 67–94.

Hoffman, M.L. (1984). 'Empathy, social cognition and moral action.' In: W. Kurtines and J. Gerwitz (Eds), *Moral Behaviour and Development: Advances in Theory, Research and Applications*. New York: Wiley.

Hollin, C. (1989). *Psychology and Crime: An Introduction to Criminological Psychology*. London: Routledge.

Hollin, C.R. (1999) Treatment programs for offenders. Meta-analysis, 'What Works' and beyond. *International Journal of Law and Psychiatry*, 22, 361–372.

Hollin, C.R. (Ed.) (2001). *Handbook of Offender Assessment and Treatment*. Chichester: Wiley.

Holmes, R.M., and DeBurger, J. (1998). *Serial Murder: Studies in crime, law and justice, Vol. 2*. Newbury Park, CA: Sage.

Holmes, R.M., and Holmes, S.T. (1998a). *Serial Murder* (2nd Ed.). Thousand Oaks, CA: Sage.

Holmes, R.M., and Holmes, S.T. (1998b). *Contemporary Perspectives on Serial Murder*. Thousand Oaks, CA: Sage.

Holmes, T.H., Rae, R.H. (1967). The social readjustment rating scale. *Journal of Psychosomatic Research*, 11, 213–218.

Holtzworth-Munroe, A., and Stuart, G.L. (1994). Typologies of male batterers: Three subtypes and the differences among them. *Psychological Bulletin*, 116, 476–497.

Home Office and Department of Health (1999). *Managing Dangerous People with Severe Personality Disorder: Proposals for Policy Development*. London: Home Office and the Department of Health. Available online from www.homeoffice.gov.uk

Home Office (1996). *Report of the Inquiry into Prison Escapes and Security* (The Mountbatten Report). London: HMSO.

Home Office (1997). *Women in prison – a thematic review*. London: Home Office.

Home Office (2003). *Prison Statistics England and Wales 2002*. London: Stationery Office.

Home Office (2005a). *Domestic Violence: A National Report*. Home Office: London.

Home Office (2005b). *National Policing Plan 2005–2008. Safer, Stronger Communities.* http://police.homeoffice.gov.uk/national-policing-plan/policing-plan-2008.html

Home Office (2006a). *A Five Year Strategy for Protecting the Public and Reducing Re-offending.* London: The Stationery Office, CM6717. Available online from www.homeoffice.gov.uk

Home Office (2006b). *Achieving Best Evidence In Criminal Proceedings: Guidance for vulnerable or intimidated witnesses, including children.* London: Home Office.

Honey, P. and Mumford, A. (1996) *Using your learning styles.* Maidenhead: Peter Honey.

Horncastle, P., and Bull, R. (1986). *Metropolitan Police Recruit Training: Phase 1.* London: Police Foundation.

Howitt, D. (2006). *Forensic and Criminological Psychology.* Essex: Pearson Prentice Hall.

Hudson, W., and McIntosh, S.R. (1981). The assessment of spouse abuse: Two quantifiable dimensions. *Journal of Marriage and the Family*, 43, 873–888.

Huesmann, L.R. (1988). An information processing model for the development of aggression. *Aggressive Behaviour*, 14, 13–24.

Huesman, L.R., and Eron, L.D. (1989). Individual differences and the trait of aggression. *European Journal of Personality*, 3, 95–106.

Hutchings, B., and Mednick, S.A. (1975). 'Registered criminality in the adoptive and biological parents of registered male criminal adoptees.' In: R.R. Fieve, D. Rosenthal and H. Brill (Eds), *Genetic Research in Psychiatry.* Baltimore, MD: John Hopkins University Press.

International Centre for Prison Studies (2007). Retrieved 12 September 2007 from www.kcl.ac.uk/depsta/rel/icps/worldbrief/europe.html

Inwald, R.E., and Shusman, E.J. (1984). The IPI and MMPI as predictors of academy performance for police recruits. *Journal of Police Science and Administration*, 12, 1–11.

Inwald, R.E., Knatz, H., and Shusman, E. (1982). *Inwald Personality Inventory Manual.* Kew Gardens, NY: Hilson Research.

Izzo, R.L., and Ross, R.R. (1990). Meta-analysis of rehabilitation programmes for juvenile delinquents. *Criminal Justice and Behaviour*, 17, 134–142.

Jackson, C., and Foshee, V.A. (1998). Violence-related behaviours of adolescents: Relations with responsive and demanding parenting. *Journal of Adolescent Research*, 13, 343–359.

Jamieson, E., and Taylor, P.J. (2004). A re-conviction study of special (high security) hospital patients. *British Journal of Criminology*, 44, 783–802.

Jenkins v. United States (1962). 307 F.2d 637 (D.C. Cir. 1962) en banc.

Jenkins, P. (1988). Serial Murder in England, 1940–1985. *Journal of Criminal Justice*, 16, 1–15.

Johnson, M.P. (1995). Patriarchal terrorism and common couple violence: Two forms of violence against women. *Journal of Marriage and the Family*, 57, 283–294.

Johnson, S., and Bowers, K. (2004). The stability of space-time clusters of burglary. *British Journal of Criminology*, 44, 55–65.

Jones, J.S., Wynn, B.N., Kroeze, B., Dunnuck, C., and Rossman, L. (2004). Comparison of sexual assault by strangers versus known assailant in a community-based population. *American Journal of Emergency Medicine*, 22, 454–459.

Joseph, J. (2003). *The Gene Illusion: Genetic Research in Psychiatry and Psychology under the Microscope.* Ross-on Wye: PCCS Books.

Kahneman, D., and Tversky, A. (1979). Prospect theory: An analysis of decisions under risk. *Econometrica*, 47, 313–327.

Kapardis, A. (1997). *Psychology and Law: A Critical Introduction.* Cambridge: Cambridge University Press.

Karmen, A. (2001). *Crime Victims: An Introduction to Victimology*, (4th Ed.). London: Wadsworth.

Kazemian, L., and Farrington, D. (2005). Comparing the validity of prospective, retrospective, and official onset for different offending categories. *Journal of Quantitative Criminology*, 21, 127–147.

Kebbell, M.R., and Wagstaff, G.F. (1999). *Face Value? Evaluating the Accuracy of Eyewitness Information*. Police Research Series: Paper 102. Available online at www.homeoffice.gov.uk/rds/prgpdfs/fprs102.pdf

Kelly, L., Lovett, J., and Regan, L. (2005). A Gap or Chasm? Attrition in Reported Rape Cases. *Home Office Research Study, 293*. London: Home Office.

Kennedy, A.M. (2008). 'Psychological syndrome evidence.' In: J.D. Lieberman and D.A. Kraus (Eds), *Psychology in the Courtroom*. Aldershot: Ashgate, 123–137.

Kennedy, D.B., and Sakis, J.R. (2008). 'From crime to tort: Criminal acts, civil liability and the behavioral science.' In: D. Canter and R. Zukauskiene (Eds), *Psychology and Law: Bridging the Gap*. Aldershot: Ashgate, 119–142.

Keppel, R. (Ed.) (2004). *Offender Profiling: Readings in Crime Assessment and Profiling*. London: Thomson/Custom Publishing.

Keppel, R.D., and Walter, R. (1999). Profiling killers: A revised classification model for understanding sexual murder. *International Journal of Offender Therapy and Comparative Criminology*, 43, 417–437.

Kerr, E., Cottee, C., Chowdhury, R., and Welch, J. (2003). The Haven: a pilot referral centre in London for cases of serious sexual assault. *British Journal of Obstetrics and Gynaecology*, 111, 267–271.

Kershaw, C., Budd, T., Kinshott, G., Mattinson, J., Mayhew, P., and Myhill, A. (2001). *The 2000 British Crime Survey*. London: HMSO (HO Statistical Bulletin 18/00).

Kirkman, M. (2002). What's the plot? Applying narrative theory to research in psychology. *Australian Psychologist*, 37, 30–38.

Klein, G.A. (1993). 'A recognition primed decision (RPD) model of rapid decision making.' In: G.A. Klein, J. Orasanu, R. Calderwood and C.E. Zsambok (Eds), *Decision Making in Action: Models and Methods*. Norwood, NJ: Ablex.

Knight, R.A. (1999). Validation of a typology for rapists. *Journal of Interpersonal Violence*, 14, 303–330.

Kohlberg, L. (1976). 'Moral stages and moralisation: The cognitive-developmental approach.' In: T. Lickona (Ed.), *Moral Development and Behaviour*. New York: Holt, Rinehart and Winston.

Kolstad, A. (1996). Imprisonment as rehabilitation: Offenders' assessment of why it does not work. *Journal of Criminal Justice*, 24, 323–335.

Krebs, V. (2002). Mapping networks of terrorist cells. *Connections*, 24, 43–52.

Kropp, R., and Hart, S.D. (2000). The Spousal Assault Risk Assessment Guide (SARA): Reliability and validity in adult male offenders. *Law and Human Behavior*, 24, 101–118.

Kropp, P.R., Hart, S.D., Webster, C.D., and Eaves, D. (1995). *Manual for the Spousal Assault Risk Assessment Guide*. Vancouver: The British Columbia Institute Against Family Violence.

Kumho Tire Co. v. Carmichael, 526 U.S., 119 S. Ct. 1167 (1999).

Kunda, Z. (1999). *Social Cognition: Making Sense of People*. Cambridge, MA; MIT Press.

Kuznetsov, A., Pierson, T., and Harry, B. (1992). Victim age as a basis for profiling sex offenders. *Federal Probation*, 56, 34–38.

Lamers-Winkelman, F. (1999). Statement Validity Analysis: Its application to a sample of Dutch children who may have been sexually abused. *Journal of Aggression, Maltreatment and Trauma*, 2, 59–81.

Lane, G., and Russell, T. (1989). 'Second-order systemic work with violent couples.' In: P.L. Caesar and L.K. Hamberger (Eds), *Treating Men Who Batter: Theory, Practice and Programs*. New York: Springer, 134–162.

Lange, J.S. (1931). *Crime as Destiny*. London: Allen and Unwin.

Lea, S.J., Lanvers, U., and Shaw, S. (2003). Attrition in rape cases; developing a profile and identifying relevant factors. *British Journal of Criminology*, 43, 583–599.

LeBeau, J.L. (1987). The journey to rape: Geographic distance and the rapist's method of approaching the victim. *Journal of Police Science and Administration*, 15, 129–136.

Lester, D. (1995). *Serial Killers: the Insatiable Passion*. Philadelphia, PA: The Charles Press.

Levin, J., and Fox, J.A. (1985). *Mass Murder: America's Growing Menace*. New York: Plenum.

Leyton, E. (1995). *Compulsive Killers: The Story of Modern Multiple Murder*. New York: New York University Press.

Lieberman, J.D., and Kraus, D.A. (Eds) (2008). *Psychology in the Courtroom*. Aldershot: Ashgate.

Lipsey, M.W. (1992). 'Juvenile delinquency treatment: a meta-analytical inquiry into the variability of effects.' In: H. Cooper, D.S. Cordray, et al (Eds), *Meta-Analysis for Explanation: A Casebook*. New York: Russell Sage Foundation.

Lipton, D.S., Pearson, F.S., Cleland, C., and Yee, D. (1998). How do cognitive skills training programmes for offenders compare with other modalities? A meta-analytic perspective. Presented at the Stop and Think Conference, Her Majesty's Prison Service, York, UK.

Lipton, D.S., Thornton, D., McGuire, J., Porporino, F.J., and Hollin, C.R. (2000). Program accreditation and correctional treatment. *Substance Use and Misuse*, 35, 705–734.

Lobato, A. (2000). 'Criminal weapon use in Brazil: A psychological analysis.' In: D.V. Canter and L.J. Alison (Eds). *Profiling Property Crimes. Offender Profiling Series, Vol IV*. Dartmouth: Aldershot.

Loftus, E.F. (1979). *Eyewitness Testimony*. Cambridge, MA: Harvard University Press.

Loftus, E.F. (1981). 'Eyewitness testimony: Psychological research and legal thought'. In: M. Tonry and N. Morris (Eds), *Crime and Justice: An Annual Review of Research (3)* . Available online at www.jestor.org

Loftus, E.F. (1991). *Witness for the Defense*. New York: St Martin's Press.

Loftus, E.F. (2003). Make believe memories. *American Psychologist*, 58, 867–873.

Loftus, E.F., and Palmer, J. (1974). Reconstruction of automobile destruction: An example of the interaction between language and memory. *Journal of Learning and Verbal Behaviour*, 13, 585–589.

Lombroso, C. (1876). *L'uomo Delinquente*. Milan: Torin.

Lombroso, C. (1887). *L'Homme Criminel. Atlas*. Paris: F. Alcan.

Lord, W., Boudreaux, M., Jarvis, J.P., Waldvogel, J., and Weeks, H. (2002). Comparative patterns in life course victimisation. *Homicide Studies*, 6, 325–347.

Lösel, F., and Köferl, P. (1989). 'Evaluation research on correctional treatment in West Germany: a meta-analysis.' In: H. Wegener, F. Lösel and J. Haisch (Eds), *Criminal Behaviour and the Justice System: Psychological Perspectives*. New York: Springer-Verlag.

Louisiana v. Code (1993). 627 So. 2d 1373.

Luedtke, G. (1970). *Crime and the Physical City: Neighbourhood Design Techniques for Crime Prevention*. Springfield, VA: National Technical Information Service.

Ly, L., and Foster, S. (2005). *Statistics of Mentally Disordered Offenders 2004: England and Wales*. London: Home Office Statistical Bulletin 22/05. Available online from www.homeoffice.gov.uk/rds

MacDonald, T.M. (1963). The threat to kill. *American Journal of Psychiatry*, 120, 125–130.

Maguire, M., and Bennett, T. (1982). *Burglary in a Dwelling: The Offence, the Offender and the Victim*. London: Heinemann.

Maguire, M., and Corbett, C. (1987). *The Effects of Crime and the Work of Victim Support Schemes*. Aldershot: Gower.

Marshall, W.L. (1989). Intimacy, loneliness and sexual offenders. *Behavioral Research in Therapy*, 27, 491–503.

Martin, C.A. (2005). *Juvenile Justice: Process and Systems*. London: Sage.

Masters, F., and Greaves, D. (1969). The Quasimodo complex. *British Journal of Plastic Surgery*, 20, 204–210.

Mawby. R.I. (2001) *Burglary*. Cullompton, Devon: Willan.

McCabe, K., Hough, R., Wood, P., and Yeh, M. (2001). Childhood and adolescent onset conduct disorder: A test of the developmental taxonomy. *Journal of Abnormal Child Psychology*, 29, 305–316.

McCarty, D.G. (1929). *Psychology for the Lawyer*. New York: Prentice-Hall.

McCluskey, K., and Wardle, S. (2000). 'The social structure of robbery.' In: D. Canter and L. Alison (Eds), *The Social Psychology of Crime: Groups, Teams and Networks*. Dartmouth: Ashgate, 247–285.

McCormick, A. (1984). Good cop/bad cop: The use of the MMPI in the selection of law enforcement personnel. Paper presented at the 19th annual symposium on recent developments in the use of the MMPI, Tampa, Florida.

McGuire, J. (Ed.) (1995). *What Works: Reducing Reoffending – Guidelines from Research and Practice*. Chichester: Wiley.

McGuire, J. (2000). *An Introduction to Theory and Research: Cognitive-Behavioural Approaches*. HM Inspectorate of Probation Report. London: Home Office.

McGuire, J., and Priestley, P. (1995). 'Reviewing "What Works': past, present and future." In: J. McGuire (Ed.), *What Works: Reducing Reoffending. Guidelines from Research and Practice*. Chichester: Wiley.

McGuire, J., Mason, T., and O'Kane, A. (Eds) (2000). *Behaviour, Crime and the Legal Processes: A Guide for Forensic Practitioners*. Chichester: Wiley.

McIntosh, M. (1975). *The Organisation of Crime*. London: MacMillan.

McKenry, P.C., Julian, T.W., and Gavazzi, S.M. (1995). Toward a biopsychosocial model of domestic violence. *Journal of Marriage and the Family*, 57, 307–320.

McKenzie, C. (1995). A study of serial murder. *International Journal of Offender Therapy and Comparative Criminology*, 39, 3–10.

McLean, I., and Balding, V. (2003). Some characteristics of 7289 cases of rape and sexual assault seen at St. Mary's Sexual Assault Referral Centre since 1986. Health Psychology Update, 12, 56–61.

Mednick, S.A., Gabrielli, W.F., and Hutchings, B. (1984). Genetic influences in criminal convictions: Evidence from an adoption cohort. *Science*, 224, 891–894.

Medoff, D. (2003). The scientific basis of psychological testing: Considerations following Daubert, Kuhmo, and Joiner. *Family Court Review*, 41, 199–213.

Meehl, P.E. (1989). Law and the fireside inductions: Some reflections of a clinical psychologist. *Behavioral Sciences and the Law*, 7, 521–550.

Meehl, P.E. (1996). *Clinical versus statistical prediction: A theoretical analysis and a review of the evidence*. Northvale, NJ: Jason Aronson. (Original work published 1954).

Megargee, E.I. (1966). Undercontrolled and overcontrolled personality types in extreme antisocial aggression. *Psychological Monographs*, 80(3).

Megargee, E.I. (1982). Psychological determinants and correlates of criminal violence. In: M.E. Wolfgang and N.A. Weiner (Eds), *Criminal Violence*. Beverly Hills, CA: Sage.

Meloy, R.J. (1996). Stalking (obsessional following): a review of some preliminary studies. *Aggression and Violent Behaviour*, 1, 147–162.

Meloy, J.R. (1998). 'The psychology of stalking.' In: J.R. Meloy (Ed.), *The Psychology of Stalking: Clinical and Forensic Perspectives*. San Diego: Academic Press, 1–23.

Meloy, J.R. (2000). The nature and dynamics of sexual homicide: an integrative review. *Aggression and Violent Behaviour*, 5, 1–22.

Meloy, R.J., and Gothard, S. (1995). Demographic and clinical comparison of obsessional followers and offenders with mental disorders. *American Journal of Psychiatry*, 152, 258–263.

Melton, G.B., Petrila, J., Poythress, N.G., and Slobogin, C. (2007). *Psychological Evaluations for the Courts: A Handbook for Mental Health Professionals and Lawyers* (3rd Ed.). New York: Guilford.

Memon, A., and Stevenage, S. (1996). Interviewing witnesses: What works and what doesn't? *Psychology*, 7 (6).

Memon, R. (2006). Legal theory and case law defining the insanity defence in English and Welsh law. *Journal of Forensic Psychiatry and Psychology*, 17, 230–252.

Mendelsohn, B. (1940). Rape in criminology. Translated and cited in S. Shafer (1968), *The Victim and his Criminal*. New York: Random House.

Mendelsohn, B. (1956) The victimology. *Etudes Internationales de PsychoSociolgie Criminelle*, (July) 23–26.

Merry, S. (1995). *Breaking the Castle Walls: Facets of the House Burglary*. Unpublished MSc Dissertation, The University of Liverpool.

Merry, S., and Harsent, L. (2000). 'Intruders, pilferers, raiders and invaders: The interpersonal dimensions of burglary.' In: D.V. Canter and L.J. Alison (2000), *Profiling Property Crimes*. Aldershot: Ashgate.

Merton, R. (1969). 'Social structure and anomie.' In: D.R. Cressey and D.A. Ward (Eds), *Delinquency, Crime and Social Process*. New York: Harper and Row, 254–284.

Messner, S., and Tardiff, K. (1985). The social ecology of urban homicide: An application of routine activities approach. *Criminology*, 23, 241–267.

Miller, G.R., and Stiff, J.B. (1993). *Deceptive Communication*. Newbury Park, CA: Sage.

Miller, L. (1995). Tough guys: Psychotherapeutic strategies with law enforcement and emergency services personnel. *Psychotherapy*, 32, 592–600.

Mitchell, E.W. (1997). *The Aetiology of Serial Murder: Towards an Integrated Model*. Unpublished Masters in Philosophy thesis, University of Cambridge, Cambridge, England.

Moffitt, T.E. (1993). Adolescence-limited and life-course-persistent antisocial behavior: A developmental taxonomy. *Psychological Review*, 100, 674–701.

Moir, A., and Jessel, D. (1995). *A Mind to Crime*. London: Michael Joseph.

Monahan, J. (1981). *Predicting violent behavior: An assessment of clinical techniques*. Beverly Hills, CA: Sage.

Monahan, J., and Walker, L. (1988). Social science research in law: A new paradigm. *American Psychologist*, 43, 465–472.

Moore, C. (1907). Yellow psychology. *Law Notes*, 11, 125–127.

Moore, J W. (1991). *Going Down to the Barrio*. Philadelphia: Temple University Press.

Moore, J.W., and Hagedorn, J. (2001). *Female Gangs: A Focus on Research*. Office of Juvenile Justice and Delinquency Prevention, March 2001.

Morey, L.C., Warner, M.B., and Hopwood, C.J. (2007). 'The personality assessment inventory: Issues in legal and forensic settings.' In: A.M. Goldstein (Ed.), *Forensic Psychology: Emerging Topics and Expanding Roles*. Hoboken, NJ: Wiley, 97–126.

Morselli, C., Tremblay, P., and McCarthy, B. (2006). Mentors and criminal achievement. *Criminology*, 44, 17–43.

Mullins, S. (2008). 'Terrorist networks and small group psychology.' In: D. Canter (Ed.), *Faces of Terrorism: Cross-Disciplinary Explorations*. Chichester: Wiley-Blackwell.

Mullins, S., and Alison, L. (2008). 'Towards a taxonomy of police decision making in murder enquiries.' In: L. Alison and J. Crego (Eds), *The Psychology of Critical Incident Management*. Cullompton, Devon: Willan.

Munsterberg, H. (1908). *On the Witness Stand: Essays on Psychology and Crime*. New York: McClure.

Myhill, A., and Allen, J. (2002). *Rape and sexual assault of women: findings from the British Crime Survey*. Home Office Findings, 159. London: Home Office.

National Health Service (2006). *In-Patients Formally Detained in Hospitals under the Mental Health Act 1983 and other Legislation, England: 1994–95 to 2004–05*. London: The Information Centre: Mental Health Statistics. Available online from www.ic.nhs.uk

National Research Council (2003). *The polygraph and lie detection. Committee to Review the Scientific Evidence on the Polygraph*. Washington, DC: The National Academic Press.

Nee, C., and Taylor, M. (2000). Examining burglars' target selection: Interview, experiment or ethnomethodology? *Psychology, Crime and Law*, 6, 45–59.

Needs, A., and Towl, G.J. (2003). *Applying Psychology to Forensic Practice*. Oxford: Blackwell.

Nettler, G. (1982). *Killing One Another*. Cincinnati, OH: Anderson.

Neumann, C.S., Vitacco, M.J., Hare, R.D., and Wupperman, P. (2005). Reconstructing the 'reconstruction' of psychopathy: A Comment on Cooke, Miche, Hart, and Clark. *Journal of Personality Disorders*, 19, 624–640.

New Jersey v. Fortin (2000). 162 N.J. 517.

Nicholas, S., Povey, N., Walker, A., and Kershaw, C. (2005). *Crime in England and Wales 2004/05*. Home Office Statistical Bulletin 11/05. London: Home Office.

Ogloff, J.R.P. (2000). Two steps forward and one step backward: The law and psychology movement(s) in the 20th century. *Law and Human Behavior*, 24, 457–483.

Ogloff, J.R.P., and Davis, M.R. (2004). Advances in offender assessment and rehabilitation: contributions of the risk-need-responsivity approach. *Psychology, Crime and Law*, 10, 229–242.

Ogloff, J.R.P., and Otto, R.K. (2003). 'Psychological autopsy and other reconstructive mental state evaluations: Clinical and legal perspectives.' In: I.Z. Schultz and D.O. Brady (Eds), *Psychological Injuries at Trial*. Chicago, IL: American Bar Association Press, 1186–1230.

Ogloff, J.R.P., and Polvi, N.H. (1998). 'Legal evidence and expert testimony.' In: D. Turner and M. Uhlemann (Eds), *A Legal Handbook for the Helping Professional*, (2nd Ed.). Victoria, BC: The Sedgewick Society for Consumer and Public Education, 379–401.

Ogloff, J.R.P., Tomkins, A.J., and Bersoff, D.N. (1996). Education and training in psychology and law/criminal justice. *Criminal Justice and Behavior*, 23, 200–235.

O'Reilly-Fleming, T. (1992). From Beasts to Bedlam: Hadfield, the Regency Crisis, M'Naghten and the 'Mad' Business in Britain, 1788–1843. *Journal of Psychiatry and Law*, 20, 167–190.

Ormerod, D. (1999). 'Criminal profiling: Trial by judge and jury, not criminal psychologist.' In: D.V. Canter and L.J. Alison (Eds), *Offender Profiling Series: Vol. 2. Profiling in Policy and Practice*. Aldershot: Ashgate, 207–261.

Ormerod, D. (2005). *Smith and Hogan: Criminal Law*, (11th Ed.). Oxford: Oxford University Press.

Osborn, S.G., and West, D.J. (1979). Conviction records of fathers and sons compared. *British Journal of Criminology*, 19, 120–133.

Otto, R.K., and Heilbrun, K. (2002). The practice of forensic psychology: A look toward the future in light of the past. *American Psychologist*, 57, 5–18.

Ozbay, O., and Ozcan, Y.Z. (2006). A test of Hirschi's social bonding theory – Juvenile delinquency in the high schools of Ankara, Turkey. *International Journal of Offender Therapy and Comparative Criminology*, 50, 711–726.

Parker, A., and Brown, J. (2000). Detection of deception: Statement validity analysis as a means of determining truthfulness or falsity of rape allegations. *Legal and Criminological Psychology*, 5, 237–259.

Pearson, M., and West, P. (2003). Drifting smoke rings: Social network analysis and Markov processes in a longitudinal study of friendship groups and risk-taking. *Connections*, 25, 59–76.

Pease, K. (1998). *Repeat Victimisation: Taking Stock*. Crime Detection and Prevention Series, Paper 90. London: Home Office.

People v. Hawthorne (1940). 293 Mich. 15, 291 N.W. 205.

Pfeifer, J.E., and Brigham, J.C. (1993). Ethical concerns of nonclinical forensic witnesses and consultants. *Ethics and Behavior*, 3, 329–343.

Phillips, S.L., Heads, T.C., Taylor, P.J., and Hill, G.M. (1999). Sexual offending and antisocial sexual behaviour among patients with schizophrenia. *Journal of Clinical Psychiatry*, 60, 170–175.

Piaget, J. (1959). *Language and Thought of the Child*. London: Routledge and Kegan Paul.

Pillman, F., Rohde, A., Ullrich, S., Draba, S., Sannemuller, U., and Marneros, A. (1999) Violence, criminal behaviour and the EEG: Significance of left hemispheric focal abnormalities. *Journal of Neuropsychiatry and Clinical Neuroscience*, 11, 454–457.

Piquero, A.R., and Buka, S.L. (2002). Linking juvenile and adult patterns of criminal activity in the Providence cohort of the National Collaborative Perinatal Project. *Journal of Criminal Justice*, 30, 259–272.

Piquero, A.R., Brame, R., and Lynam, D. (2004). Studying criminal career length through early adulthood among serious offenders. *Crime and Delinquency*, 50, 412–435.

Police and Criminal Evidence Act (1984). Home Office. Available online at www.homeoffice.gov.uk/documents/PACE-cover

Police Skills and Standards Organisation (PSSO) (2002). *Developing skills in the Police Sector. Strategic Plan 2001–2004*.

Porporino, F.J., and Fabiano, E.A. (2000). Theory Manual for Reasoning and Rehabilitation. Prepared for the Joint Prison Probation Service Accreditation Panel.

Porter, L., and Alison, L. (2001). A partially ordered scale of influence in violent group behaviour: An example from gang rape. *Small Group Research*, 32, 475–497.

Porter, L., and Alison, L. (2006a). Behavioural coherence in group robbery: A circumplex model of offender and victim interactions. *Aggressive Behaviour*, 32, 330–342.

Porter, L., and Alison, L. (2006b). Leadership and hierarchies in criminal groups: scaling degrees of leader behaviour in group robbery. *Legal and Criminological Psychology*, 11, 245–265.

Porter, S., Woodworth, M., Earle, J., Drugge, J., and Boer, D. (2003). Characteristics of sexual homicides committed by psychopathic and nonpsychopathic offenders. *Law and Human Behavior*, 27, 459–470.

Powis, B. (2002). *Offenders' Risk of Serious Harm: A Literature Review*. London: Home Office RDS Occasional Paper 81. Available online from www.homeoffice.gov.uk/rds

Price, D. (2000). *The Origins and Durability of Security Categorisation: A Study in Penological Pragmatism or Spies, Dickie and Prison Security*. British Criminology Conference, Selected Proceedings. Volume 3.

Prison Statistics (Sept. 2007). HMPS Website www.hmprisonservice.gov.uk

Pynes, J., and Bernardin, H.J. (1992). Mechanical vs. consensus-derived assessment center ratings: A comparison of performance job validities. *Public Personnel Management*, 21, 17–28.

Quinsey, V.L., Harris, G.T., Rice, M.E., and Cormier, C.A. (1998). *Violent Offenders: Appraising and Managing Risk*. Washington, DC: American Psychological Association.

R v. Sally Lorraine Emery (and Another) (1993). Cr.App.R. (S) 394.

R. v Turnbull and Others (1977).

R v. Turner (1975) Q.B. (C.A.) 834.

Rappaport, R. (1988). The serial and mass murderers. *American Journal of Forensic Psychiatry*, 9, 39–48.

Reicher, S., Stott, C., Cronin, P., and Adang, O. (2004). An integrated approach to crowd psychology and public order policing. *Policing: An International Journal of Police Strategies and Management*, 27, 558–572.

Reiss, A. (1988). Co-offending and criminal careers. *Crime and Justice*, 10, 117–170.

Rengert, G., and Wasilchick, J. (1985). *Suburban Burglary. A Time and a Place for Everything*. Springfield, IL: Charles C. Thomas.

Reppetto, T. (1974). *Residential Crime*. Ballinger, Cambridge.

Ressler, R.K., and Schachtman, T. (1992). *Whoever Fights Monsters*. New York: St. Martin's Press.

Ressler, R.K., Burgess, A.W., Douglas, J.R., Hartman, C.R., and D'Agostino, R.B. (1986). Sexual killers and their victims: identifying patterns through crime scene analysis. *Journal of Interpersonal Violence*, 1, 288–308.

Ressler, R.R., Burgess, A.W., and Douglas, J.E. (1988). *Sexual homicide*. Lexington: Lexington Books.

Rhodes, W.M., and Conly, C. (1981). 'Crime and mobility: An empirical study.' In: P.J. Brantingham and P.L. Brantingham (Eds), *Environmental Criminology*. Beverley Hills, CA: Sage, 167–188.

Richards, P. (1999). *Homicide Statistics. Research paper no. 99/56*. London: House of Commons Library.

Riggs, D.S., Caulfield, M.B., and Street, A.E. (2000). Risk for domestic violence: Factors associated with perpetration and victimisation. *Journal of Clinical Psychology*, 56, 1289–1316.

Riggs, N., Houry, D., Long, G., Markovchick, V., and Feldhaus, K.M. (2000). Analysis of 1,076 cases of sexual assault. *Annals of Emergency Medicine*, 35, 358–362.

Risinger, D.M., and Loop, J.L. (2002). Three card monte, monty hall, modus operandi and 'offender profiling': Some lessons of modern cognitive science for the law of evidence. *Cardozo Law Review*, 24, 193–285.

Roediger, H.L. III, and McDermott, K.B. (1995). Creating false memories: Remembering words that were not presented in lists. *Journal of Experimental Psychology: Learning, Memory and Cognition*, 21, 803–814.

Roesch, R., and McClachlan, K. (Eds) (2007). *Clinical Forensic Psychology and Law*. Aldershot: Ashgate.

Rogers, R., and Shuman, D.W. (2005). *Fundamentals of Forensic Practice*. New York: Springer.

Rose, V.G. (2001). 'An introduction to law and the Canadian legal system.' In: R.A. Schuller and J.R.P. Ogloff (Eds), *Introduction to Psychology and Law: Canadian Perspectives*. Toronto: University of Toronto Press, 29–56.

Rosenfeld, J.P. (2005). 'Brain fingerprinting:' A critical analysis. *Scientific Review of Mental Health Practice*, 4, 20–37.

Ross, L., and Alison, L. (1999). Critical incident stress debriefing and its effects on coping strategies and anger in a sample of Australian police officers in shooting incidents. *Work Stress*, 13, 144–161.

Ross, R.R., and Fabiano, E. (1985). *Time to think. A cognitive model of delinquency prevention and rehabilitation*. Johnson City, TN: Institute of Social Sciences and Arts.

Ross, R.R., Fabiano, E.A., and Ewles, C.D. (1988). Reasoning and rehabilitation. *International Journal of Offender Therapy and Comparative Criminology*, 32, 29–35.

Rossmo, D.K. (1997). 'Geographic profiling.' In: J.L. Jackson and D.A. Beckerian (Eds), *Offender Profiling Theory and Practice*. Chichester: Wiley, 159–176.

Rotter, J.B. (1954). *Social Learning and Clinical Psychology*. Englewood Cliffs, NJ: Prentice-Hall.

Rotter, J.B. (1966). Generalised expectancies for internal versus external control of reinforcement. *Psychological Monographs*, 80, whole no. 609.

Rowe, D.C. (2001). *Biology and Crime*. Los Angeles: Roxbury.

Ruperal, C. (2004). *The Nature of Rape in Females in the Metropolitan Police District*. Home Office Research Study No. 247. London: Home Office.

Rutter, M. (1971). Parent-child separation: Psychological effects on the children. *Journal of Child Psychology and Psychiatry*, 12, 233–260.

Rutter, M., and Giller, H. (1983). *Juvenile Delinquency: Trends and Perspectives*. Harmondsworth: Penguin.

Ryan, K.M. (2004). Further evidence for a cognitive component of rape. *Aggression and Violent Behaviour*, 9, 579–604.

Salfati, C.G. (2000). Profiling homicide: A multidimensional approach. *Homicide Studies*, 4, 265–293.

Salfati, C.G. (2001). A European Perspective on the study of homicide. *Homicide Studies*, 5, 286–291.

Salfati, C.G., and Canter, D. (1999). Differentiating stranger murders. Profiling offender characteristics from behavioural styles. *Behavioural Sciences and the Law*, 17, 391–406.

Salfati, C.G., and Dupont, F. (2001). Canadian homicide: An investigation of crime scene actions. *Homicide Studies*, 10, 118–139.

Salfati, C.G., and Harastis, E. (2001). Greek homicide. A behavioural examination of offender crime-scene actions. *Homicide Studies*, 5, 335–362.

Sampson, R., and Laub, J. (1990). Crime and deviance over the life course: The salience of adult social bonds. *American Sociological Review*, 55, 609–627.

Sampson, R.J. (2001). 'Sociology of delinquency.' In: N.J. Smelser and P.B. Baltes (Eds), *International Encyclopedia of the Social and Behavioral Sciences*. Oxford: Elsevier Science, 3380–3384.

Sandberg, A.A., Koepf, G.F., Ishiara, T., and Hauschka, T.S. (1961). An XYY human male. *Lancet*, 262, 488–489.

Santtila, P., Junkkila, J., and Sandnabba, N.K. (2005). Behavioural linking of stranger rapes. *Journal of Investigative Psychology and Offender Profiling*, 2, 87–103.

Sarason, I.G. (1968). Verbal learning, modelling, and juvenile delinquency. *American Psychologist*, 23, 254–266.

Saunders, D.G. (1992). A typology of men who batter: Three types derived from cluster analysis. *American Journal of Orthopsychiatry*, 62, 264–275.

Scarr, H.A. (1973). *Patterns of Burglary*. Washington DC: National Institute of Law Enforcement and Criminal Justice, Government Printing Office.

Schmidt, F.L., and Hunter, J.E. (1998). The validity and utility of selection methods in personnel psychology: practical and theoretical implications of 85 years of research findings. *Psychological Bulletin*, 124, 262–274.

Schrenck-Notzing, A. (1897). *Uber Suggestion und Erinnerungsfalschung in Berthold Prozess*. Leipzig: Johann Ambrosius Barth.

Schuler, R. (1980). Definition and conceptualisation of stress in organizations. *Organizational Behaviour and Human Performance*, 25, 184–215.

Schuller, R.A., and Ogloff, J.R.P. (2001). 'An introduction to psychology and law.' In: R.A. Schuller and J.R.P. Ogloff (Eds), *Introduction to Psychology and Law: Canadian Perspectives*. Toronto: University of Toronto Press, 3–28.

Schwartz-Watts, D., and Morgan, D.W. (1998). Violent versus non-violent stalkers. *Journal of the American Academy of Psychiatry and Law*, 25, 541–545.

Scogin, F., Schumacher, J., Gardner, J., and Chaplin, W. (1995). Predictive validity of psychological testing in law enforcement settings. *Professional Psychology Research and Practice*, 26, 68–71.

Scottish Executive (2001). *Homicide in Scotland*. Statistical Bulletin Criminal Justice Series, November. Edinburgh.

Scully, D., and Marolla, J. (1985). 'Riding the Bull at Gilley's': Convicted rapists describe the rewards of rape. *Social Problems*, 32, 251–263.

Seidman, B.T., Hudson, S.M., and Robertson, P.J. (1994). An examination of intimacy and loneliness in sex offenders. *Journal of Interpersonal Violence*, 9, 518–534.

Selye, H. (1956). *The Stress of Life*. New York: McGraw-Hill.

Sewell, J.D. (1983). The development of a critical life events scale for law enforcement. *Journal of Police Science and Administration*, 11, 113–114.

Shaw, J., Hunt, I.M., Flynn, S., et al. (2006). Rates of mental disorder in people convicted of homicide: National clinical survey. *British Journal of Psychiatry*, 188, 143–147.

Sheldon, W.H. (1942). *The varieties of temperament: A psychology of constitutional differences*. New York: Harper.

Shover, N. (1973). The social organisation of burglary. *Social Problems*, 20, 499–514.

Shover, N. (1991). 'Burglary.' In: M. Taylor (Ed.), *Crime and Justice. A Review of Research*. Chicago: Chicago Press.

Shusman, E.J., and Inwald, R.E. (1991). Predictive validity of the Inwald Personality Inventory. *Criminal Justice and Behaviour*, 18, 419–426.

Silva, F., Martorell, C., and Clemente, A. (1986). Socialisation and personality: Study through questionnaires in a preadult Spanish population. *Personality and Individual Differences*, 7, 355–372.

Silverman, R.A., and Mukherjee, S.K. (1997). Intimate homicide: an analysis of violent social relationships. *Behavioural Sciences and the Law*, 5, 37–47.

Singleton, N., Meltzer, H., Gatward, R., Coid, J., and Deasy, D. (1998). *Psychiatric Morbidity Among Prisoners in England and Wales*. London: The Stationery Office. Available online from www.statistics.gov.uk

Singleton, N., Bumpstead, R., O'Brien, M., Lee, A., and Meltzer, H. (2001). *Psychiatric Morbidity Among Adults Living in Private Households, 2000*. London: The Stationery Office. Available online from www.statistics.gov.uk

Skinner, B.F. (1953). *Science and Human Behaviour*. New York: Macmillan.

Smith, A.D. (2000). Motivation and psychosis in schizophrenic men who sexually assault women. *Journal of Forensic Psychiatry*, 11, 62–73.

Smith, A.D., and Taylor, P.J. (1999). Serious sex offending against women by men with schizophrenia. *British Journal of Psychiatry*, 174, 233–237.

Smith, D.A., and Paternoster, R. (1987). The gender gap in theories of deviance: Issues and evidence. *Journal of Research in Crime and Delinquency*, 24, 140–172.

Smith, D.J. (2002). 'Crime and the life course.' In: M. Maguire, R. Morgan and R. Reiner (Eds), *The Oxford Handbook of Criminology*, (3rd Ed.). Oxford: Oxford University Press, 702–755.

Smith, D.J. (2006). *Social Inclusion and Early Desistance from Crime*. Edinburgh: University of Edinburgh Centre for Law and Society.

Stattin, H., and Magnusson, D. (1991). Stability and change in criminal behaviour up to age 30. *British Journal of Criminology*, 31, 327–346.

Stephens, C., Long, N., and Miller, I. (1997). The impact of trauma and social support on posttraumatic stress disorder: A study of New Zealand police officers. *Journal of Criminal Justice*, 25, 303–314.

Stott, C., and Pearson, G. (2007). *Football Hooliganism: Policing and the War on the English Disease*. London: Pennant.

Straus, M.A. (1979). Measuring intrafamily conflict and violence: The Conflict Tactics (CT) Scales. *Journal of Marriage and the Family*, 41, 75–88.

Straus, M.A., and Gelles, R.J. (1990). *Physical violence in American families: Risk factors and adaptations to family violence in 8,145 families*. New Brunswick: Transaction Publishers.

Straus, M.A., Gelles, R.J., and Steinmetz, S.K. (1980). *Behind Closed Doors: Violence in the American Family*. Garden City, NY: Anchor/Doubleday.

Stromwall, L.A., Granhag, P.A., and Hartwig, M. (2004). 'Practitioners' beliefs about deception.' In: P.A. Granhag and L.A. Stromwall (Eds), *Deception Detection in Forensic Contexts*. Cambridge: Cambridge University Press, 229–250.

Stuesser, L. (2005). Experts on eyewitness identification: I just don't see it. *International Commentary on Evidence*, 3, 1–15.

Sugar, N.F., Fine, D.N., and Eckert, L.O. (2004). Physical injury after sexual assault: Findings of a large case series. *American Journal of Obstetrics and Gynaecology*, 190, 71–76.

Sutherland, E.H. (1947). *Principles of Criminology*, (4th Ed.). Philadelphia, PA: Lippincott.

Svensson, R. (2002). Strategic offences in the criminal career context. *British Journal of Criminology*, 42, 395–411.

Sykes, G.M., and Matza, D. (1957). Techniques of neutralisation: A theory of delinquency. *American Sociological Review*, 22, 664–673.

Tajfel, H. (1982). *Social Identity and Intergroup Relations*. Cambridge: Cambridge University Press.

Tapp, J.L. (1976). Psychology and the law: An overview. *Annual Review of Psychology*, 27, 359–347.

Taylor, P.J. (1985). Motives for offending among violent and psychotic men. *British Journal of Psychiatry*, 147, 491–498.

Taylor, P.J. (2002). *Expert Paper: Mental Illness and Serious Harm to Others.* London: NHS National Programme on Forensic Mental Health Research and Development. Available online from www.nfmhp.org.uk/expertpaper.htm

Taylor, P.J., Leese, M., Williams, D., Butwell, M., Daly, R., and Larkin, E. (1998). Mental disorder and violence: A special (high security) hospital study. *British Journal of Psychiatry*, 172, 218–226.

Terry, W.C. (1981). Police stress: The empirical evidence. *Journal of Police Science and Administration*, 9, 61–75.

Thompson, D. (2001). *The Decision to Burgle: An Action System Model of Target Selection in Burglary.* Unpublished PhD thesis, Department of Psychology, The University of Liverpool.

Thompson, K.M. (1990). Refacing inmates: A critical appraisal of plastic surgery programs in prison. *Criminal Justice and Behavior*, 17, 448–466.

Thornhill, R., and Palmer, C. (2000). *A Natural History of Rape: Biological Bases of Sexual Coercion.* Cambridge: MIT Press.

Thornhill, R., and Thornhill, N.W. (1987). 'Human rape: The strengths of the evolutionary perspective.' In: C.B. Crawford, M. Smith and D. Krebs (Eds), *Sociobiology and Psychology: Ideas, Issues and Applications.* Hillsdale, NJ: Lawrence Erlbaum, 269–291.

Thornton, D., and Reid, R.L. (1982). Moral reasoning and type of criminal offence. *British Journal of Social Psychology*, 21, 231–238.

Tilley, N. (Ed.) (2005). *Handbook of Crime Prevention and Community Safety.* Cullompton, Devon: Willan.

Tjaden, P., and Thoennes, N. (1998). *Stalking in America: Findings from the National Violence Against Women Survey.* Washington, DC: National Institute of Justice.

Toch, H. (2002). *Stress in Policing.* Washington, DC: American Psychological Association.

Towl, G.J. (Ed.) (2006). *Psychological Research in Prisons.* Oxford: Blackwell.

Towl, G.J., and Crighton, D.A. (1996). *The Handbook of Psychology for Forensic Practitioners.* London: Routledge.

Turco, R.N. (1990). Psychological profiling. *International Journal of Offender Therapy and Comparative Criminology*, 34, 147–154.

Turner, J., Hogg, M., Oakes, P., Reicher, S., and Wetherell, M. (1987). *Rediscovering the Social Group: A Self-Categorisation Theory.* Oxford: Blackwell.

Ullman, S.E., Filipas, H.H., Townsend, S.M., and Starzynski, L.L. (2006). The role of victim-offender relationship in women's sexual assault experiences. *Journal of Interpersonal Violence*, 21, 798–819.

Undeutsch, U. (1989). 'The development of statement reliability analysis.' In: J. Yuille (Ed.), *Credibility Assessment.* Norwell, MA: Kluwer Academic.

Virkkunen, M. (1986). Reactive hypoglycaemic tendency among habitually violent offenders. *Nutrition Reviews Supplement*, 44, 94–103.

Von Hentig, H. (1948) *The Criminal and his Victim.* New Haven, CT: Yale University Press.

Vrij, A. (2000). *Detecting Lies and Deceit: The Psychology of Lying and the Implications for Professional Practice.* Chichester: Wiley.

Vrij, A. (2004). Why professionals fail to catch liars and how they can improve. *Legal and Criminological Psychology*, 9, 151–181.

Vrij, A. (2008). *Detecting Lies and Deceit: Pitfalls and Opportunities*, (2nd Ed.). Chichester: Wiley.

Vrij, A., Edward, K., and Bull, R. (2001). People's insight into their own behaviour and speech content while lying. *British Journal of Psychology*, 92, 373–389.

Wagstaff, G. (1984). The enhancement of witness memory by hypnosis: A review and methodological critique of the experimental literature. *British Journal of Experimental and Clinical Hypnosis*, 2, 3–12.

Walby, S., and Allen, P. (2002). *Rape and Sexual Assault of Women: The Extent and Nature of the Problem. Findings from the British Crime Survey Home Office Research study No. 237*. London: Home Office.

Walker, A., Kershaw, C., and Nicholas, S. (2006). *Crime in England and Wales 2005/06*. London: Home Office (Home Office Statistical Bulletin). Available online at www.homeoffice.gov.uk/rds/pdfs06/hosb1206.pdf

Walker, L., Hennig, K., and Krettenauer, T. (2000). Parent and peer contexts for children's moral reasoning development. *Child Development*, 71, 1033–1048.

Walklate, S. (2001). *Gender, Crime and Criminal Justice*. Cullompton, Devon: Willan.

Wallace, C., Mullen, P., and Burgess, P. (2004). Criminal offending in schizophrenia over a 25-year period marked by deinstitutionalization and increasing prevalence of comorbid substance use disorders. *American Journal of Psychiatry*, 161, 716–727.

Walsh, D. (1980). Break-ins: Burglary from Private Houses. London. Constable.

Warr, M. (1996). Organisation and instigation in delinquent groups. *Criminology*, 34, 11–37.

Warren, J., Hazelwood, R., and Dietz, P. (1996). The sexually sadistic serial killer. *Journal of Forensic Sciences*, 41, 970–974.

Wasserman, S., and Faust, K. (1997). *Social Network Analysis: Structural Analysis in the Social Sciences*. Cambridge: Cambridge University Press.

Wayte, T., Samra, J., Robbennolt, J.K., Heuer, L., and Koch, W.J. (2002). 'Psychological issues in civil law.' In: J.R.P. Ogloff (Ed.), *Taking Psychology and Law into the Twenty-First Century*. New York: Kluwer Academic/Plenum, 323–369.

Webb, E.J., Campbell, D.T., Schwartz, R.D., and Sechrest, L. (1966). *Unobtrusive Measures: Non-reactive Research in the Social Sciences*. Chicago: Rand McNally.

Webster, C.D., Douglas, K.S., Eaves, D., and Hart, S.D. (1997). *HCR-20: Assessing Risk for Violence, Version 2*. Burnaby: Mental Health, Law, and Policy Institute, Simon Fraser University.

Weerman, F. (2003). Co-offending as social exchange: Explaining characteristics of co-offending. *British Journal of Criminology*, 43, 398–416.

Wells, G.L., and Olson, E.A. (2003). Eyewitness testimony. Annual Review of Psychology, 54, 277–295.

Wells, G.L., Small, M., Penrod, S., Malpass, R.S., Tulero, S.M., Brinacombe, C.A.E. (1998). Eyewitness identification procedures: Recommendations for line-ups and photospreads. *Law and Human Behaviour*, 22, 603–647.

West, D.J. (1982). *Delinquency: Its Roots, Careers and Prospects*. London: Heinemann.

West, D.J., and Walk, A. (1977). *Daniel McNaughton: His Trial and the Aftermath*. London: Gaskell Books.

Whyte, W.H. (1956). *The Organisational Man*. Garden City, NY: Doubleday.

Wigmore, J.H. (1909). Professor Munsterberg and the psychology of testimony: Being a report of the case of Cokestone v. Munsterberg. *Illinois Law Review*, 3, 399–445.

Wiles, P., and Costello, A. (2000). *The 'road to nowhere': the evidence for travelling criminals*. Home Office Research Study 207. London: Home Office.

Wilson, M., and Daly, M. (2006). Are juvenile offenders extreme future discounters? *Psychological Science*, 17(11), 989–994.

Witkin, H.A., Mednick, S.A., Schulsinger, F., et al. (1976). Criminality in XYY and XXY men. *Science*, 193, 547–555.

Witt, R., Clarke, A., and Fielding, N. (1999). Crime and economic activity: A panel data approach. *British Journal of Criminology*, 39, 391–400.

Witte, A.D. (1993). Some thoughts on the future of research in crime and delinquency. *Journal of Research in Crime and Delinquency*, 30, 513–524.

Wolfgang, M., and Ferracuti, F. (1967). *The Subculture of Violence*. New York: Tavistock.

Wolfgang, M.E. (1958). *Patterns in Criminal Homicide*. Philadelphia, PA: University of Philadelphia Press.

Wolpe, P.R., Foster, K.R., and Langleben, D.D. (2005). Emerging neurotechnologies for lie-detection: promises and perils. *The American Journal for Bioethics*, 5, 39–49.

Wrightsman, L.S., Nietzel, M.T., and Fortune, W.H. (1998). *Psychology and the Legal System*, (4th Ed.). London: Brooks/Cole.

Yllö, K.A. (1993). 'Through a feminist lens: Gender, power, and violence.' In: R.J. Gelles and D.R. Loseke (Eds), *Current Controversies on Family Violence*. Newbury Park, CA: Sage, 47–62.

Yochelson, S., and Samenow, S. (1976). *The Criminal Personality, Vol.1: A Profile for Change.* New York: Jason Aronson.

Young, H.S. (1984). Practicing RET with lower class offenders. Special Issue: The work of Howard Young. *British Journal of Cognitive Psychology*, (84), 2(2), 33–59. In: Home Office, Enhanced Thinking Skills Theory Manual. London: Home Office.

Youngs, D. (2004). Personality correlates of offence style. *Journal of Investigative Psychology and Offender Profiling*, 1, 99–120.

Youngs, D. (2008). 'Contemporary challenges in investigative psychology: Revisiting the Canter Offender Profiling equations.' In: D. Canter and R. Zukauskiene (Eds), *Psychology and Law: Bridging the Gap.* Aldershot: Ashgate.

Youngs, D., Canter, D. and Cooper, J. (2004). The facets of criminality: A cross-modal and cross-gender validation. *Behaviormetrika*, 31, 1–13.

Zeedyk, M.S., and Raitt, F.E. (1998). Psychological evidence in the courtroom: Critical reflections on the general acceptance standard. *Journal of Community and Applied Social Psychology*, 8, 23–39.

Zuckerman, M., DePaulo, B.M., and Rosenthal, R. (1981). 'Verbal and nonverbal communication of deception.' In: L. Berkowitz (Ed.), *Advances in Experimental Social Psychology*, Vol. 14. New York: Academic Press, 1–57.

Index